PATRIOTIC AND HISTORICAL PLAYS
FOR YOUNG PEOPLE

Patriotic

and

Historical Plays

for

Young People

Royalty-free plays and programs
about the people and events
that made America great

Edited by

SYLVIA E. KAMERMAN

Publishers   **PLAYS, INC.**   *Boston*

Library of Congress Cataloging in Publication Data

Main entry under title:
Patriotic and historical plays for young people.
    1. United States—History—Revolution, 1775–1783—Juvenile drama. I. Kamerman, Sylvia E. E295.P29   973.3   75-22196
ISBN 0-8238-0195-0

This . . . will signal not just to the people of America, but to all the peoples of the world, the Bicentennial of an event that changed the course of man's development. . . .

We need so urgently now a new dedication and a new expression of our freedom, a new welling up of our pride and spirit. We need now . . . a new signal. . . .

We will light a Third Lantern, a new signal that will call us to a new spirit in our Third Century, a new signal that we hope will be repeated in the homes, and the farms, and the factories, and the schools . . . across America.

—Reverend Robert W. Golledge, Vicar
Old North Church, Boston
April 18, 1975

★ TABLE OF

CONTENTS ★

PATRIOTIC AND HISTORICAL PLAYS FOR YOUNG PEOPLE

Foreword

America's early years are rich with exciting events and the achievements of the illustrious men and women who participated in them. The one-act, royalty-free plays and programs in this new collection dramatize the most memorable episodes that shaped our nation's history, and are especially suitable for performance by young people.

Here are stirring historical dramas with the full flavor of Revolutionary times, featuring such heroic figures as George Washington, Thomas Jefferson, Benjamin Franklin, Thomas Paine, Molly Pitcher, Paul Revere, and Betsy Ross. Such special events as the signing of the Declaration of Independence, the Boston Tea Party, and the birth of the Constitution are brought to life in these authentic plays. Other great moments in American history are re-created—George Washington crossing the Delaware, the trials of the Continental Army at Valley Forge, the courageous stand of Peter Zenger in defense of freedom of the press.

Also included in this book are comedies, spoofs, and parodies which present a lighthearted and fanciful look at history. The lively plays in this special section use modern stage techniques and humor in ways that will delight young actors and 'their audiences.

To provide for variety and flexible programming, PATRIOTIC AND HISTORICAL PLAYS FOR YOUNG PEOPLE also includes reading plays which require no memorization and only a minimum of rehearsal. These scripts may be tape-recorded or broadcast over a public-address system, or used as part of the reading curriculum. With slight adaptation, they may also be successfully staged as "spot-

1

light" productions, with or without scenery, special costumes, etc. The short choral readings are ideal for informal classroom use and may also serve as effective "curtain-raisers" in combination with a longer play for a complete assembly program.

Production notes suggesting simple settings, costumes, and properties are given for all of the dramas and comedies to make them easy for amateurs to stage. These performance-tested stage and reading plays offer a wide variety of material for young actors, teachers, and drama directors to dramatize our nation's heritage.

—S. E. K.

Author of Liberty

Thomas Jefferson and the Declaration of Independence

by Mildred Hark and Noel McQueen

Characters

MRS. GRAFF, *a young German woman*
SOPHIE, *15, a neighbor*
JACOB GRAFF
THOMAS JEFFERSON, *33*
JOHN ADAMS
ROGER SHERMAN
BENJAMIN FRANKLIN, *70*
CAESAR RODNEY

TIME: *Monday, July 1, 1776. Evening.*
SETTING: *The parlor of Mr. Jefferson's lodgings on the second floor of the Graff home in Philadelphia.*
AT RISE: MRS. GRAFF *is busy straightening up the room and dusting. She comes to the table upstage and dusts a book, then lifts book to dust underneath it.*

MRS. GRAFF: Books, books, books—such a man for books. (*She puts the book down and picks up some papers and fans herself with them.*) Ach, the heat. (*Sound of doorknocker is heard from offstage. She goes to door right and calls.*) Yes, who is it?
SOPHIE (*From offstage, calling*): It is Sophie, Mrs. Graff.
MRS. GRAFF: Ah, Sophie. I am busy upstairs—come on up. (*She stands waiting at the door.*) Do not hurry so, child. It is too hot. (SOPHIE *appears in doorway.*)
SOPHIE: It is cooler outside after the rain.
MRS. GRAFF: So? Well, it didn't help much in here. Come in, child, come in.

SOPHIE (*Entering a few steps and looking around*): Mr. Jefferson will not mind?

MRS. GRAFF: Mind your coming into his rooms? Why should he?

SOPHIE: I—I don't know. It's just that—well, he is such an important man, and such a fine gentleman.

MRS. GRAFF: That he is. But what has that to do with the case? Are you not a fine young lady?

SOPHIE (*With a little laugh*): For a moment the other day I felt like one. When you introduced me to him in the hall downstairs, and he bowed so low, I tried to curtsy as Mother taught me, but I felt clumsy, and I know my face got red.

MRS. GRAFF (*Smiling*): Ah, Sophie. A little modest blushing never hurt a girl. You looked sweet, and on the way to the door he said to me, "A charming child, Mrs. Graff."

SOPHIE (*Pleased*): He said that about me?

MRS. GRAFF: Of course about you. Oh, Mr. Jefferson may be a fine Virginia gentleman and we just plain folks, but it makes no difference to him. Again and again I have heard him say, "All people are created equal," and that is what he and his friends keep telling the other gentlemen in Congress.

SOPHIE (*Remembering*): Congress. That reminds me what I came for, Mrs. Graff. Mother sent me to get the latest news.

MRS. GRAFF: I know no more than you do. Mr. Jefferson is not home yet. My, my, those poor gentlemen. If it is hot here, think how it must be in the State House—and with all that talk, talk, talk. All day they've been at it, nine hours steady. (*Suddenly remembering her work*) And a good thing, perhaps. I am so behind with my work. (*She returns to table and starts dusting again.*) All day neighbors keep running in to ask me if I have news, and we stop and gossip.

SOPHIE: That's what comes of having such a famous lodger in your house. (*Worried*) But we don't mean to trouble you, Mrs. Graff, asking for news.

MRS. GRAFF: No, no, Sophie, I did not mean that. I like to talk as well as the next one. And it was not only the neighbors who kept me from my work. The baby has been fretful.

SOPHIE: Little Frederick? He isn't ill?

MRS. GRAFF: No. The heat, I think, and cutting another tooth maybe.

SOPHIE (*Admiringly*): Another tooth. Oh, Mrs. Graff, may I see him before I go?

MRS. GRAFF: Certainly you may. As soon as I've finished here we'll go down. (*She dusts for a moment,* SOPHIE *watching.*)

SOPHIE (*Touching table*): Is this where Mr. Jefferson does all his writing?

MRS. GRAFF: Yes. Hour after hour he sits. My, I should think his fingers would give out.

SOPHIE (*Picking up a small doll*): But what is this? A doll!

MRS. GRAFF: Yes, a present for his daughter. He often shows me things he has bought to take home. Gloves for his wife, and strings for his fiddle—

SOPHIE: He plays on the violin?

MRS. GRAFF: Both he and his wife love music. My, so many things that man can do. Play music and draw sketches—he is an inventor, too. (*Pointing to portable desk on table*) See this desk? He had it made so that it folds up, and he carries it with him when he travels. He can rest it on his knees and write as he rides in a carriage. So he wastes no time.

SOPHIE: But what is it that he writes so much? Not just letters, surely.

MRS. GRAFF: No, child, important papers. Legal things. Most of it is over my head. Whereas this and whereas that. But my husband, Jacob, has talked to him, and he says that Mr. Jefferson puts his ideas in much clearer form than most lawyers. Now, you take this latest paper he has been working on. (*Indicating papers propped up on desk*) I have read parts, and it is easy to understand. Now here, look—as I was telling you about people being equal. (*She runs her finger along paper as she reads.*) "We hold these truths to be self-evident, that all men are created equal." See? He calls this the Declaration of Independence.

SOPHIE: The Declaration? Is that not what Congress is voting on?

MRS. GRAFF: No, not yet. As my Jacob explains it to me, they are voting on a resolution made by Mr. Lee. That will decide whether Mr. Jefferson's Declaration will be read.

SOPHIE (*Looking at paper, too*): It will be hard to read with so many crossing outs.

MRS. GRAFF: Oh, this is not the one they will read in Congress.

Mr. Jefferson penned one out neatly. The good copy is already there and waiting.

SOPHIE (*With her finger on the paper*): And here is the part you were reading.

MRS. GRAFF (*Looking too and picking up paper*): Yes, and it goes on. "That they"—that means all men—"are endowed by their Creator with in—inherent and inalie—inalien—" well, anyway, with "rights, that among these are life, liberty and the pursuit of happiness."

SOPHIE: The pursuit of happiness. It sounds like a beautiful fairy tale.

MRS. GRAFF: According to Mr. Jefferson, it is no fairy tale. He says we will have it here in our own country.

GRAFF (*From offstage, calling*): Liebchen, Liebchen, I am home.

MRS. GRAFF (*Still holding paper*): Ah, it is my Jacob.

GRAFF (*From offstage*): Wife, wife, where are you?

MRS. GRAFF (*Calling and starting toward door right*): Upstairs, Jacob. Ah, it is so good to hear your voice. (JACOB GRAFF *enters, dressed in working clothes.*)

GRAFF (*As he enters, smiling*): So? Well, it is good to be home. (*He kisses his wife and then nods to* SOPHIE.) Good evening, Sophie.

SOPHIE: How are you, Mr. Graff?

MRS. GRAFF: I am late, Jacob—with cleaning Mr. Jefferson's rooms. Supper is not ready.

GRAFF: Never mind, Liebchen. We are not the only ones late for supper. As I passed the State House, crowds still stood there waiting for the posting of the latest news.

MRS. GRAFF: Did you hear anything, Jacob?

GRAFF: No, I did not stop. Why should I stand there in the heat when Mr. Jefferson will tell us all about it? (*Sound of a baby crying from off right is heard.* GRAFF *smiles.*) Ah, Frederick. He must have heard me come in. He wants to see his papa.

MRS. GRAFF (*Teasing*): Maybe so, Jacob, but I think it is the new tooth.

GRAFF: New tooth? Another since this morning?

MRS. GRAFF: No, Jacob, the same one.

SOPHIE (*Laughing*): May I go down and quiet him, Mrs. Graff?

MRS. GRAFF: Of course, Sophie. There is some milk on the table. Just heat it on the stove a little—you know how.

SOPHIE: Yes, Mrs. Graff.

MRS. GRAFF: Oh, and Sophie, maybe you would like to stay and eat with us, spend the evening. Then you could watch me put little Frederick to bed.

SOPHIE: Oh, I would like that so much! But I would have to ask Mother.

MRS. GRAFF: Good. Settle the baby, and then run home and ask her.

SOPHIE: I will. It won't take me long. (*She goes off right.*)

MRS. GRAFF: You must be hungry, Jacob, and tired, too.

GRAFF: Oh, a little. We almost finished the foundation today.

MRS. GRAFF: So? It is good work you do, Jacob. Laying bricks, building new homes in this new country. I am almost finished here—then we will have supper. (*She goes to table and puts paper back on desk.*)

GRAFF: Why do you move Mr. Jefferson's papers?

MRS. GRAFF: Oh, I was reading part to Sophie.

GRAFF: Since when are a gentleman's papers your business?

MRS. GRAFF: You need not scold, Jacob. It is the Declaration. That will soon be everybody's business.

GRAFF: Not unless Congress passes Mr. Lee's resolution.

MRS. GRAFF (*Earnestly*): But they must pass it, Jacob. We have all suffered enough from unjust laws. Our country must be free so that little Frederick can grow up and be somebody in his own right.

GRAFF (*Sighing*): Even if it means a long war.

MRS. GRAFF: Maybe it won't be necessary. Perhaps the gentlemen in Congress will find other ways.

GRAFF (*Shaking his head*): I don't know. All that fighting near Boston, and General Washington is taking his army to New York. (THOMAS JEFFERSON *appears in doorway right.*)

JEFFERSON: Good evening, Mrs. Graff. Good evening, Jacob. (*They both turn toward doorway.*)

MRS. GRAFF: Mr. Jefferson. You're home at last, sir. I must apologize for being in your rooms so late, but I was cleaning, and then Jacob came home and we—

GRAFF (*Smiling*): We were talking, Mr. Jefferson, about the news from Congress.

JEFFERSON (*Smiling tiredly*): And who talks of anything else today? Well, I'm glad to see you both, but I'm sorry to say that there is no more news now than there was this morning. The resolution did not pass.

MRS. GRAFF: But, sir, we heard that Maryland had changed over and was voting for it.

JEFFERSON: That is true, Mrs. Graff. They had a meeting Friday night, and today they announced the change.

GRAFF: How about New York?

JEFFERSON: The New York delegates declared they were for it themselves and were assured their constituents were for it, but they refrained from voting.

MRS. GRAFF: But Mr. Jefferson, it makes no sense.

JEFFERSON (*Laughing a little*): So it seems, but the New York delegates are bound by instructions nearly a year old. However, they will vote for it in the end. We know New York is safe, but still there is Delaware—South Carolina—and your own Pennsylvania. They are still in the halfway house of Dickinson.

GRAFF: I know Mr. Dickinson is one of our delegates, sir. But what do you mean by halfway house?

JEFFERSON (*Smiling*): Oh, just that your Mr. Dickinson is a persuasive talker, Jacob. For hours we have listened to him. He keeps the doubtful ones from going either one way or the other. That's why I say they are in his halfway house. (*He sits wearily in large chair at right.*)

MRS. GRAFF: It is such a shame. You are tired, sir.

JEFFERSON (*Wearily*): Yes, I am. All day long we have debated, without refreshment, without pause, only to have the delegates from South Carolina ask that the final decision might be put off until tomorrow so they might weigh in their own minds their ultimate vote.

GRAFF: But why must they weigh it longer? Have we not already gone so far that there is no turning back?

JEFFERSON (*Wearily*): Yes, Jacob. That is the irony of it. But it seems that statesmen hate to put facts into words. They are like ostriches refusing to see what is before them.

MRS. GRAFF (*With spirit*): I'm afraid I would lose patience and tell them a thing or two. But Mr. Jefferson, you say you did not eat all day. Did you stop somewhere on the way home?

JEFFERSON: No. Some of the gentlemen went to the city tavern, but I'm afraid the long speeches have dulled my appetite. (*Laughs*)

MRS. GRAFF: But you should eat. I will get you something.

JEFFERSON: No, thank you, not just now. But I would appreciate it if you could arrange some light refreshments for a little later. I am expecting a few gentlemen.

MRS. GRAFF: Of course. I'll be glad to.

JEFFERSON: I am sorry to trouble you at such short notice, but we feel we ought to put our heads together before tomorrow's session.

MRS. GRAFF: It is no trouble, Mr. Jefferson. I have some fresh cakes and biscuits—and in the springhouse some cheeses to go with them.

JEFFERSON: Excellent, Mrs. Graff. And perhaps a cool drink?

GRAFF: Of course, Mr. Jefferson. I shall fetch some punch.

JEFFERSON: Ah, but Jacob, you have already worked hard today.

GRAFF (*Smiling*): But I was only working on the foundation for one house while you have been laying the foundation for a whole country.

MRS. GRAFF: That's right, and that concerns all of us, Mr. Jefferson, so why should we not all help? (SOPHIE *appears in doorway right.*)

SOPHIE: Mrs. Graff, Mother says I may stay—(*Seeing* JEFFERSON, *she stops.*) Oh, excuse me.

MRS. GRAFF: It's all right, child.

JEFFERSON (*Nodding*): Good evening, Miss Sophie.

SOPHIE (*Bobbing a curtsy*): Good—good evening, Mr. Jefferson. (*Embarrassed*) Well, I—I'll look after the baby again, Mrs. Graff. (*She runs off.*)

MRS. GRAFF (*Smiling*): Sophie is in awe of you, Mr. Jefferson.

JEFFERSON (*Surprised*): In awe of me? Bless her pretty soul. (*With a laugh*) I wish I could have that effect on some of the gentlemen in Congress.

MRS. GRAFF: She is a good child, and she will help us prepare for the gentlemen, too. So, it is all settled, you see. (*Smiling*) We have more help than we need. (*She turns toward doorway.*)

JEFFERSON (*Rising*): One moment, Mrs. Graff. While you are both here, there is something I want to say. I have not told you how much I appreciate all you have done for me while I have been staying with you.

GRAFF (*Protesting*): But we have done nothing—

MRS. GRAFF: You pay us for everything, Mr. Jefferson. Your lodgings and—

JEFFERSON: One cannot pay for kindness, Mrs. Graff. You have made me feel at home. Why, you have even let me share your little Frederick. In the evenings you have let me look in on him.

GRAFF: Ach, little Frederick, he is so fond of you, Mr. Jefferson.

MRS. GRAFF: The way he smiles when you bounce him on your knee!

JEFFERSON (*Smiling*): A fine boy—a fine boy. And to see both of you so happy, so much in accord—well, I am reminded of my own home, my own family. (*He sighs.*) They seem not so far away.

GRAFF: I know it has been difficult for you, Mr. Jefferson, working so hard here when you have been worried about your family. I know your wife's health has not been good.

JEFFERSON: Yes, that is always on my mind. But whenever I have not heard, or the post has not come, Mrs. Graff has cheered me.

GRAFF (*Patting* MRS. GRAFF's *shoulder*): See, my liebchen, I do not call you my sunshine for nothing.

MRS. GRAFF (*Embarrassed*): Ach, Jacob.

JEFFERSON: No, he is right. You both have a—a sunshine—a cheerfulness about your new home here, and it makes me feel less lonely for my own—my Monticello.

GRAFF: Monticello. It must be beautiful. I have liked hearing you tell about it.

JEFFERSON: One night soon, Jacob, when we have more time, I want to show you a sketch I've made. I want your advice on an addition I'm planning.

GRAFF (*Pleased*): But I am just a bricklayer, sir.

JEFFERSON: And being a bricklayer, you know construction. Sometimes I make plans and what I put on paper is not practical. That's where your knowledge will help.

GRAFF: Then I surely will try. (*Happily*) There is nothing I like better than a problem to do with building.

JEFFERSON: And I, too. My happiest times are when I am making plans for my house. Often I feel I would be more content to be occupied in such personal pursuits than in the building of governments.

MRS. GRAFF: Well, houses or governments, either one takes strength, and I had best be getting on with preparing our supper and the refreshments for you and your visitors. (*She moves books from small table right and puts them on table upstage.*) I'll just go to fetch a nice white cloth for the table.

JEFFERSON: But attend to your supper first, Mrs. Graff.

MRS. GRAFF: No, if I get it now, then all will be ready when I bring up the things later. (*She exits right.*)

JEFFERSON (*Starting left*): Well, Jacob, I must get ready.

GRAFF (*Hesitantly*): There was one thing, sir, I've been wanting to ask you. (JEFFERSON *stops and turns toward* GRAFF.) Sometimes I think our women folks do not realize what may be in store for them, and now that Mrs. Graff is gone I can mention it.

JEFFERSON: You mean the war?

GRAFF (*Worried*): Yes, sir. We are so lately settled in our new home here I would hate to lose it.

JEFFERSON: It's a danger we all face. Even now Lord Dunmore, the royal governor, is arming slaves to attack the homes in Virginia. I can only pray that my Monticello is safe. But I must stay *here* to work for its protection in the only way I know. We must establish a free government, Jacob. A home is nothing unless one is free.

GRAFF: I know that, sir. And if necessary we must fight for that freedom. (*Sighing deeply*) But if we lose—that is the thought that plagues me, Mr. Jefferson.

JEFFERSON (*Firmly*): We dare not think of that possibility, Jacob.

GRAFF: But, sir, the British are bringing my own countrymen— the Hessians—over to fight for them. (*Shaking his head, worried*) The Hessians are well-trained soldiers, you know.

JEFFERSON: But they will not be fighting for their country, Jacob. Their hearts will not be in it. (*Proudly*) We shall be fighting for what we love—for what is right. With Providence to help us, we will surely win. (MRS. GRAFF *enters with white cloth and spreads it on table right.*)

MRS. GRAFF: There. That will do. It is getting dark, Mr. Jefferson. Would you like the lamps lighted?

JEFFERSON: Yes, thank you. (*Sound of knocker is heard from off.*) That will be one of the gentlemen from the Congress, and I have not even tidied myself. (*Starts toward exit left*)

MRS. GRAFF: There is fresh water in your pitcher. I'll show the gentlemen in and say you'll be ready in a minute.

JEFFERSON: Thank you.

GRAFF: And I will take care of the lamps. (JEFFERSON *opens door and exits left, leaving door open.*)

MRS. GRAFF: There is a taper in the hall, Jacob. (*They both exit right. After a moment,* GRAFF *enters right with lighted taper and goes from table to table lighting lamps.* MRS. GRAFF *enters right followed by* JOHN ADAMS.) Mr. Jefferson asks that you make yourself at home, sir. He will be with you shortly.

ADAMS: Thank you. Good evening, Jacob. (MRS. GRAFF *exits.*)

GRAFF: Good evening, Mr. Adams. Mr. Jefferson tells us it was quite a day for long speeches in the Congress.

ADAMS (*Sitting in chair right*): True. (*Smiling*) And did he also tell you that I was responsible for one of the longest ones?

GRAFF: No, sir, he didn't.

ADAMS: Well, it was a matter of self-defense. The opposition had been going on and on. So I gave them a little of their own medicine. I swear, Jacob, if it hadn't been for the flies we'd be there still.

JEFFERSON (*Appearing in doorway left, in shirtsleeves*): Oh, it's you, Adams. I'll be with you shortly.

ADAMS: My dear Jefferson, don't hurry on my account. I am satisfied to sit and rest.

JEFFERSON: I know how you feel. (*He exits again.*)

GRAFF (*Puzzled*): Mr. Adams, if I may ask, sir, what did you mean about the flies?

ADAMS (*Laughing*): Why, the horseflies, Jacob. That livery stable just next to the hall sends swarms of them through the open windows and I think some of the honorable Congressmen cut short their speeches because while standing they couldn't slap the beasts from their silk-stockinged legs.

GRAFF (*Laughing*): One case when the fly in the ointment was a good thing.

ADAMS: Yes, indeed. (GRAFF *exits right, as* JEFFERSON *enters left, now wearing a different coat.*) Well, Thomas, have you heard the latest from South Carolina? (JEFFERSON *sits down in chair near* ADAMS.)

JEFFERSON: Nothing since the meeting broke up, but I am eager to hear.

ADAMS: Well, from what I gathered at the tavern, the delay may be a good thing.

JEFFERSON: That sounds like good news, then? (*He closes door left, then sits again.*)

ADAMS: Rumor has it that they were practically agreed toward the last and by morning will be with us.

JEFFERSON: I hope it's true. Perhaps, John, our patience is bearing fruit. (*Nodding*) We do well not to listen to those who would rush things through just because we have the majority.

ADAMS: Yes, majority rule is all right in most things, but in this case we must have unanimity. If one or two states decided to secede, it would ruin us.

JEFFERSON (*Seating himself at left with a wry laugh*): I hope future generations will thank us for listening to so many dull speeches.

ADAMS (*With irritation*): Someone should thank us. Of all the idle use of time! Nothing was said but what had been repeated and hackneyed in that room before, a hundred times, for six months past. (*Sound of doorknocker is heard from off right.*)

JEFFERSON (*Laughing*): I suppose everyone has to have his say in a democracy. (SOPHIE *enters right. She now wears a frilly apron over her dress. She curtsies.*)

SOPHIE: Mr. Roger Sherman. (*She steps back and exits, as* ROGER SHERMAN *enters.*)

SHERMAN: Good evening, gentlemen.

ADAMS: Evening, Roger.

JEFFERSON (*Rising*): Good evening, Sherman. Do come in and sit down, won't you? (*Indicates chair. They sit down.*)

SHERMAN (*Very businesslike*): Well, Jefferson, you asked me here, and I am glad to come. But to be honest, I take a very dim view of things. If we couldn't swing the doubtful states today, what makes anyone think we can do it tomorrow?

ADAMS: But have you heard the rumor about South Carolina?

SHERMAN (*Sourly*): That's just a rumor, and there is still Pennsylvania—and Delaware. You know as well as I that we need every state. (*Sound of doorknocker is heard off.*)

ADAMS (*Heatedly*): But it's so ridiculous. Why can't they see that we are only seeking to declare what is already an established fact? We are already separated from Great Britain. The King has declared us out of his protection. We are already at war.

SHERMAN: But we cannot expect to win the war without every state to back us up.

JEFFERSON (*Seriously*): I agree to that. Liberty must be the wish of all. Each man's heart must be in it.

SOPHIE (*Entering and curtsying*): Doctor Benjamin Franklin.

JEFFERSON (*Rising and going right*): Ah, the good Doctor. (*He goes off right, followed by* SOPHIE. *After a slight pause,* JEFFERSON *re-enters, leading* BENJAMIN FRANKLIN *in by the arm.*)

FRANKLIN (*Trying to free himself from* JEFFERSON'S *grasp*): No, no, Jefferson, you need not hold my arm. I may be a bit slow now that I am seventy, but I'm not so old that I cannot mount the stairs or walk without aid. (*As* JEFFERSON *walks left with* FRANKLIN, ADAMS *and* SHERMAN *rise.*)

ADAMS: Good evening, Doctor Franklin.

SHERMAN: Good evening, Doctor.

FRANKLIN: Good evening, gentlemen. Jefferson seems to think that because a man is in his seventies, he must be treated like a babe in arms.

ADAMS (*Laughing*): I'm sure, sir, that his solicitude is from love for our elder statesman. (*Indicating chair he has been sitting in*) Won't you be seated, sir?

FRANKLIN: Oh, by all means, before I fall over. (*He sits down, laughing.*) But I assure you, Adams, that after sitting through that oration of yours this afternoon, I thought I would never want to sit again. (*They all laugh.*)

JEFFERSON (*Returning to his chair*): That should put you in your place, Adams. (*They all sit down again,* ADAMS *in a chair upstage from* FRANKLIN.) At any rate, Doctor Franklin, I am honored that you should trouble to find your way to my humble lodgings after dark.

FRANKLIN: I had no difficulty. The lamps are evenly spaced, and there is one directly across the street.

JEFFERSON: Yes, Philadelphia is ahead of other cities I have visited when it comes to lighting.

SHERMAN: And who should know that better than Doctor Franklin? He was responsible for the street lamps in the first place.

JEFFERSON: Indeed?

FRANKLIN: No, the honor of that public benefit has been ascribed to me, but it belongs truly to a Mr. John Clifton. I entered the first bill in the Assembly for the paving of streets and he added the provision for lighting them. I can claim some credit for an improvement to the lamps we were getting from London. But it was a simple thing. Just a long funnel above to draw up the smoke, and crevices below to facilitate the ascent of the air through the lamp. By this means they were kept clean and did not get dark as London lamps do.

SHERMAN: So, sir, you are responsible for better lighting everywhere.

FRANKLIN: No, not everywhere. In London they still use the old kind, and as a result, their streets are very poorly illuminated.

ADAMS (*Acidly*): It seems to be the fashion over there, to be poorly illuminated. Heaven knows we have been trying to make them see the light long enough. (*They all laugh.*)

JEFFERSON: And I do believe we are about to strike a light that will be seen right across the broad Atlantic.

SHERMAN: Oh, if we could only persuade the rest of them!

FRANKLIN: Patience, my friend. Men should not be persuaded against their will or honest judgment. Remember we are founding a free country. And besides, with South Carolina safe, we are a large step forward.

ADAMS (*Excitedly*): Safe? That is news, sir. You know for certain then?

FRANKLIN: Yes, I listened as I passed their delegation on the way out. They were holding a meeting on the floor and doubtless thought these aging ears could not catch their words. But one was saying: "It's settled then. Tomorrow we vote for the resolution." And the rest cheered.

JEFFERSON (*Pleased*): Good—good. If only the others would listen to reason there would be something to cheer for indeed. (So-PHIE *enters right, holding a note, and walks over to* JEFFERSON.)

SOPHIE (*Handing note to* JEFFERSON): A messenger brought this note for you, Mr. Jefferson. (*He rises.*)

JEFFERSON (*Taking note*): Thank you, Sophie. (SOPHIE *exits.* JEFFERSON *goes to table upstage, picks up paper knife and opens note.*) A note by special messenger—it may be good news. (*He unfolds paper and reads a moment.*) It is news—great news. Pennsylvania will be with us in the morning.

ADAMS (*Rising, eagerly*): Can you be certain? Who sent the note?

JEFFERSON: James Wilson. (*Glancing at paper again*) He says that every post all day has brought word from every corner of the state, in favor of the resolution. So Dickinson and Morris will absent themselves in the morning. Wilson will change his vote, and Pennsylvania is with us.

FRANKLIN: Well, gentlemen, it would seem that only the state of Delaware stands between us and Mr. Jefferson's Declaration.

ADAMS (*Sighing*): Just one small state.

JEFFERSON: But, sirs, it is not *my* Declaration alone. You talk as though you had no part in it.

FRANKLIN (*Waving his hand in denial*): What part did we have? You did all the writing. The few paltry changes I suggested made no material difference.

ADAMS: Nor mine. We all insisted that you undertake the drafting of the Declaration because we recognized your ability.

SHERMAN: He's right, Jefferson.

ADAMS: Your reputation for a masterly pen, for literary writing— your happy talent for composition, your felicity of expression—

JEFFERSON (*Half laughing*): Oh, Adams, enough, enough.

ADAMS: No, I insist. It is a great work, and future generations will call it yours.

JEFFERSON (*Humbly*): I only intended it to be an expression of the American mind, and to give to that expression the proper tone and spirit called for by the occasion. The form was less important to me than the content.

ADAMS: The Declaration of Independence is a masterpiece, and once the resolution to read it is passed, it should meet with prompt approval. Don't you agree, Doctor?

FRANKLIN: That Mr. Jefferson has written a masterpiece, yes. That all of it will meet with prompt approval, I am not so sure.

JEFFERSON (*Puzzled*): What do you mean "all of it"? That Declaration is fashioned from the very principles for which we stand. (*Heatedly*) It is a whole cloth. Pull out a thread and it will be in shreds.

FRANKLIN (*Smiling*): So it seems to you, my friend. Have you a copy at hand? Perhaps I can show you what I mean.

JEFFERSON (*Stepping to table and taking papers from desk*): Here is the draft you saw. (*He hands them to* FRANKLIN.) If something should be taken out or changed, let us do it now.

SHERMAN: I would not change a word.

FRANKLIN (*Calmly*): Gentlemen, gentlemen, not so fast. It is not *we* who will make changes, but the Congress. It has been my experience that when papers are reviewed by a public body, they invariably undergo a certain amount of mutilation. (*Looking at paper*) Now you take this part to do with slavery. My guess is it will be stricken out.

JEFFERSON (*Excitedly*): But that can't be, sir. How can we say "Life, liberty and the pursuit of happiness" and not have it apply to all human beings?

FRANKLIN: I know, I know, but we are only human ourselves, Jefferson. We cannot change the inner selves of others. This slavery is an evil thing, feeding on man's selfishness, greed, and love of power. And I fear it has become so deep rooted, it cannot be plucked out at once.

JEFFERSON (*Earnestly*): But nothing is more certainly written in the book of fate than that these people are to be free. Eventually some step must be taken.

FRANKLIN: Eventually, yes. That is the point I am making. But it will take time, Jefferson.

JEFFERSON (*Sighing*): Time. (*He pauses.*) Your words are wise, good Doctor. Will you forgive me for my momentary temper?

FRANKLIN: There is nothing to forgive. But take an old man's advice. (*He holds up papers.*) Be sure to keep this original copy of the Declaration of Independence, Jefferson. Future citizens of our great country should know that Thomas Jefferson stood for the equal rights of *all* men. (*He puts papers down on table behind him.*)

SOPHIE (*Entering right*): Excuse me again, sir.

JEFFERSON: Yes, Sophie?

SOPHIE: A gentleman wishes to speak with you, sir. A Mr. Caesar Rodney.

JEFFERSON (*Going right*): Your pardon, gentlemen. (*He exits, followed by* SOPHIE.)

ADAMS: I don't recall anyone by the name of Caesar Rodney having anything to do with our cause.

FRANKLIN: Nor I. (*Laughing*) And we certainly would have remembered a name like Caesar! (JEFFERSON *re-enters, followed by* CAESAR RODNEY.)

JEFFERSON (*As he walks center*): It is a pleasure, sir. Do come and meet my friends. You will be most welcome to our little gathering. (*Gesturing as he makes introductions*) Here we have Doctor Franklin, Mr. Adams and Mr. Sherman. May I present Mr. Caesar Rodney of the state of Delaware?

ADAMS: Delaware? (*He stands.*)

JEFFERSON: Yes, an additional delegate. Mr. Rodney, I would like these gentlemen to hear from your own lips how you will vote tomorrow.

RODNEY: It is a pleasure for me to announce that I will cast my vote *for* the resolution.

ADAMS (*Stepping forward and shaking hands*): Congratulations, sir. You do not know with what fond eyes we look upon you. Be seated, sir. (RODNEY *sits upstage right where* ADAMS *had been sitting.*)

SHERMAN (*Rising*): Mr. Rodney, this is the news we have been waiting for. (JEFFERSON *moves upstage center and half sits on the table.*)

RODNEY: I bring it gladly.

FRANKLIN (*Solemnly*): My friend, you have supplied the final link in the chain of liberty.

SHERMAN: Hear! Hear!

ADAMS (*Pacing about and gesturing*): Tomorrow, the resolution will pass, and the second day of July, 1776, will begin the most memorable epoch in the history of America. I am inclined to believe that this day will be celebrated by succeeding generations as a national holiday. It should be marked with pomp and parades, with shows, games, sports, guns, bells, bonfires, and illuminations, from one end of this continent to the other, from this time forward, forevermore!

FRANKLIN: Hear, hear! (*Laughing*) For a moment I thought you were off on another speech, Adams. (*They all laugh.*) I agree with all you say except the date.

ADAMS: But tomorrow is July the second.

FRANKLIN: I am inclined to think that the day to celebrate will be the one on which the Declaration of Independence is *adopted* by Congress.

ADAMS: Perhaps you are right, but that should come on the third or at the latest, the fourth of July. (MRS. GRAFF enters right, carrying tray with food. She is followed by GRAFF, who carries tray with jug of punch and glasses. They place trays on table right.)

JEFFERSON (*Stepping forward*): Ah, refreshments. And just at the right moment. Have you heard the good news, Jacob?

GRAFF (*All smiles*): Yes. When Mr. Rodney came in, sir.

JEFFERSON: Then fill up the glasses, for you and your wife as well. (GRAFF *fills glasses rapidly from jug.* MRS. GRAFF *takes two, handing one to* ADAMS *and one to* RODNEY.)

ADAMS (*Holding glass up*): May heaven prosper the new Republic and make its future bright!

RODNEY (*Rising and raising glass*): Long live the United States of America! (JEFFERSON, *who has taken two more glasses, passes one to* SHERMAN *and one to* FRANKLIN.)

SHERMAN (*Rising*): At last we stand as free men and women. (MRS. GRAFF *hands* JEFFERSON *a glass. He stands near center and raises it.* MR. *and* MRS. GRAFF *take glasses and stand near table right.*)

JEFFERSON: And now, gentlemen—(*Then bowing to* MRS. GRAFF) and Mrs. Graff—do we all have glasses? (*He looks about.*) I think the time has come that we should drink a toast together. And so may I ask our friend, our beloved elder statesman, Doctor Franklin, to put into words the thoughts which are overflowing from our hearts? (*He bows to* FRANKLIN.)

FRANKLIN (*Rising, with a glass in one hand and a sheet from the Declaration in the other*): Thank you, Jefferson. I shall be honored. And I think it only fitting and proper that we should have a toast to the Declaration of Independence. This great new document—(*Flourishing the paper, then indicating desk*) written upon a new desk, in this new house belonging to this new young couple (*He bows slightly to* GRAFFS.)—establishes a new government. (*Sound of baby crying is heard from offstage.* FRANKLIN *pauses and smiles.*)

MRS. GRAFF: Ach, the baby. He should not interrupt.

FRANKLIN (*Smiling*): Why not? He is an American. He raises his voice with the rest of us. May that new little American grow up in a free country. And now (*Raising glass*) to the Declaration of Independence. I can do no better than to quote the words of its author—(*Raising paper and reading*) "For the support of this Declaration, we mutually pledge to each other our lives, our fortunes, and our sacred honor." (*All raise their glasses, as the curtain falls.*)

THE END

Incident at Valley Forge

A time of trial, a time of courage

by Walter Hackett

Characters

GENERAL NATHANAEL GREENE
TOM BAILEY
PARDON MILLER
JOB WESCOTT
MRS. CATHERINE GREENE
MARTHA WASHINGTON
ETHAN JONES
OFFICER

SCENE 1

BEFORE RISE: *A Continental* OFFICER *enters. He reads from a sheet of paper.*

OFFICER (*Reading*): "Headquarters. Valley Forge, December 24, 1777. To all regimental and company commanders of the Continental Army. It is with deep regret that we inform you that tomorrow, Christmas Day, will be no different from any other routine day of the week. Because of our inability to gather provisions, the entire army will continue on short rations. This restriction, of course, affects commissioned officers as well as non-commissioned officers and privates. We realize that this unfortunate circumstance may be the cause of discontent among the men, many of whom are at low ebb; but we ask that you explain matters to them. We ask that you inform them that as soon as supplies come through, they will benefit. Signed, Nathanael Greene, Commissary General, Continental Army." (*Exits*)

SETTING: *General Nathanael Greene's quarters at Valley Forge.*

AT RISE: MRS. GREENE *and* MARTHA WASHINGTON *are sitting at a small table. Both are sewing on clothes.*

MRS. GREENE: I'm so pleased you came over this afternoon, Martha. I do need help. I have so much work to do, I don't know where to begin.

MARTHA: I couldn't put my time to better advantage. I am sure that our poor boys will appreciate our efforts. (*She places sewing on table and picks up a long strip of cloth.*) I believe I'll start to roll bandages. It's important that we have a big supply of them.

MRS. GREENE: You had better not remove your cloak, Martha. The fire is quite low; and goodness knows when we will get more wood. It's as precious as gold.

MARTHA: A little cold won't hurt us. We are fortunate to have even a little wood to burn. There are thousands of our men, living in those little hovels outside your door, who have none. (*Pause*) Is General Greene still away?

MRS. GREENE: Yes—poor Nat. He's still off foraging for supplies. He's in Chester, I believe. I'm expecting him back late tonight.

MARTHA: I hope he is successful.

MRS. GREENE: I'm inclined to doubt it.

MARTHA: And so am I, with all due respect to your husband. After all, the Pennsylvania farmers aren't willing to exchange supplies for worthless American certificates.

MRS. GREENE: Of course Nat could force them to hand over what food supplies they have on hand, but he won't. He's too honest for that. (*Pause*) How is General Washington? I haven't seen him in nearly a fortnight.

MARTHA: Worrying, still worrying . . . sick at heart. An army of but eleven thousand men, and over three thousand unfit for any kind of duty.

MRS. GREENE: And the remainder slowly freezing and starving to death. It has been a terrible winter. So cold that the sentries freeze to death on their posts. Sometimes I wonder what will happen. I wonder if we can last. But I immediately put away such thoughts, because I am positive that the thirteen Colonies will win out in the long run.

MARTHA: We will win because we are fighting for something that is dearer to us than life itself. We are fighting for democracy.

MRS. GREENE: A few days ago I received a letter from a dear friend in Rhode Island. I wish you could have read it. I wish our poor troops could read it. It would open their eyes to the fact that the folks back home are counting heavily on them to win this struggle.

MARTHA: On the other hand, if the people at home could see what is going on here at Valley Forge—misery, suffering, sickness—perhaps they might contribute more heavily to the cause. The other evening, my husband said to me: "Martha, we need more than spirit to win. We need more men, more money, more supplies." (*She sighs.*)

MRS. GREENE: Desertions are mounting higher and higher—men leaving to go to their families. (*Knock on door is heard.*) I wonder who that can be at this hour? (*Calling*) Yes? Come in. (ETHAN JONES, *wearing ragged uniform and rags wrapped around his feet, enters.*)

JONES: Mrs. Washington.

MARTHA: Yes—what is it?

JONES (*In a surly tone*): Got a message from General Washington. He left word that he wants you to invite Mrs. Greene for supper tonight at his quarters.

MARTHA: Kindly inform the General's aide that Mrs. Greene will be there. (*Turning to* MRS. GREENE) I presume it is all right, Catherine? You said you didn't expect General Greene until late this evening.

MRS. GREENE: I'll be delighted.

MARTHA: That will be all, private. (JONES *turns to leave.*)

MRS. GREENE: Private. (JONES *stops.*)

JONES: Yes, ma'am?

MRS. GREENE: What is your name?

JONES: Ethan Jones, private, First Rhode Island Regiment.

MRS. GREENE: One of our Rhode Island boys. Where in Rhode Island is your home?

JONES: Providence. I was a carpenter afore this war. (*Bitterly*) Now I'm just—just a . . . a—

MRS. GREENE: A what, Private Jones? (JONES *stands there in sullen silence.*) Ethan Jones, do you see that pair of boots standing there by the door?

JONES (*Following her gaze*): Yes, ma'am.

MRS. GREENE: Take them along with you on your way out. (JONES *stares at her in amazement.*) Yes—take them.

JONES (*Unbelieving*): You—you mean they're for me to wear? They're mine?

MRS. GREENE: Yes, Ethan Jones, they're yours. They belong to you. (JONES *snatches up boots.*)

JONES (*Hesitantly*): That's mighty good of you, Mrs. Greene— mighty good of you. (*Overcome, he starts to leave.*)

MRS. GREENE: Ethan Jones. (JONES *turns.*)

JONES: Yes, Mrs. Greene?

MRS. GREENE: Please don't mention where you got the boots.

JONES: No, ma'am, I certainly won't. Thank you again, Mrs. Greene. (*He exits.*)

MARTHA: That was a most charitable gesture, Catherine.

MRS. GREENE: It was more than a gesture, Martha . . . much more. Did you notice his feet? He wasn't wearing boots. His feet were wrapped in strips of cloth—bloody cloth. There are hundreds of other men here at Valley Forge without boots. Their bare feet leave trails of blood wherever they walk in the snow. I wish I had more boots to give away. (*She suddenly starts to laugh.*)

MARTHA: Why are you laughing?

MRS. GREENE: I was just trying to picture the expression on General Greene's face when I tell him that I've given away his favorite pair of boots. (*Curtain*)

*   *   *   *   *

SCENE 2

SETTING: *The woods at Valley Forge. If desired, this scene may be played in front of the curtain.*

AT RISE: TOM BAILEY, PARDON MILLER *and* JOB WESCOTT, *three ragged Continental soldiers, stand together, talking.*

WESCOTT (*Timidly*): But I'm not sure that we should do it, Tom. I'm not sure that it's right.

BAILEY: What's the matter? Are you afraid, Job Wescott?

MILLER: Of course he is. He's scared of the reckoning.

WESCOTT: I am not scared. I'm just as brave as you two. And maybe a heap wiser.

MILLER: You've got no gumption.

WESCOTT: You listen to me, Pardon Miller and Tom Bailey, I'm just as brave as you two think you be; but I'm not anxious to get myself court-martialed and maybe hanged. Perhaps you two haven't thought of that. Suppose we're caught.

BAILEY: Looky here, Job. I been thinking this over for the past month, and I have it all figured out smooth as silk. We joined the army to fight. Isn't that right?

WESCOTT: Of course we did.

MILLER: No one can say we haven't fought long and hard. Look at Brandywine, Princeton.

BAILEY: Look at Long Island.

MILLER: We fought in those battles. And what happened?

BAILEY: If it hadn't been for General Greene, we'd have been wiped out. It was him that saved the day every time.

WESCOTT: Why are you telling me all this? I was there. Didn't I pick up a bullet at Brandywine?

BAILEY (*Going on*): Look at us now. What's happened? Here we are stuck in this hole. Here we are freezin' to death in this neck of the woods.

MILLER: Why, I haven't had a decent feed in so long, I wouldn't know how to eat it if it was suddenly put in front of me.

BAILEY: It's so cold that we can't even drill. Look at our own regiment. There's not a half-dozen decent pair of boots among the lot.

MILLER: The scarecrow army—that's us. Well, I'm sick of it; and I'm going to do something about it.

BAILEY: I've got a wife and three children back in Rhode Island. I haven't seen them in months. Then there's my farm. (*Proudly*) Once it was the nicest little strip of land in the whole of Portsmouth, but now . . . (*Bitterly*), it's probably all overgrown!

MILLER: My place down in Warwick has eighty acres—forty of it under cultivation. (*Sadly*) Probably running to ruin, what with only my wife and boy to tend to it. My wife's not strong enough to do that sort of work; it's a man's job.

WESCOTT (*Uneasily*): I know, everything you say is true. But I still don't think we should desert. It's a mighty serious offense. I don't want to find myself with a rope round my neck and my heels kicking in the wind. It's either that or a firing squad.

BAILEY (*Bitterly*): Which is better—hanging or starving? At least hanging is a lot quicker.

WESCOTT: Suppose everyone in the army felt that way. If they did, we'd soon lose this war.

MILLER: Are you with us or not? Better make up your mind—and make it up fast.

WESCOTT: I suppose I may as well join you. (*He rubs his hand nervously over his face.*) When do you plan to make a run for it?

MILLER: Tonight.

BAILEY: As soon as the camp is quiet.

WESCOTT (*Unhappily*): Christmas Eve, and we're deserting.

MILLER (*Roughly*): What difference does that make?

BAILEY: We have to make sure the coast is clear. I figure the best time is ten o'clock. That's when they change the outposts. We can sneak out and dodge right between them.

MILLER: Then we'll skirt Philadelphia and travel on foot through Jersey. In New York we can pick up a coastal trader that'll drop us off either at Newport or Providence.

WESCOTT: You two have forgotten one important thing.

BAILEY: What's that?

WESCOTT: We haven't any food or any money to buy it with.

BAILEY: That's all taken care of. We're going to raid the commissary afore we leave.

WESCOTT (*Upset*): But that's stealing. It be plain stealing from them who need it just as bad as we do—maybe even more. No—I don't like that idea.

MILLER: Look, Job, all we're going to take is what we can carry. They won't miss it.

WESCOTT (*Urgently*): This army is so short of rations that even a kernel of corn is important.

BAILEY (*Grabbing* WESCOTT *by his coat collar*): Looky here, you want to go with us, don't you?

WESCOTT (*Uncertainly*): Y—yes, I . . . I guess I do.

BAILEY (*Thrusting him aside*): Then you'll do as I say, and you'll like it. And if you be wise, Job Wescott, between now and the time we leave, you won't say a word to anyone. Understand? No one! Now, let's get out of here. (*All three exit. After a slight pause*, ETHAN JONES *enters and stands looking in the direction of the three departed soldiers. Curtain*)

* * * * *

SCENE 3

SETTING: *General Greene's quarters.*

AT RISE: GENERAL GREENE *is seated at table. He is writing a re-*

port. MRS. GREENE *is seated in chair, knitting.* GENERAL GREENE *puts quill down and yawns.*

MRS. GREENE: You had better go to bed, Nat. You look very tired. Your eyes are so heavy with sleep that you can scarcely keep them open. Besides, this is Christmas Lve.

GREENE (*Stretching*): These foraging expeditions take a lot out of a man. Tramp, tramp, fifteen, eighteen hours a day with hardly any rest. Makes a man so dog-tired he could lie down in the snow and sleep forever. I'll be glad when spring breaks so that we can leave Valley Forge.

MRS. GREENE: What then?

GREENE: We'll probably march on New York. I hope that General Washington relieves me of this business of Commissary General. I want to get back into active duty.

MRS. GREENE (*Scolding slightly*): Nat, you'll stay on your present post just as long as the General wants you. (*He stands.*)

GREENE: Just as you say, Cathy.

MRS. GREENE: After all, collecting food and clothing and making a few pennies go a long way are just as important as commanding troops in actual battle. General Washington knows that you'd rather see active duty; and when he has a mind to transfer you to your old post, he'll do it.

GREENE (*Crossing to her and putting an arm around her shoulder*): Cathy, I may be a general, but at home I obey your orders. (*He goes back to the table and sits down, taking up quill.*)

MRS. GREENE: Back home tonight, friends and relatives will be together . . . celebrating Christmas Eve.

GREENE (*Sympathetically*): I hope you're not too homesick, Cathy. (*Making a sweeping motion with his hand*) I know all this is pretty crude. I know you're not used to this rough life. Perhaps you had better go home for a while.

MRS. GREENE: Is that an order, General Greene?

GREENE: No.

MRS. GREENE: Then I'll stay. When I think of our men out there tonight, I have no right to complain. (*Heavy rapping on the door is heard.*)

GREENE: I wonder who that can be at this time of night? (*Rapping continues.*)

MRS. GREENE: I'll get it, Nat. (*She crosses to door and opens it.* ETHAN JONES *rushes in.*)

JONES: Mrs. Greene, is the General here? I have to—(*He stops, catching sight of* GENERAL GREENE, *who rises to meet him.*) General, I have to see you. It's very important.

GREENE: Let me see—you're Jones.

JONES: Yes, sir. Ethan Jones from the First Rhode Island.

MRS. GREENE: You're the soldier to whom I gave the boots.

JONES: That's right, Mrs. Greene.

GREENE: Well, a Rhode Islander is doubly welcome in my house. (*He shoves a chair toward* JONES.) Sit down.

JONES: I can't, General. I ran all the way over here to tell you. I wasn't going to at first, then I got thinking it over, and I knew . . . I just knew I had to. . . .

GREENE: Take your time, man. (*Pauses*) Now, tell me what's bothering you. Speak up, man!

JONES: Nothing's bothering me, sir. But something's going to be bothering you, unless you hurry.

GREENE (*Sharply*): Get to the point, Jones. (MRS. GREENE. *drops into a chair, and sits, listening.*)

JONES: Early tonight I overheard a conversation. (*He pauses.*)

GREENE: Well?

JONES: Three of your own Rhode Island boys are going to desert.

GREENE: Desert!

JONES: Yep—desert.

MRS. GREENE: That's dreadful news.

JONES: I'm not a squealer. I usually don't believe in it. But this is different. It's for their own good. I thought maybe you might talk them out of it.

GREENE: Who are they?

JONES: Tom Bailey, Pardon Miller, and Job Wescott.

MRS. GREENE: Do you know them, Nat?

GREENE: Yes. I know them. They're among our best men, too. (*He paces back and forth.*) Poor devils! They're probably half-crazed with hunger and cold. If they were in their right senses, they wouldn't think of taking such a step; desertion would be the last thing on their minds.

JONES (*Eagerly*): That's just what I figured, General Greene. And that's why I rushed here to see if you couldn't do something . . . maybe talk them out of it. If I thought they'd listen to me, I'd have done it myself. But they might listen to you where they wouldn't pay attention to me.

GREENE: Where are they now?

JONES: I think you'll find them over at the commissary. They're planning on raiding it. (GREENE *stops his pacing. He pounds one hand into the other.*)

MRS. GREENE: Will it mean court-martial, Nat? (GREENE *nods.*) But isn't there something you can do?

JONES (*Crossing to* GREENE): General Greene, you have to do something. I'm speaking to you as a man now, not as my superior officer. I knew if I came here that you'd help. The army can't lose men, not even half-starved ones. We need them, every last one, if we're going to win this war.

GREENE: If those men leave the boundaries of this camp, there is nothing I can do. It will be out of my hands.

JONES: But can't you stop them afore they leave?

GREENE: I can try, Ethan Jones. I can try mighty hard. (*Rushes off, followed by* JONES, *as curtain falls.*)

*   *   *   *

SCENE 4

SETTING: *A storeroom in the Commissary.*

AT RISE: BAILEY *and* WESCOTT *are busy untying sacks and piling up supplies, then stuffing them into two large sacks.* MILLER *stands on guard, near the door. He has a pistol in his hand.*

MILLER (*Turning to them*): Hurry up, you two. Work fast or we won't be able to get away by ten o'clock. We don't want to get caught in here.

WESCOTT: I still say it's wrong to raid the storehouse.

MILLER: Keep your mouth shut and get to work. (WESCOTT *accidentally overturns a box.*) You clumsy ox. Keep quiet or you'll have the guard on top of us.

BAILEY (*Picking up various food items*): There doesn't seem to be much to pick from. Back home I wouldn't give this food to my dog. (*He starts to break open a crate with an ax.*)

MILLER: Didn't I say not to make so much noise? (BAILEY *stops pounding.*)

BAILEY: This barrel has cornmeal in it. We can use some.

MILLER: Let it go. You're making too much noise. (MILLER *puts ax down and starts to help* WESCOTT.)

BAILEY: I'll be glad when we get out on the Post Road. I'm getting fidgety.

WESCOTT: Might be worse on the Post Road. Likely to run across a passel of Britishers.

MILLER (*Roughly*): What's the matter with you two—losing your gumption?

WESCOTT: As far as this business is concerned, guess I never had any. (*A slight offstage sound is heard.*)

MILLER (*Nervously*): What was that?

BAILEY: Must have been the wind. (*The door starts to open.*)

MILLER (*Raising pistol*): Keep out, whoever you are. (GENERAL GREENE *enters.*)

GREENE (*Pleasantly*): Good evening, men. Sorry to disturb you. I didn't know there was anyone in here. Let me see. Don't I know you three? (*He walks over to them.* MILLER *strives to conceal the pistol.*) Of course. Job Wescott.

WESCOTT: Yes, sir. (MILLER *and* WESCOTT *stand stiffly at attention, their hands behind them.*)

GREENE: Pardon Miller and Tom Bailey. It's been some time since I've talked to you men. How have you been?

WESCOTT: All right, General.

BAILEY: Getting along, General. (WESCOTT *endeavors to drop a small package he is holding, but he is unable to do so without having* GREENE *notice.*)

GREENE: Pleased to hear it. Mind if I sit down and talk to you for a spell?

MILLER: Er—no, General, not at all. (GREENE *sits down on a bag of potatoes.*)

GREENE: Ah! There! Of course maybe I shouldn't be sitting on such a precious object as a bag of potatoes. Food isn't exactly plentiful around camp, is it?

BAILEY (*Uncomfortably*): Guess not.

GREENE: For example, tonight Mrs. Greene and I each had a baked potato for our supper. Wasn't bad at that. I've even managed to get Mrs. Greene to eat her skins. She's gotten so she likes them. But we won't be eating potato skins much longer. We'll soon be getting some decent food.

MILLER (*Bitterly*): You mean you officers will be getting it.

GREENE: We officers? You're mistaken, Miller. These new supplies are for everyone. Everyone is to share alike. Of course, perhaps I shouldn't be telling you men all this; but I feel so good about it that I just can't keep quiet. So we'll call it sort of a Christmas present. All of us deserve something better than we've been getting for the past few months. Been hard on all of us, eh?

BAILEY (*Bitterly*): Mighty hard, General.

GREENE: You Rhode Island men have taken it with good grace. I'm proud of you, and I want to take this opportunity to thank you personally. You, Miller, I haven't forgotten how gallantly you behaved at Princeton. When this is over, Congress will reward you for your courage.

MILLER (*Uneasily*): It wasn't anything.

GREENE: You, Wescott, I recall that you were wounded at the Brandywine. And you, Bailey, you've always been a first-rate soldier. Would that the Continental Army had more men of your calibre.

WESCOTT: Thankee, General.

BAILEY: Yes, sir.

GREENE: I'm glad to learn that you three men haven't become discouraged. We still have a long hard row ahead. It's going to take a lot more self-sacrifice to win, but we'll come through. By the way, you three are all married, aren't you? (*All three men nod.*) I thought so. Well, that means that all three of you have more to fight for. It means that you are fighting not only for personal liberty, but also the liberty of your children. None of us here may benefit to any great degree by this liberty; but our children will.

BAILEY: I pray that that is so.

WESCOTT: But we're paying a mighty big price for our liberty.

MILLER (*Sadly*): Farms going to pieces. No one to tend to them.

GREENE: We're all sacrificing something. Back home my own business has gone to nothing. Financially, I'm almost ruined. But what matter! That places me in the same boat as you three men.

MILLER: Maybe it does.

GREENE: I'm glad that you men have kept your heads and haven't attempted to desert. Tonight they brought in a deserter. Poor chap! He was half frozen.

WESCOTT: What will they do to him, General?

GREENE: Ordinarily he'd either be shot or hanged. But I'm going to intercede with General Washington in his behalf. The poor lad must have been temporarily out of his head. Yes, I think I can get him off with a light punishment. It would be a shame to see such a young life snuffed out because of one heedless act on his part. After all, we need every man.

MILLER: That's right, sir.

GREENE: I'm mighty glad that this deserter I speak of wasn't from your regiment.

BAILEY: How do you mean that, General Greene?

GREENE: If he had been, and I had interceded for him, my brother officers would have said that I was prejudiced just because he was a Rhode Islander.

BAILEY: So they would have.

WESCOTT: That's so.

MILLER: And that would have put you in a bad light.

GREENE (*Starting to leave*): Well, I must be getting back. (*He turns and pauses.*) I have an idea. This is Christmas Eve, a time to celebrate. Suppose the four of us repair to my quarters. It's much warmer there. We can talk in comfort. How does that strike you? (*The three soldiers stare at each other in uncertainty.*) Fine! Suppose we go. (GREENE *starts again for door, followed by the men. He pauses and turns to* WESCOTT.) Oh, Job Wescott?

WESCOTT: Yes, sir?

GREENE: I'm sure all of us would enjoy a steaming mug of something warm to drink. You may as well take along that sack of tea you're holding. (*Quick curtain*)

THE END

Paul Revere of Boston

A man of many talents

by Eleanora Bowling Kane

Characters

READER
PAUL REVERE, *as a boy of 12*
ABIGAIL, *a neighbor's child*
DEBORAH REVERE, *16*
FRANCES REVERE, *11*
THOMAS REVERE, *8*
JOHN REVERE, *6* ⎬ *Paul's sisters and brothers*
MARY REVERE, *4*
ELIZABETH REVERE, *3*
MR. APOLLOS REVERE, *Paul's father*
MRS. DEBORAH REVERE, *Paul's mother*
PAUL REVERE, *as a man*
DR. JOSEPH WARREN, *leading patriot*
MRS. WARREN, *his wife*
JOHN GRISWOLD
JAMES ⎬ *members of Sons of Liberty*
MAN

SCENE 1

BEFORE RISE: *Lights dim, as dramatic music and sound of galloping hoofs are heard. Spotlight falls on* READER *at lectern, down left, as the music fades.*

READER (*Reading from book on stand*):
Listen, my children, and you shall hear
Of the midnight ride of Paul Revere,

On the eighteenth of April, in Seventy-five;
Hardly a man is now alive
Who remembers that famous day and year.

(READER *closes book and speaks to audience*.) You all know the beginning of Henry Wadsworth Longfellow's famous poem, "Paul Revere's Ride." But Paul Revere was more than a patriot, a messenger of freedom. He was a versatile craftsman who contributed much to early America. He was a silversmith, engraver, publisher, and manufacturer of such different products as church bells and picture frames. Even as a boy, Paul was clever. (*Curtains open, as* READER *exits.*)

* * *

TIME: *1747.*

SETTING: *The kitchen of the Revere house in Boston. There is a window at rear next to a large fireplace. Several chairs, one large sofa or wing chair are beside fireplace, and a spinning wheel and various accessories of the Colonial period stand right. Gun, bowl and pipe are on mantel. There is a door right, leading outside, and a door left leading to rest of house.*

AT RISE: PAUL REVERE, *as a boy, is stretched out on floor next to spinning wheel, trying to repair it. He pushes treadle with his hands, nods, and then rises and tries the spinning wheel, adjusting it as he uses it. From offstage, voices of* PAUL's *brothers and sisters are heard. Then they pass window, singing "On the Bridge of Avignon." Door bursts open, right, and* DEBORAH, FRANCES, THOMAS, JOHN, MARY *and* ELIZABETH REVERE *enter, followed by* ABIGAIL, *a neighbor's child.* DEBORAH *empties nuts from her apron into bowl.* THOMAS *stirs fire.* FRANCES *gets her sampler, sits, and starts to embroider. Other children flop onto chairs or floor.*

ABIGAIL: Paul, you did it! You repaired my mother's spinning wheel. I told her you could, but she said no child could fix it. Won't she be surprised?

THOMAS: Why should she be? Paul can fix anything, even the back bar in this fireplace. It fell down while Father was in the shop and Paul took care of it, and he mended the iron pot in the fireplace, too.

DEBORAH (*Holding up bowl of nuts*): Look, Paul, we gathered these nuts, but there really aren't very many of them.

JOHN (*Coming over and shaking the bowl*): I'm afraid Mother will be disappointed. I think she expected more than this.

FRANCES: It's all *your* fault, Paul.

PAUL: My fault? Why, I wasn't even there.

ABIGAIL (*Laughing*): That's why it's your fault. If you had been with us we'd have found more. You always know where the best nut trees are.

THOMAS: Oh, let's forget those stupid things. (*Goes over to mantel and picks up gun*) What I want is to learn about shooting, but Father won't let me. He says I'm just a little too young. But, Paul, you are a very good shot. Father's proud of you.

PAUL: You'll learn, Thomas. In this New World all boys and men must know how to shoulder a musket—it's necessary. By the way, speaking of Father, I heard you singing that old French song Father loves. But he likes to hear you sing it in French, not in English.

FRANCES: It's too hard for the little ones to sing in French. We need your help to teach it to them.

PAUL: And you have it. Is everyone ready to sing the Bridge of Avignon? (*Children, laughing and ad libbing, form a circle and dance as they sing "Sur le Pont d'Avignon" in French, with* PAUL *leading them. During the end of the song,* MR. *and* MRS. REVERE *enter right.*)

ELIZABETH: It's Papa and Mama! (ELIZABETH, MARY, JOHN *and* THOMAS *clamor excitedly around their parents.*)

DEBORAH: Here, Mother, let me take your shawl. (MR. *and* MRS. REVERE *sit and children gather around them.*)

MR. REVERE: Ah, *mes enfants,* it's nice to hear your happy singing, and in the tongue of my country, too. I do not hear it often.

MARY: Paul is teaching us how to sing in French.

MRS. REVERE (*Sternly*): I trust, my dears, that your singing game meant that you have finished your chores. (*Children nod.*)

THOMAS: We finished dipping the candles, Mother.

ELIZABETH: And they smell *so* good—like bayberries!

JOHN: The candles are hanging in the shed, Mother.

DEBORAH: And we finished the churning.

MARY: But my arms are tired, Mother. Churning is hard work.

ABIGAIL (*Going to spinning wheel*): Mistress Revere, did you know that Paul mended my mother's spinning wheel? 'Twas a difficult thing to do.

MRS. REVERE: Indeed it was. We're very proud of Paul.

MR. REVERE: And of all of our little Reveres. They have been very good children today.

ELIZABETH (*Hugging* MR. REVERE): Since we have been good, Father, will you tell us a story, please?

THOMAS: The old story, Father, about how you came over here.

MR. REVERE: What, that old story again?

PAUL: Yes, Father, please.

FRANCES: Don't leave any out—the name part, too, Father.

MR. REVERE (*Groaning in mock despair*): If I must, I must. But you know, I am a much better silversmith than I am a story-teller. (*Children arrange themselves comfortably on floor.* PAUL *gets wooden bowl from mantel, sits, and starts carving a design on it.*) Well, now. Once upon a time, there was a family in France called de Rivoire. They lived very happily, this family, in a chateau most elegant, situated on a shining river. *Enfin.* Because they were Huguenots, they were badly treated by some of their countrymen, and they had to flee from their beloved France because of their religion.

THOMAS (*Interrupting*): And one of them named Simon de Rivoire went to an island in the English Channel.

MR. REVERE: And to him came his nephew—just a young lad— named Apollos.

FRANCES: That was you, Father.

JOHN: Of course, it was. Stop interrupting the story.

MR. REVERE: Do not speak so harshly to your sister, my son.

JOHN: I'm sorry, but please hurry, Father, and get to the part where you went on the big ship.

PAUL: Now who's interrupting? Go on, Father.

MR. REVERE: *Eh bien,* the lad, only fourteen, crossed the gray, angry seas to a city in the colonies, called Boston. Here he learned the trade of a silversmith and came to like Boston.

PAUL: So he decided to stay.

DEBORAH: But he changed his name from Rivoire to Revere.

MR. REVERE (*Laughing*): So the bumpkins might pronounce it better.

MRS. REVERE: And then he met a beautiful young lady . . .

PAUL: Named Deborah . . .

MR. REVERE: And he married her.

PAUL: And lived happily ever after . . . !

ELIZABETH (*Jumping up*): With seven *beautiful* girls and boys! (*All laugh, as children stand and drift offstage, humming "Sur le Pont d'Avignon."* PAUL *and* FRANCES *remain.*)

FRANCES: Will you help me with my sampler, Mother? (FRANCES *and* MRS. REVERE *examine the sampler.* MR. REVERE *gets his pipe at the mantel, and strolls back to watch* PAUL *at his carving.*)

MR. REVERE: Paul, that leaf pattern you are carving is quite good. Did you make a drawing first?

PAUL: Yes, Father. I did just what you told me to do. But I'm tired of carving *wood.* I want to work with you in the shop. I want to make lovely things out of *silver,* the way you do. I want to stand in the shop when the ladies come and hear them say (*Mockingly*), "What a perfectly exquisite teapot, Master Revere!" I want to make the most beautiful silver in America.

MR. REVERE: You have many talents, my little Paul, and some-day—yes, I think someday, you will carve yourself a place in this new world. (*Curtain*)

* * * * *

SCENE 2

TIME: *Spring of 1775.*

SETTING: *Paul Revere's silversmith shop. The window has a sign reading,* P. REVERE, SILVERSMITH. *On the mantel are pieces of silver: trays, candlesticks, bowls, etc. There is a counter at right with other silver pieces, including a teapot and tray. There is a bench behind counter. A fireplace is at rear, and a door at right leads outside.*

AT RISE: PAUL REVERE, *as a man, is behind counter.* MRS. WARREN, *in front of counter, holds tray.*

MRS. WARREN: Yes, Master Revere, I like it very much. Very much indeed. It's a beautiful piece of work.

PAUL: Thank you, Mrs. Warren. I had a good teacher, my father. I entered this shop for my training at the age of 19, and since my father's death, I have continued the business.

MRS. WARREN: Indeed you have, and most successfully, too. Yours is the most beautiful silver in the colonies.

PAUL: Then you are satisfied with the tray?

MRS. WARREN: Quite satisfied, Master Revere. (*She puts down tray and picks up teapot.*) You know, I did want a new teapot, but with the present tax on tea, I don't know when we'll be drinking it again. (*She puts it down.*) Will the tray be ready next week?

PAUL: It will be ready, Mrs. Warren.

MRS. WARREN: I shall ask my husband to stop by for it. That is, if I can tear him away from his meetings. He's always meeting with somebody—the Sons of Liberty . . . the Sons of This . . . the Sons of That. I vow, I do believe he lives at "The Green Dragon" these days.

PAUL: "The Green Dragon" is more than an inn. It is a very cradle of liberty, Mrs. Warren, and your husband is a leader we are proud of. With men like him, John Hancock, and Samuel Adams, we need not fear the British!

MRS. WARREN: Which reminds me. My husband told me that you are being sent to Philadelphia today by the Sons of Liberty. Do you expect to bring us exciting news?

PAUL: In these times, madam, all of the news is exciting. In Philadelphia I shall hear what is happening in the other colonies. (*He puts on his tricorn hat and looks around the shop as he prepares to leave.*) Will you tell your husband that I am on my way?

MRS. WARREN: I certainly will. Off to Philadelphia!

PAUL: Yes, Mrs. Warren. Off to Philadelphia! (*They exit, as curtain closes.*)

* * * * *

SCENE 3

TIME: *Night, several weeks later.*

SETTING: *The same as Scene 2.*

AT RISE: JOHN GRISWOLD *and* JAMES *enter. They take off their cloaks and hats and pretend to light fire.*

JAMES (*Rubbing his hands*): Well, John Griswold, that's better. Now we can see. All we have to do is wait for Revere and the others.

JOHN: Do you think Revere will get here in time for this meeting?

JAMES: Undoubtedly. Dr. Warren very definitely expects him. He should bring dispatches of interest to the Sons of Liberty.

JOHN: I'm glad I could come tonight. I shouldn't like to miss Revere's news. He has worked hard as express rider for the Sons of Liberty.

JAMES: With little pay, too. I understand that he is hard put to make money to support his family.

JOHN (*Picking up a piece of silver*): He is devoting most of his time to the patriotic cause, and his business suffers.

JAMES (*Looking off*): Here come the others. Now we'll hear some news. (DR. WARREN *enters with* MAN.)

JOHN: Good evening, gentlemen.

DR. WARREN: Good evening, John Griswold. Any sign of Revere? I have news for him and all of us, of the utmost importance.

JOHN: No word as yet, sir.

MAN: Don't be too sure of that. I've news of him, right here. (*They become excited and* MAN *laughs and waves a newspaper.*) Oh, not the kind of news you mean. It's a notice in the *Gazette*. Our friend Paul Revere announces to the city of Boston that he will design and make *artificial* teeth! Now, that's what I call a strange occupation for a silversmith.

JOHN: Not at all. Paul Revere can do anything!

JAMES: Except get to the Sons of Liberty meeting on time.

DR. WARREN: It is absolutely imperative that Revere be here tonight. I have news of such importance that I must tell you all immediately. I shall not wait for him. (PAUL *enters hastily, flinging off his coat and hat.*)

PAUL (*Moving forward*): And you won't have to wait, Dr. Warren. I bring messages from the Sons of Liberty in Philadelphia—one for Mr. Adams, and this one for you, sir. (PAUL *hands the message to* DR. WARREN.)

DR. WARREN: Good work, Paul, but there is something of even greater importance brewing. Listen: Adams and Hancock are at Lexington. We have definite word that the British plan to move inland, capture our leaders, and seize our supplies at Concord. The country folk must be warned. You are our express rider, Paul. We rely on you for this. (*There are ad lib exclamations of excitement.*)

PAUL (*Quickly*): How will the British go?

DR. WARREN: They have a choice. They may go by Roxbury Neck—a long march. They may cross the Charles River in boats to Cambridge.

PAUL (*Frowning*): Hm-m . . . it will be necessary for me to know their route. Can you find a way to let me know?

DR. WARREN: We'll arrange a signal for you as soon as we learn which way they are going.

PAUL: Good! Let it be by lantern. We'll do it this way. I'll watch the tower of the North Church. If they go by land, burn one lantern in the belfry. If they go by sea, light *two*. I shall be off as soon as I see your signal. (*Curtain closes and lights dim. Sound of galloping horse is heard.*)

* * * *

SCENE 4

BEFORE RISE: READER *stands in front of curtain as lights come up. A clock is heard striking twelve.* NOTE: *While poem is being read, several actors may enter and pantomime the action, if desired.*

READER:

And lo! as he looks, on the belfry's height
A glimmer, and then a gleam of light!
He springs to the saddle, the bridle he turns,
But lingers and gazes, till full on his sight
A second lamp in the belfry burns. . . .
   (*Sound of galloping starts and then fades.*)

It was twelve by the village clock
When he crossed the bridge into Medford town.
He heard the crowing of the cock,
And the barking of the farmer's dog,
And felt the damp of the river fog
That rises after the sun goes down.

It was one by the village clock
When he galloped into Lexington.
He saw the gilded weathercock
Swim in the moonlight as he passed,
And the meeting-house windows, blank and bare,
Gazed at him with a spectral glare . . . .

It was two by the village clock
When he came to the bridge in Concord town.
He heard the bleating of the flock,
And the twitter of birds among the trees,

And felt the breath of the morning breeze
Blowing over the meadows brown . . . .

You know the rest; in the books you have read,
How the British regulars fired and fled—
How the farmers gave them ball for ball,
From behind each fence and farmyard wall,
Chasing the red-coats down the lane,
Then crossing the fields to emerge again
Under the trees at the turn of the road,
And only pausing to fire and load.

So through the night rode Paul Revere,
And so through the night went his cry of alarm
To every Middlesex village and farm,—
A cry of defiance, and not of fear,
A voice in the darkness, a knock at the door,
And a word that shall echo for evermore!
(READER *exits and curtain rises.*)

*   *   *

TIME: *After the Revolution.*

SETTING: *Revere's shop, as in Scene 2, but with another counter,
displaying hardware, as well as lengths of fabric, necklaces,
lockets, bracelets, etc. Sign in the window now reads,* P. REVERE,
SILVERSMITH, HARDWARE.

AT RISE: REVERE, *now 51, is arranging his stock.* JOHN GRISWOLD
enters.

JOHN: Good morrow, Paul. Getting your new merchandise ready,
I see.

PAUL: Yes, I thought that running a hardware store would be
much more profitable than just silversmithing.

JOHN: There's room for all kinds of businesses in this new land
of ours, Paul (*Proudly*); our new country, free from England,
ours! And what a lively part *we* played to make it so, eh, Paul?

PAUL (*Laughing*): We were busy—no denying that.

JOHN: Especially you. All that you did for the Sons of Liberty—
your ride to warn the farmers. Now, there's something that'll
go down in history.

PAUL: I don't know why, but to tell you the truth, John, I rather
fancy some of my other jobs during the late war.

JOHN: Like that gunpowder mill you built? That was quite a feat, I'll admit.

PAUL: Do you know what I was really proud of? The order to print currency from copper plates so the soldiers could be paid. And I'm working right now on establishing a mill for rolling copper into flat sheets. This should be a most interesting development.

JOHN: Well, you're the one to do it. You can do anything. Remember that time that General Washington ordered you to go to Fort Castle William to repair some damaged cannon?

PAUL (*Going to silversmith bench*): Ah, yes. That was quite a challenge. The General wanted me to devise a new type of carriage for those cannon. It was a most unusual assignment. (*He starts rubbing a piece of silver with a cloth.*) But there will be many new challenging things to do in our country, now that the struggle is over. I shall look forward to them most eagerly.

JOHN: And you will do them successfully, I'm sure. You always have. Even when we were children, we always said it was you who could do anything. Yes, Paul, there's no doubt about it. You'll become famous as Paul Revere, the versatile citizen! (*PAUL laughs and shakes his head, then goes back to polishing, as curtain closes.*)

THE END

An Imaginary Trial of George Washington

The Father of Our Country takes the stand

by Diana Wolman

Characters

JUDGE, *appointed by the King of England*
BAILIFF
LORD NORTH, *attorney for the Crown*
JOHN ADAMS, *attorney for the defense*
GEORGE WASHINGTON, *the defendant*
TOM PAINE
JOHN HANCOCK
RICHARD HENRY LEE
THOMAS JEFFERSON
PATRICK HENRY
BENEDICT ARNOLD
PAUL REVERE ⎫ *witnesses*
MARY HAYES (MOLLY PITCHER)
ETHAN ALLEN
RACHEL SALOMON
MARQUIS DE LAFAYETTE
DEBORAH GANNET
BENJAMIN FRANKLIN
CITIZENS

SCENE 1

TIME: *1780.*

SETTING: *A courtroom in Colonial America. Judge's bench, a large table, is at right. There is a chair behind table, and a British flag stands beside chair. The witness stand is at center. Several rows of chairs at left, facing center, represent the gallery. In front of first row of chairs are two tables, each with papers and documents on it, one for the defense and the other for the Crown.*

AT RISE: JUDGE *sits at bench. Witnesses and* CITIZENS *sit in gallery.* ADAMS *and* WASHINGTON *sit in first row, at one table.* LORD NORTH *stands center, holding document.* BAILIFF *holds long wooden staff.*

BAILIFF (*Striking floor with long wooden staff*): Hear ye, hear ye! The trial of George Washington for treason against the British Crown is now in session.

JUDGE (*Striking gavel on table*): Lord North, as lawyer for the Crown, will you please read the bill of particulars?

NORTH (*Reading from legal document*): First: After pledging loyalty to his country and his king, as subject and officer, George Washington has taken up arms against his government in an effort to overthrow it. Second: He has conspired with other subjects of His Majesty to overthrow the rightfully established government of England by force and violence. Third: He has surrounded himself with people of low character—anarchists, robbers, smugglers—who have incited the people to riot and he has made treasonous statements in public. (NORTH *places document on* JUDGE's *table*)

JUDGE: George Washington, step forward. (WASHINGTON *steps forward to face* JUDGE.) How do you plead, guilty or not guilty?

WASHINGTON: Before God and man, as history is my witness, I am *not* guilty!

JUDGE: Take the stand. (WASHINGTON *walks to witness stand, sits.* NORTH *approaches witness stand.*)

NORTH: Your full name, please.

WASHINGTON: George Washington.

NORTH: Where and when were you born?

WASHINGTON: February 22, 1732, at Bridges Creek, Virginia.

NORTH: Occupation?

WASHINGTON: Farmer.

NORTH (*Surprised*): A farmer, did you say?

WASHINGTON (*Proudly*): Yes. To me there is nothing more rewarding than to plant and watch living things grow. I would like above all to be able to return to my beloved Mt. Vernon.

NORTH (*With sarcasm*): And can you explain just how you, a

lover of the land, became Commander-in-Chief of this handful of rebellious subjects?

WASHINGTON: This honor came to me by default, so to speak. *All* of us are farmers, or workers, or merchants. We are not soldiers by training or desire. I, at least, had some experience as an officer under General Braddock in the recent French and Indian War. In the spring of 1775, five years ago, the Second Continental Congress appointed me Commander-in-Chief of the Continental Army, and this responsibility I undertook with great humility and a sense of duty.

NORTH (*Interrupting angrily*): May I interpose here, Your Lordship, that this man is most responsible for all our troubles today. I can show that it was Washington and probably Washington alone who kept the Revolution alive. He was the only man among these rebels who combined military experience with a sense of organization and an ability to deal with men. Oh, I am willing to admit his personal superiority of character and love for justice. But, in the year and a half from November 1776 to the spring of 1778, the Revolution would have collapsed on many occasions had we killed or captured this one man.

PAINE (*In gallery; rising*): Aye, those were the times that tried men's souls. I remember well that bitter winter at Valley Forge. The summer soldier and the sunshine patriot will always shrink from service to his country.

JUDGE (*Looking up over his spectacles at* PAINE): You, there, what is your name?

PAINE: Tom Paine. And I wish to say that—

JUDGE (*Angrily*): Your turn will come. Indeed, it will! (PAINE *sits.* NORTH *takes seat in first row of gallery at left.* JUDGE *turns to* ADAMS) Mr. Adams, as lawyer for George Washington, do you have anything to say at this time?

ADAMS (*Rising*): I would like to ask the defendant some questions, if I may. (*Approaches witness stand*) General Washington, what duties have you performed in the past?

WASHINGTON: I have been a surveyor, a soldier, an officer. . . .

ADAMS: And how did you carry on these activities?

WASHINGTON: Very faithfully, Mr. Adams. I have always been loyal to my work and to my superiors.

ADAMS: What was your attitude toward the conflict with the English government at first?

WASHINGTON (*Slowly*): At first I never dreamed of separation from our mother country. Even after I became Commander-in-Chief, we officers would nightly toast King George's health. (*Soberly*) But now I am convinced that separation is the only possible solution.

ADAMS: Thank you. That will be all. (*Nods to* WASHINGTON, *who leaves stand and returns to seat.* NORTH *rises, walks over to stand before* JUDGE.)

NORTH: Your Lordship, I intend to prove to you that Washington has surrounded himself with men of low and treasonous character and I have witnesses to prove it. I now call to the stand John Hancock. (HANCOCK *comes to witness stand.* NORTH *picks up copy of Declaration of Independence and approaches* HANCOCK.) You are a smuggler by trade. Is that not correct?

HANCOCK: No, sir, a merchant, a rather wealthy merchant, I am glad to say, but one who respectfully disregards the hated duties imposed on our imports.

JUDGE (*Sarcastically*): I see. I shall write down—John Hancock, smuggler. (*Picks up pen*)

HANCOCK (*Angrily*): You may write what you please, but I, too, have written, knowing full well what the consequences might be. I was the first to sign the Declaration of Independence, and I signed it in large bold letters to make sure that George the Third could read it without his spectacles. (*Laughter from gallery*)

JUDGE (*Striking table with gavel*): Order in the court!

NORTH: That will be all, Mr. Hancock. (HANCOCK *leaves witness stand, returns to his seat.*) Indeed, I wish to speak about that hateful document, which I now hold in my hand. Will Richard Henry Lee please take the stand? (LEE *rises and walks to witness stand.*) Mr. Lee, can you identify the document that I am now holding?

LEE: Certainly. That is the Declaration of Independence.

NORTH: And what was your connection with this piece of treachery?

ADAMS (*Jumping up*): I object, Your Lordship, to the prosecutor's use of such prejudiced language to describe this noble expression of the free spirit of man.

JUDGE (*Dryly*): Objection overruled. (ADAMS *sits*.)

LEE: I am proud to state here that I am the one who made the original motion concerning independence, at the Continental Congress. May I read it to you? (*Takes paper from pocket and reads*) "RESOLVED: that these united colonies are, and ought to be, free and independent states; that they are absolved from all allegiance to the British Crown, and that all political connection between them and the state of Great Britain, is, and ought to be, totally dissolved."

NORTH (*Angrily*): You will live to regret this rash notion of yours.

LEE (*Proudly*): On the contrary, I am proud of what I said on that momentous occasion (*Continues reading*), "Let this happy day give birth to a new nation." In my opinion, July 4th will, in the future, be regarded as the birthday of these United States.

NORTH (*With disgust*): That is quite enough.

ADAMS (*Stepping forward to witness chair as* NORTH *sits down*): Now I would like to ask the witness: What is your opinion of General Washington?

LEE (*Admiringly*): Washington is more than a general. He is the embodiment of all that is noblest and best in the American people. Not only has he willingly served without pay, but from his own pocket he has bought clothing for his men and sent aid to the destitute families of his companions in battle. I prophesy that Washington will go down in history as first in war, first in peace, and first in the hearts of his countrymen.

ADAMS: Thank you, Mr. Lee. (*Spontaneous applause from gallery as* LEE *returns to seat.* ADAMS *follows.* NORTH *rises.*)

NORTH: I call Thomas Jefferson to the stand. (JEFFERSON *walks up to stand, sits down.*) I ask you, sir, whether you recognize this paper.

JEFFERSON: Yes, I do.

NORTH: Will you read the opening words?

JEFFERSON (*Reading*): "In Congress, July 4, 1776, Unanimous Declaration of the United States of America . . ."

NORTH: Would you please state briefly in your own words, Mr. Jefferson, the purpose of that Declaration.

JEFFERSON: We wished to make known to the world why we moved to declare our independence from the government of

Great Britain. We listed the reasons for our act, including the tyrannical action of the present British king. We presented also—

NORTH (*Interrupting; impatiently*): Would you say, Mr. Jefferson, that the words of the Declaration of Independence are, in truth, *your* very own words? Is it not true that *you,* in fact, are the author of this treacherous paper? (*Brandishes paper*)

JEFFERSON: Sir, I had the honor to be chosen by my colleagues at the Continental Congress to help in the writing of this document.

NORTH: Do you accept the doctrines announced in the paper?

ADAMS (*From seat*): Objection!

JUDGE (*Reluctantly*): Lord North, this line of questioning should not be continued, since Mr. Jefferson is not now on trial.

NORTH (*To* JUDGE): Very well. I wish, sir, to submit this Declaration to be marked Exhibit A.

JUDGE: Is there evidence that the defendant, George Washington, signed this document?

NORTH: No, sir, he did not sign it, but we shall introduce conclusive evidence that the defendant in fact supported the views of the Declaration.

JUDGE: Admitted. (NORTH *hands document to* JUDGE.)

NORTH (*To* JUDGE): I have no further questions for the witness, Your Lordship. (JEFFERSON *leaves stand and returns to his seat.*)

JUDGE: Who is your next witness, Lord North?

NORTH: Patrick Henry, of Virginia.

JUDGE: Patrick Henry, step forth! (HENRY *stands up at his seat.*) Take the stand. (*He goes to witness stand.*)

NORTH: You are a Virginian?

HENRY: The distinction between New Yorkers, New Englanders, Virginians, and Pennsylvanians, is no more. I am not a Virginian, sir. I am an American.

JUDGE: Yes, I hear you've been inventing that word lately. And you have been making treasonous statements, haven't you?

HENRY: What I said is merely that Caesar had his Brutus, Charles the First his Cromwell, and George the Third . . .

JUDGE (*Striking gavel on table*): Treason!

HENRY (*Continuing calmly*): . . . and George the Third may profit by their example. If *this* be treason, make the most of it.

JUDGE: Do you realize what you are saying, you bold young man? You shall hang for this!

HENRY: Is life so dear or peace so sweet as to be purchased at the price of chains and slavery? Forbid it, Almighty God! I know not what course others may take, but as for me, give me liberty or give me death!

JEFFERSON (*Speaking from his seat*): He speaks the way Homer wrote.

JUDGE: You will hang, all right, you may be sure of that. (*To* JEFFERSON) And you, too, Mr. Jefferson.

FRANKLIN (*From his seat*): We must all hang together, or assuredly we shall all hang separately. (*Applause from gallery*)

JUDGE (*Enraged*): Order in the court, or I shall clear the room!

NORTH: Your Lordship, I can prove that the rebels who follow Washington are not only traitors to their king and government, lawbreakers and men of low character, but they are godless creatures, unnatural in their behavior and blasphemous to God himself. In proof, I now call forth the next witness, Thomas Paine. (PAINE *goes to witness stand, faces* JUDGE. JUDGE *holds up book.*)

JUDGE: I have here a copy of an abominable piece of writing called *The Age of Reason,* by one Thomas Paine, in which the author denies all religion and all established churches of God. Are you the author of this, Mr. Paine?

PAINE: I am. And if I am on trial for having written it, then I say that I am guilty of believing that this is an age of reason— that human beings should use their common sense and not merely follow what other generations before them believed or said.

NORTH: What do you believe in exactly, Citizen Paine?

PAINE: As I have written: The world is my country. All mankind are my brethren. To do good is my religion. I believe in one God and no more.

NORTH: You have only recently come to this land, haven't you?

PAINE: Four years ago, in 1776.

NORTH: And what was your work in England?

PAINE: At various times I have been a stay-maker, a cobbler, a civil servant, and a laborer in a weaver's shop.

NORTH: How did you get to America?

PAINE: I was fortunate enough to secure a letter from Benjamin Franklin when he was in England.

NORTH: And you have been preaching armed rebellion ever since, have you not?

PAINE: It is my belief that the period of debate is closed. Arms, as the last resort, must decide the contest.

NORTH: You admit that, then, do you?

PAINE: Admit, indeed! I boast of it. Why, it is only common sense. Why should a huge continent be tied to a little island thousands of miles away? Why should the colonists submit to laws which hurt their trade and industry? Why—

JUDGE: And just what do you think will happen when rabble like you take over and make your *own* government?

PAINE: Independence would result in a democratic form of government and establish in America an asylum for mankind, a haven of refuge for the oppressed peoples of the world. We have every opportunity and encouragement before us to form the noblest, purest constitution on the face of the earth. We have it in our power to begin the world all over again.

NORTH: If you are finished, Mr. Paine, you may leave the stand! (PAINE *leaves witness stand and returns to his seat.*)

JUDGE: Who is your next witness, Lord North?

NORTH: The next witness will be someone who actually heard George Washington incite soldiers to fight their king, someone who saw him make plans to rebel against the rightful government of these colonies, one who can identify him as the chief ringleader of the rebellion—a man who only last week had breakfast with him. I now call to the stand—Benedict Arnold. (BAILIFF *crosses left.*)

BAILIFF (*Calling offstage*): Benedict Arnold! (ARNOLD *enters, as witnesses and* CITIZENS *stare at him in surprise.*)

CITIZENS (*Ad lib; shouting*): Traitor! Informer! (*Etc.* JUDGE *pounds gavel angrily.*)

JUDGE: Order in the court! (ARNOLD *takes witness stand.* CITIZENS *are quiet.*)

NORTH: What is your name?

ARNOLD: Benedict Arnold.

NORTH: Have you ever seen the defendant before?

ARNOLD: Many times.

NORTH: What do you know about him?

ARNOLD: I have heard him make plans for the defeat of the British Army. I heard him order that Paine's book, *Common Sense,* be read aloud to all his troops to make them more willing to fight.

NORTH: Is there anything else?

ARNOLD: One time, when the officers and the soldiers had not been paid for a long period and their wives and families were close to starving, a number of Continental officers were ready to revolt. They were stopped from doing so by a letter from George Washington, asking them to act for the good of their cause and not according to their personal desires.

NORTH: Thank you. You have done a real service to His Majesty today.

ARNOLD: I am glad to have this chance to serve my king and to make amends for my former disloyalty.

ADAMS (*From seat; sarcastically*): *And* to get paid 6,000 British pounds.

JUDGE (*Sharply*): You are out of order, Mr. Adams. Proceed, Lord North.

NORTH: Mr. Arnold, what was your position with Washington?

ARNOLD: I was a commanding officer. I took part in the famous battle of Saratoga and was largely responsible for Burgoyne's surrender.

NORTH: How do you feel about those activities now?

ARNOLD: I am willing to speak freely of the days when I erred. Truly I was a dupe. I now realize that I was wrong when I worked for the overthrow of His Majesty, King George the Third. I was blinded and full of false ideas. I wish to atone for those days and will eagerly identify any of the rebels you may wish me to point out.

NORTH: Thank you, Mr. Arnold. That is all for now. (BENEDICT ARNOLD *steps down from stand and takes a seat in gallery.* CITIZENS *glare at him.*) Your Lordship, the Crown rests. (NORTH *crosses to sit in first row of gallery, behind prosecution table.* JOHN ADAMS *rises, crosses center.*)

JUDGE: As attorney for the defense, you may now proceed, Mr. Adams. (ADAMS *approaches* JUDGE.)

ADAMS: On trial today stands a man whose name will go down in history as the father of his country, whose picture will be revered throughout the civilized world as the image of liberty and freedom. He is guilty only of following the Lord's will that truth should be told and that freedom be proclaimed throughout the land. I will show you that the colonies suffered long and grievously before they took the extreme measure of armed rebellion, and that they took this step only after all other measures failed because of the obstinacy of the British government. I will show that the followers of Washington are men and women from all walks of life, from town and country, from north, south and even the frontier. They are Presbyterians, Jews, Frenchmen, Germans, Poles, black men and white, frontiersmen and housewives.

JUDGE (*Testily*): Yes, yes, Mr. Adams—get on with your case.

ADAMS: Your Lordship, allow me to present character witnesses who will explain in their own words why they support George Washington and his struggle, of their own accord, without hope of award or glory. First I call to the stand that outstanding citizen of Boston, Paul Revere.

REVERE (*Walking up to stand*): I am glad to appear here on Washington's behalf and also to correct a false impression that the court may be getting.

JUDGE: What impression is that, Mr. Revere?

REVERE: Perhaps you have assumed up to now that all of us in the Revolution are merchants—or smugglers, as you choose to call them—or even rich farmers. As a matter of fact, the majority of us are workers, and it is we—mechanics, carpenters, rope makers, printers and joiners—who organized the Sons of Liberty.

JUDGE: I have heard of you. What is your trade—that is, when you are not riding a horse?

REVERE: Silversmith, sir . . . and as for the incident you are referring to, I was acting for the North End Club of the Sons of Liberty, and I am proud to say that it was our organization that prevented your men from capturing John Hancock at Lexington.

NORTH (*Jumping up*): Your Lordship, this insurrection has been brewing for a long time. Before you sits a member, nay, a leader of this mob, this mixed rabble of Scotch, Irish and other foreign vagabonds.

ADAMS: I object, Your Lordship. Paul Revere and his type are the very strength of our community. It is the firm patriotism of these workers that will save our country. (NORTH *sits down*.)

REVERE: Indeed it will. (*Boldly*) We are determined to fight up to our knees in blood rather than be ruled by tyrants, foreign or domestic. As our song goes (*Chants*)—

Come, rally, Sons of Liberty,
Come all with hearts united,
Our motto is "We Dare Be Free,"
Not easily affrighted!

ADAMS: Thank you, Mr. Revere. (REVERE *leaves stand, and returns to his seat.*) Allow me to present one such person who is not easily affrighted—Mrs. Mary Hayes! (MOLLY PITCHER *goes to witness stand.*) Please tell the court your full name.

MOLLY: Mary Ludwig Hayes, sir.

ADAMS: By what name are you better known?

MOLLY: Molly Pitcher.

ADAMS: And I am sure our grandchildren will remember you as Molly Pitcher. Tell me, how did you acquire this unusual nickname?

MOLLY: It was at the Battle of Monmouth, in New Jersey. As you will remember, the day of the battle was very hot. Our noble patriots, fighting for independence, naturally suffered from the heat. I moved among them, offering water from my pitcher.

ADAMS: And a brave thing that was, too. But I also know that you did even more. Tell the court about the rest of your action in that battle.

MOLLY: My husband was firing a cannon. Suddenly, he fell to the ground. Immediately, I ran to his cannon and continued to fire it. (*Proudly*) For this action George Washington gave me the rank of sergeant.

ADAMS (*Admiringly*): It was well deserved, and the cause must be a noble one to inspire a woman like you to take such drastic action. Thank you. That is all. (MOLLY PITCHER *bows and leaves stand, returning to her seat.*)

JUDGE: Who is your next witness?

ADAMS: Your Lordship, I wish to call to the stand Mr. Ethan Allen of Vermont. (ETHAN ALLEN *goes to witness stand.*)

JUDGE: Proceed with this witness.

ADAMS (*To* ALLEN): Tell the court your full name and place of birth.

ALLEN: My name is Ethan Allen, and I was born at Litchfield, Connecticut, on January 10, 1738.

ADAMS: Do you know the defendant, George Washington?

ALLEN: Yes, Mr. Adams, quite well.

ADAMS: Please tell us what you did during the years of 1771 through 1775 that brought you into contact with George Washington.

ALLEN: I was the leader of the Green Mountain Boys of New Connecticut, now called Vermont. It was our boys who captured Fort Ticonderoga on May 10, 1775.

ADAMS: What happened later?

ALLEN: On September 25, 1775, I was captured by the British near Montreal, and I remained their prisoner until I was exchanged on May 6, 1778.

ADAMS: Do you think your sacrifice worthwhile?

ALLEN (*Fervently*): I would do it all over again, if I had to, for the cause of the Revolution and for George Washington.

ADAMS: Your opinion of Washington is evidently high.

ALLEN (*Firmly*): The highest. He is a man of great courage and conviction to leave his comfortable home at Mt. Vernon to risk danger in war.

ADAMS: Thank you, Mr. Allen. (ETHAN ALLEN *returns to his seat.*)

JUDGE: Have you more witnesses?

ADAMS (*To* JUDGE): Yes, Your Lordship. My next witness is not a man of war but a woman who came here of her own free will, to explain how she and others like her feel about George Washington. I call to the stand Mrs. Rachel Salomon. (RACHEL SALOMON *approaches witness stand.*)

RACHEL: Thank you, Mr. Adams.

ADAMS: Will you explain why you came here today?

RACHEL: My husband, Haym, is now in jail, but I know that he wants me to tell the world why he and other Jews, like Benjamin Nones, for instance, have gladly supported the Revolutionary cause.

ADAMS: Tell us something about your husband.

RACHEL: My husband was born in Poland. Ten years ago, we were forced to flee that country because of the large part he was taking in the struggle for Polish independence. In 1772 we went to New York, where Haym became a financier. He gradually grew wealthy and became interested in the cause of independence. In 1776 he was arrested by the British and was supposed to be put to death, but he was released by the Hessians, whose language he could speak. Then, two years ago, he was put in jail again.

ADAMS: And does he believe in American independence?

RACHEL: Deeply. My husband is not a fighting man, but he has helped the cause by giving of his own money and by helping to raise more. I'll never forget that Yom Kippur night. Yom Kippur, Mr. Adams, is the holiest of holidays for us. Nothing in the world, I had always thought, would ever make my husband interrupt these services. But a messenger came right into the synagogue, informing us that Washington needed money desperately for his army. Right then and there, my husband took up a collection, and Washington had the funds he needed to carry on.

ADAMS: Why has Mr. Salomon been willing to risk his life, his wealth, all he has worked so hard to attain?

RACHEL: Perhaps the court will understand better when I read a part of a letter that George Washington sent to the Jewish community of Newport, Rhode Island. (*She takes letter from pocket.*) In his own words he has stated that (*Reads*) "the government of the United States will give to bigotry no sanction, to persecution no assistance." He has pledged to make America, once it is independent, a haven for all people of different faiths. At last Jews will have one country in which they can live and bring up their children without fear of persecution and banishment.

ADAMS: I am sure that your sentiments are shared by thousands of our fellow Americans. You may step down, Mrs. Salomon. (*She returns to her seat.*)

JUDGE (*To* ADAMS): Who is your next witness?

ADAMS: Your Lordship, our patriots have come from all over Europe. People who love mankind and hate oppression have come to our shores to help the cause of liberty. My next witness is the Marquis de Lafayette. (LAFAYETTE *goes to witness stand.*) Will you give your full name, please?

LAFAYETTE: Marie Joseph Paul Yves Roch Gilbert du Motier, Marquis de Lafayette.

ADAMS: Why did you leave your home and family to come to America?

LAFAYETTE: I came to America in 1778, at the age of nineteen, in defiance of my own king, because I wanted to help the cause of human freedom. At the first news of this quarrel, my heart was in it.

ADAMS: How did you manage to get here?

LAFAYETTE: I fitted out a ship which carried eleven other officers and myself to these shores.

ADAMS: Who were some of the people who came with you, or some other Europeans you met here?

LAFAYETTE: With me came the Baron de Kalb, who since died of his wounds at the battle of Camden. Also from Europe came Baron von Steuben of Prussia. From Poland came Thaddeus Kosciusko, an excellent artillery officer, and Count Casimir Pulaski, who unfortunately died at the battle of Savannah.

ADAMS: What happened to your ship?

LAFAYETTE: We were captured by the King of France, but managed to escape and resume our journey. After we landed at Georgetown, I traveled to Philadelphia and offered my services as a volunteer.

ADAMS: Tell us about your career in Washington's army.

LAFAYETTE: I immediately was made a major-general and was fortunate enough to become one of Washington's most trusted men. It was then that I came to respect and honor him. As a military man he was a genius, but even more important, he is the soul of fairness and humility.

ADAMS: I am glad that a man of your distinction was able to come to this courtroom today to speak in behalf of the defendant, George Washington. (LAFAYETTE *leaves stand.*)

LAFAYETTE (*As he returns to his seat*): I consider it an honor to speak for George Washington.

ADAMS: I now call Miss Deborah Gannet to the stand. (DEBORAH GANNET, *a young black woman, comes to witness stand.*) Will you give the court your full name, please?

DEBORAH: Deborah Gannet.

ADAMS: What is your occupation, Miss Gannet?

DEBORAH: Fighting for my country's freedom is my favorite one, sir, although I used to be a slave.

ADAMS: How do you know George Washington?

DEBORAH (*Proudly*): He is my commanding officer.

ADAMS: How can that be possible for you, a woman?

DEBORAH: After the Governor of Virginia offered slaves their freedom and fifty dollars to serve in the King's army, the American army gave us the same chance. I decided to disguise myself and enlist as a soldier under George Washington.

ADAMS: How long did you serve in the army?

DEBORAH: For seventeen months, I was a member of the Massachusetts regiment without anyone suspecting my real identity.

ADAMS: Do all the regiments have both white and black troops?

DEBORAH: Most of them. Only Georgia and South Carolina bar slaves from signing up. As a Bostonian, I'm sure you know that among the first to fall in the Boston Massacre was a former slave by the name of Crispus Attucks. And I am proud that it was one of my people, Peter Salem, who killed that boastful British Major John Pitcairn. And—

JUDGE (*Sharply*): That is enough!

ADAMS: Just one more question. Why were you willing to lead a hard soldier's life for so long?

DEBORAH: I can't help thinking of the words of your wife, Abigail Adams, when she wrote: "I wish most sincerely there was not a slave in the province; it always appeared a most iniquitous scheme to me to fight ourselves for what we are daily robbing and plundering from those who have as good a right to freedom as we have."

ADAMS: Thank you, Miss Gannet. That's all. (*She returns to her seat.*)

JUDGE: Who is your next witness, Mr. Adams?

ADAMS: I call Mr. Benjamin Franklin. (FRANKLIN, *wearing bifocal glasses and leaning on cane, comes up to stand.*) How old are you, Mr. Franklin?

FRANKLIN: Seventy-four years old.

ADAMS: And interesting years they have been, too—as well as useful ones.

FRANKLIN (*Modestly*): Well, you know what I say: Early to bed and early to rise makes a man healthy, wealthy and wise.

ADAMS: Tell the court something of your background, please.

FRANKLIN: I was apprenticed to my older brother in Boston, but I ran away at the age of seventeen. Since then I have been a writer, the publisher of a newspaper, and an inventor of sorts.

ADAMS: You are very modest, but this assemblage knows that you are the author of *Poor Richard's Almanac,* that you started our first public library, that you are the inventor of the famous Franklin stove, bifocal glasses—the kind Lord North is wearing (*Laughter from gallery*)—and a number of other household helps. But right now we are interested most in your official duties.

FRANKLIN: I represented the colonies in England in 1765.

ADAMS: What was your advice to the British Parliament concerning the Stamp Act?

FRANKLIN: I told them then that it could never work. It was my warning that if the British Army were sent to enforce it, a revolution might result.

ADAMS: Did you try in any other way to prevent this conflict?

FRANKLIN: Several times. The most recent was several years ago. I was negotiating with Lord Howe, on Staten Island. I suggested then that the matter could be peacefully settled by agreeing to our independence. But all he was instructed to offer was the King's clemency if we would stop fighting, with no guarantee of future liberty within the Empire. For years, Mr. Adams, I have striven to prevent just such a conflict as we are having now between brother and brother.

ADAMS: Despite your efforts, the conflict was not averted. What is your opinion of the situation today?

FRANKLIN: Once I wrote, "There never was a good war or a bad peace." Now I realize that rebellion against tyrants is obedience to God. (CITIZENS *and other witnesses cheer.*)

ADAMS: Thank you, Mr. Franklin. Two continents value your opinion. (FRANKLIN *returns to his seat.*)

JUDGE: Have you completed your case, Mr. Adams?

ADAMS: I have one final witness—the defendant, George Washington. Will you come forward, General Washington? (GEORGE WASHINGTON *goes to witness stand.*)

WASHINGTON: I appreciate this opportunity to thank the many friends of liberty who have spoken here today. (ADAMS *takes Declaration from table.*)

ADAMS: General Washington, you did not sign this Declaration of Independence. Why not? Did you think it was not justified?

WASHINGTON: No, sir. I could not sign the Declaration of Independence because I was on the battlefield with my soldiers when it was written. But I believe with all my heart in the ideas expressed in the Declaration. May I see it, please? (ADAMS *hands Declaration to* WASHINGTON.) This document specifically states (*Reads*): "Governments long established should not be changed for light and transient causes; . . . experience hath shown, that mankind are more disposed to suffer, while evils are sufferable, than to right themselves by abolishing the forms to which they are accustomed. But when a long train of abuses . . . evinces a design to reduce them under absolute despotism, it is their right, it is their duty, to throw off such government, and to provide new guards for their future security."

JUDGE (*Interrupting*): General Washington, consider for a moment to what chaos such a doctrine may lead. If a dissatisfied people can, of their own will, overthrow their established government, what rule of law and order could possibly prevail?

NORTH (*Ominously*): If the court please, we can easily foresee the terrible consequences of this traitorous doctrine. Should this doctrine spread to other lands, the kingdom of Spain might lose the allegiance of Mexicans and of the Argentine. Brazilians might declare: Brazil for Brazilians! What would the world come to?

JUDGE: Indeed, this is the very heart of their treason.

ADAMS: You both forget that there is a right higher than the right of kings over their subjects. A government exists not for the sake of the rulers but only for the good of the people, and only by the consent of the governed. Governments exist to help the people secure the rights which are theirs as human beings.

JUDGE: What rights?

WASHINGTON: In answer to your question, allow me to quote what I think is the *heart* of this Declaration of Independence (*Reads*): "We hold these truths to be self-evident, that all men are created equal, that they are endowed by their creator with certain unalienable rights, that among these are life, liberty, and the pursuit of happiness.—That to secure these rights, governments are instituted among men, deriving their just powers from the consent of the governed, that whenever any form of government becomes destructive of these ends, it is the right of the people to alter or to abolish it . . ." (WASHINGTON *returns to seat.*)

ADAMS (*To* JUDGE): The defense rests.

JUDGE: Then let the defendant, George Washington, come forward. (GEORGE WASHINGTON *rises, goes to* JUDGE'*s table and stands facing* JUDGE.) George Washington, as defendant in this trial, do you have anything further to say before we pass judgment?

WASHINGTON: Only history can pass judgment on our noble cause. But I believe firmly that history shall prove our cause was just, our path honorable, and that what we have started and fought for here and now will in the future lead this nation to greatness and leadership among the free peoples of the world. (*Music of "America the Beautiful" is played as curtains slowly close.*)

THE END

All Because of a Scullery Maid

Unlikely spies help the Revolution

by Marguerite Kreger Phillips

Characters

FELICITY, *an elderly housekeeper*
DAME WHITING, *schoolmistress*
TOLERANCE ⎫
SARAH ⎬ *young people boarding with Dame Whiting*
CHESTER ⎭
LIBBY SHIPPEN, *a young actress*
SAM, *a young indentured servant*
OLIVER PURCELL, *the old silhouette man*

TIME: *A day in May, 1777.*
SETTING: *The colonial sitting room in the home of Dame Whiting, who runs a boarding school.*
AT RISE: FELICITY *is sitting at right, looking over patches of fabric in her workbasket.* CHESTER *enters from left, and* FELICITY *hastily pushes patches into basket, as if covering something.*

CHESTER: Ah! Here you are, Felicity. Right where I hoped to find you. Could you spare me a piece of twine?
FELICITY (*Smiling*): Now why should I have twine in my basket of patches? (SARAH *enters behind* CHESTER.)
SARAH: Chester, I told you not to expect Felicity to have twine in with her precious quilt patches and patterns. (*She sits down. Sound of a door knocker is heard, and* CHESTER *runs out.*)
FELICITY (*Shaking her head at* SARAH): Dame Whiting would not approve of Chester's answering the door. That dear boy is growing so fast, I fear me the British will take him for a man one of these days when they come looking for spies.

60

SARAH: Why should they come here? Dame Whiting keeps a neutral house and teaches her students nothing of these matters.

CHESTER (*Rushing back, excitedly*): A beautiful creature at the door is asking for the famous maker of quilts. That must be you, Felicity.

FELICITY: Hadn't you the good manners to bid her to enter?

CHESTER: But she is a strolling player! You know what Dame Whiting thinks of theater folk.

FELICITY (*Surprised*): Oh! I must see her! (*Rises and exits hastily, leaving basket on chair*)

CHESTER (*Watching until* FELICITY *is off*): Aha! She's left her workbasket. When I first came in, I vow she was hiding something in it. She always guards it as if she thought the British would find a spy in it. (*Goes to stand over basket*) Sarah, do you challenge me to take a look in that basket?

SARAH (*Giggling, uncertainly*): Oh, Chester, do you think you should?

CHESTER (*Fingering patterns gingerly*): It's only quilt patterns. Who would want those? (*Plunges hand into basket and brings out small silhouette cut out of dark paper*) A silhouette?

SARAH: That's strange—let me see it. (*Takes silhouette and examines it*)

CHESTER: She always acts so odd when we have our lessons in cutting silhouettes. (*Takes silhouette back from* SARAH) Could she have cut this?

SARAH (*With a laugh*): Felicity do that? Oh, Chester, put it back. Felicity is a very good housekeeper and a dear old person, but she could never cut a silhouette. (CHESTER *shrugs and puts silhouette carelessly into basket, so that a part of it sticks up.*)

CHESTER: I still think it's a queer thing to find in her basket.

SARAH (*Shoving him toward door*): You do get such funny ideas in your head. Come along, and we'll tell Dame Whiting about the strolling player you saw at the door. (*They exit.* FELICITY *enters, followed by* LIBBY SHIPPEN, *who looks about room quizzically.*)

FELICITY (*Nervously*): I shouldn't have let you in. Dame Whiting will not like it.

LIBBY (*Smiling*): And I shouldn't have mentioned being a strolling player. Folks have strange ideas about us. I was told to expect kindness from the maker of famous quilt patterns. That is why I sought you out. (LIBBY *moves over near chair and stares at basket. She gasps as she sees the silhouette and turns quickly to* FELICITY.) Does Dame Whiting know that you have a gift for cutting silhouettes?

FELICITY (*Her voice trembling*): Who are you? (LIBBY *looks around cautiously, then reaches into her pocket and takes out a silhouette cut in halves.*)

LIBBY (*Handing silhouette to* FELICITY): Perhaps this will help. (FELICITY *examines it carefully.*)

FELICITY (*Startled*): The sign! (*Anxiously, looking at* LIBBY) Do the patriots trust one so young?

LIBBY (*Nodding*): They had to. The message came through after Oliver Purcell, the silhouette man, had left. I was the only one available, and had proved myself trustworthy in Washington's camp for a year. I am to give the message to you, and you must cut it into the silhouette and have it ready for Oliver Purcell when he stops here.

FELICITY (*Nervously*): He comes today, at any time now! He always stops to give the children a lesson in silhouette cutting. It is part of his disguise.

LIBBY: He mustn't stop to give a lesson today. (*Points at basket*) How does it happen that I found your silhouette so exposed in your workbasket? I was told that no one knew of your real work and that I must ask only for the maker of quilt patterns.

FELICITY (*Worried*): No one knows about my real work for the cause of liberty, and I thought no one in this house knew I could cut silhouettes. (*Nervously*) I am frightened now. Someone has searched in my basket, which means that someone suspects I cut silhouette messages and pass them on. (*Stops and listens*) Sh! (LIBBY *pushes her silhouette back into her pocket, and* FELICITY *hastily pulls patches over top of basket, just as* DAME WHITING *sweeps haughtily into room.*)

DAME WHITING (*Displeased*): Felicity, have I not forbidden you to admit strangers from the road? (LIBBY *crosses in front of* FELICITY.)

LIBBY (*Curtsying to* DAME WHITING): Pray do not scold this sweet old woman. I am only Libby, a poor strolling player without work because of this dreadful war.

DAME WHITING (*Coldly*): Chester has informed me that a theatrical player is in my house. Such a person has never entered here before.

LIBBY (*Pleading*): Will you not let me work for a few days' shelter? Please, let me be a scullery maid.

FELICITY (*Timidly*): She can do no harm, Dame Whiting.

DAME WHITING (*Sharply*): I must think of my young folks.

LIBBY (*Very humbly*): Dame Whiting, I wish to be a scullery maid, not a strolling player. (*Quickly*) But I could teach the young people to dance—country dances, jigs, reels—(*Stops as* DAME WHITING *snorts in disapproval.* LIBBY *curtsies, then takes a few minuet steps.*) The minuet, then? The loveliest dance of all. I can teach them to sing, to read—(*Suddenly, in a firm voice*) Do you read, Dame Whiting?

DAME WHITING (*Coldly*): Reading is not the fashion for women of breeding.

FELICITY (*Persuasively*): 'Tis better she remain in the scullery. Much as I love my task as your housekeeper, I would look kindly on a little help.

DAME WHITING (*Stiffly*): A wise decision—although her speech betrays the fact that she is no scullery maid. (*With disdain*) Felicity, you may put this—this scullery maid—in the little room off the scullery, the vegetable room. That will do quite well for her.

FELICITY (*Horrified*): With the *onions?*

DAME WHITING: What *about* the onions? There's room for both! (*Turns and exits*)

LIBBY (*Patting* FELICITY'S *arm consolingly*): Do not concern yourself for me. We have our work for the cause to keep our spirits up. At least I am safe here and can now give you the message. I think you should cut it out in the silhouette at once. Dame Whiting may change her mind and send me away.

FELICITY (*Sitting down and reaching into workbasket*): Don't worry. I will do it at once.

LIBBY (*Anxiously, looking around*): Are you sure Dame Whiting does not suspect your work for our cause?

FELICITY (*Taking scissors from basket*): She thinks me but a simple old housekeeper. Now to work. (*She takes piece of black paper from basket.*) There is time to do it now before she brings the young folks in here for their lesson.

LIBBY: Very well! Now for the message. (LIBBY *speaks slowly and cautiously, as* FELICITY *cuts silhouette.*) General Howe has sailed away from Philadelphia. Clinton is now in command of New York. General Burgoyne plans to march from Quebec straight through New York state to join Clinton. There are eight thousand British troops under Burgoyne coming down from Canada to join Howe. (*She watches as* FELICITY *finishes cutting out a face in silhouette.*) Do the forehead and long nose of the silhouette indicate the whole message, or do the curls mean something, too?

FELICITY (*Carefully*): I see they did not give the code even to you, a trusted messenger. Therefore, I cannot, either. (*Folds silhouette. Sighs*) My basket has been such a safe hiding place because of my prize quilt patterns—but it is safe no longer. If I only knew who it is that suspects me! (*Sighs*) Now to hide this silhouette until you can get it to Oliver Purcell, the silhouette man, when he comes.

LIBBY (*Surprised*): Am I to give it to him?

FELICITY: Yes. You must meet him at the door and send him on his way with the message. If I answer the door when he comes, Dame Whiting would expect me to ask him in to give the young people a lesson in cutting, and he must not be delayed.

LIBBY: I see. (*With a laugh*) The new scullery maid will not know the silhouette man gives lessons here. Clever Felicity, I see now why our dear George Washington trusts you.

FELICITY: I shall be upstairs with the linens when the silhouette man comes. You will hand him the message.

LIBBY: But I do not know the silhouette man!

FELICITY (*Pausing*): You cannot mistake Oliver Purcell. He is the only silhouette man that comes this way. He is quite old, carries a portfolio—oh, you cannot mistake him. Now I must hide this silhouette so you can get it easily when he comes. (*She walks quickly about room, lifting up various objects and replacing them as she speaks.*) No, not there. No, this is just the place the British would search if they happened by. No, that will not do. . . .

LIBBY (*Pointing to chocolate pot on shelf*): What about the chocolate pot up there?

FELICITY: The chocolate pot? Dame Whiting treasures it above all else. No one is allowed to touch it.

LIBBY (*Pleased*): 'Tis the very place then.

FELICITY (*Considering, thoughtfully*): Dame Whiting even dusts it herself. That she did this very morning, and she will not dust it again for a week.

LIBBY: Oh! Sweet, sweet chocolate pot!

FELICITY (*Carefully placing folded silhouette inside, replacing lid*): 'Tis done. Should Oliver Purcell come while the young people are in here—

LIBBY: Think not to add to our troubles. I'll get the young folk all out of the way by some clever means. Now, would it not be wise to take all pieces of paper and the silhouettes out of your basket?

FELICITY: Yes, that is essential, now that someone has seen them. (*She takes paper and some finished silhouettes from basket and puts them into her pocket. Then she holds up a piece of yellowed paper.*) This is a very special quilt pattern. There are others in the bottom. I shall leave this one to fool anyone who might seek further to spy on me. (*Voices of* SARAH *and* TOLERANCE *are heard off left.*) Come, we are finished just in time. (*She sets basket on chair. Then, they exit right, as* DAME WHITING, TOLERANCE, SARAH *and* CHESTER *enter left.* CHESTER *goes to chest and pulls out shears and parchment.* TOLERANCE *goes to high stool, sits and poses.* SARAH *goes to peer into* FELICITY'S *basket.* DAME WHITING *sits down; sees* SARAH *at basket.*)

DAME WHITING (*Sharply*): Sarah! Felicity does not wish her basket to be touched. I'm surprised at her carelessness in leaving it here.

SARAH: I was only—(CHESTER *coughs loudly and pushes shears and paper into her hands, and both sit down on stools.*)

DAME WHITING: We need an especially long lesson today. We have no silhouettes to show dear Oliver Purcell.

CHESTER (*Knowingly*): I could find one not too far from here to show him.

SARAH (*Warningly*): Chester!

TOLERANCE (*With her face turned in profile*): At least one of you could start cutting a silhouette of me.

SARAH (*Laughing*): Tolerance, you do try to sound so grown up.

TOLERANCE (*Snappishly*): I'm fifteen, and women no older than I are acting as spies. My brother told me so, and Felicity says spies for the British are very young.

DAME WHITING: Where would Felicity gain such knowledge of the British?

TOLERANCE: Oh, don't be cross with the dear old fuddy-duddy.

CHESTER (*Smugly*): Maybe she isn't such a fuddy-duddy as you think.

TOLERANCE: Oh, you and your wagging tongue.

DAME WHITING: Tolerance! Surely you did not learn that word from Felicity.

TOLERANCE: My brother told me of it. 'Tis used in the theater.

DAME WHITING: The theater? Indeed, that reminds me—I had best tell you that we have a new scullery maid. Chester, run and find Felicity, and have her bring the scullery maid to me. There is work here for her to do. (CHESTER *exits left.* SARAH *takes scissors and paper and begins to cut silhouette.*)

SARAH (*As* TOLERANCE *moves*): You would move! I was just about to cut that side of your face.

TOLERANCE: But you are so slow! Must I pose here forever?

DAME WHITING: Young ladies! (CHESTER *enters excitedly, waving a paper.*)

CHESTER: Dame Whiting, she can read!

TOLERANCE *and* SARAH: Read? Who? (FELICITY *and* LIBBY *enter.*)

LIBBY (*Holds out her hand to* CHESTER *for the paper*): Dame Whiting, I was but reading a play part. I am sorry.

CHESTER (*Grinning with admiration*): I'm not.

DAME WHITING (*Provoked*): The lesson is over. (*Rises stiffly*) We shall await Oliver Purcell in the garden. Chester, bring the materials we shall need for the silhouettes when Mr. Purcell arrives. (*Turning*) Felicity, see to the linens. (*Gesturing toward* LIBBY) Later we shall have a serious talk about that new person in our house. (*Tosses her head haughtily, looking at* LIBBY, *then hurries off, followed by* SARAH.)

TOLERANCE (*Lingering to touch* LIBBY's *sleeve*): Strange attire for a scullery maid. Silk, if I mistake not. (*Exits*)

CHESTER (*Holding parchment and shears*): Felicity, unless your scullery maid gives me a lesson in acting, I shall tell Dame Whiting how clever you are at cutting silhouettes! (*Runs off.*)

FELICITY (*Turning to* LIBBY; *excitedly*): It was Chester! He is the one who has been snooping in my basket.

LIBBY (*Laughing*): Better Chester than a British spy.

FELICITY: Chester is no spy, but he has sharp eyes. (*Worried*)

What if he sees Oliver Purcell before you have a chance to give him the silhouette and send him on his way?

LIBBY: Dame Whiting is keeping Chester busy in the garden. I shall watch for the silhouette man by the back road, and you watch from the front door. Hurry off, then! (*She exits quickly. FELICITY turns to exit. Suddenly SAM, a young indentured servant, staggers in and falls to the floor, exhausted. She gasps.*)

SAM: A thousand pardons. The door was open, and I did need to get inside.

FELICITY (*Bravely*): We want no trouble here.

SAM (*Beseechingly*): Tell me, are you Felicity, famous for quilt patterns?

FELICITY (*Puzzled*): I am Felicity, and I do make quilt patterns, but who are you?

SAM: I beg you to sit down. I am too weak to stand, and 'tis most ungentlemanly for me to sprawl if you continue to stand. (*FELICITY sits in chair and moves her basket close to her*)

FELICITY: Haste then with your story.

SAM: I am indentured to a heartless, mercenary Tory. He made me a proposal that could give me my freedom. When his wife started nagging him for carelessly burning one of her prize quilt patterns, he said I would have my freedom if I would bring back another pattern. Do you have the Hickory Nut Lane pattern?

FELICITY: Yes, I have. (*Sighing in relief*) And to think I took you for a spy.

SAM (*Suddenly alert*): A spy?

FELICITY: Well, you never know these days. (*Pause*) Now about that Hickory Nut Lane pattern.

SAM: Actually my master tricked me. As soon as he had his wife's word that she would stop nagging, he sent me off on this errand, but also sent word to the British to pick me up. I learned this from a stable boy. The British are to take the pattern from me, claiming they found it, and then return me to my master to serve out my year of bondage. I'm afraid they are close on my trail.

FELICITY (*Rising*): If this tale be false—

SAM (*Staggering to his feet*): Give me a glass of warm milk, I beg of you, and mayhap a lump of butter in it?

FELICITY (*Sharply*): You'll get lumps somewhere else, if all this be poppycock. Whoever heard of trading the bondage of a year for a quilt pattern!

SAM: You should hear my mistress nag.

FELICITY (*Chuckling*): Come along into the kitchen then. You must not remain in here. (*She and* SAM *exit left.* CHESTER *peers in at right, as if looking for something, then tiptoes in.* SARAH *hurries in after him.*)

SARAH: Chester!

CHESTER: Sh-h! I saw a ragged beggar enter our front door while I was out there at that stupid lesson. He did not go out. I'm sure he is a spy!

SARAH: Really, Chester, you are having more funny ideas today— Felicity wouldn't let anybody else in. That scullery maid made enough trouble for her! (*Mischievously*) But now that she isn't here, I'm going to look and see just what she does have in that basket. (*Begins to look through basket*)

CHESTER (*Persistently*): By all the brass buttons in the colonies, I saw him come in here, and I thought I heard Felicity, too.

SARAH (*With surprise*): Chester, there are no silhouettes in here now—just a piece of yellow paper.

CHESTER: But there were before. She must have hidden them somewhere else—where she was sure no one could find them.

SARAH (*Giggling*): You know there's no such place, Chester. *You* snoop everywhere!

CHESTER (*Gazing around room*): Everywhere indeed, Sarah— except Dame Whiting's precious chocolate pot, of course.

SARAH: No one would dare to touch that. (*Suddenly*) Of course! That would be the very place to hide something important.

CHESTER: Do you think Felicity would dare to open the chocolate pot?

SARAH (*Cunningly*): Do you think *you* would dare, Chester?

CHESTER (*Resolutely*): By jinks, I would! (*Strides over to chocolate pot and lifts lid. He puts his hand in and pulls out folded silhouette.*)

SARAH: A silhouette! (*Uneasily*) Oh, Chester, what does it mean?

CHESTER: I knew there was something mysterious about old Felicity!

SARAH: Chester, let's put one of our own silhouettes in there instead, folded—just like that one. 'Twill give Felicity a fright and serve her right when she finds it in place of her own. She is deceiving us all about her silhouette cutting.

CHESTER (*Mysteriously*): And who knows for what purpose? Now get one of ours. (SARAH *takes silhouette from chest and folds it exactly like the other.* CHESTER *puts first silhouette into his pocket, and places* SARAH's *in the chocolate pot.*) I hope we can see old Felicity's face when she finds that silhouette in place of her own. Do run along now, Sarah, and keep our secret. I want to take a look at that yellow paper.

SARAH (*As she exits*): Mayhap you'll find the ragged beggar you think you saw, too. (CHESTER *kneels near basket and is peering at yellow paper, when* LIBBY *rushes in. She does not see him. She goes straight to chocolate pot and removes silhouette. She turns, sees* CHESTER, *and gasps. Then, in control, she speaks coquettishly.*)

LIBBY: Chester, do be a good boy and don't tell on me. I'll teach you how to be a real actor, if you forget you saw me. (*She runs off.* CHESTER *stands open-mouthed for a moment, then starts after* LIBBY. TOLERANCE *enters and calls to him.*)

TOLERANCE: Chester, if you don't come at once, Dame Whiting— (CHESTER *turns to leave, but* TOLERANCE *grabs his arm.*)

CHESTER: Let go of me, Tolerance. There is something funny going on here, and I aim to investigate. I saw that new scullery maid take a folded silhouette out of the chocolate pot.

TOLERANCE: Dame Whiting's chocolate pot? Oh, Chester, nobody ever touches that. (CHESTER *pulls free and runs off.*) Chester! You hurt my arm. (FELICITY *enters.*)

FELICITY: What is going on?

TOLERANCE (*Casually*): Oh, nothing really. Felicity, Dame Whiting wants you to bring out your basket and let her see some of the quilt patterns.

FELICITY (*Unsuspecting*): All right.

TOLERANCE: Please tell her I'm still looking for Chester. (TOLERANCE *picks up basket and hangs it over* FELICITY's *arm.* FELICITY *exits. Sound of door knocker is heard, and* TOLERANCE *calls off left.*) Come in, come in. (OLIVER PURCELL *enters. He carries a portfolio, and looks anxious and weary.*) Master Purcell! We've been waiting all day for you.

OLIVER (*Excitedly clutching his portfolio*): Tolerance, I must see Felicity at once, and alone.

TOLERANCE: Why, Master Purcell, what business could you have with our dear old Felicity that is so private?

OLIVER (*Impatiently*): I must speak to her at once. (*Sees her suspicious glance and changes tone*) Ah! You forget that it is I who spread her fame as a maker of quilt patterns. I just overheard a group of British soldiers talking. They are seeking her to obtain a special pattern, and are also looking for a young man who may be hiding here.

TOLERANCE: Oh, dear. I had better get Dame Whiting.

OLIVER (*Quickly*): Just call Felicity. I sent the soldiers the other way, but someone may send them right back. I must warn Felicity.

TOLERANCE: I'll get you a glass of milk first. Sit down—you do look weary. (*Starts to exit*)

OLIVER: Has any stranger been here today?

TOLERANCE: Only a new scullery maid. (*Exits.* OLIVER *paces for a moment. Then* TOLERANCE *screams from offstage, and runs back in.*) Oh, Master Purcell, there's a strange young man out there. I'm going to find Dame Whiting! (*Runs out*)

OLIVER: Tolerance, wait—

SAM (*Hurrying in, holding a glass of milk*): I didn't mean to—I was just having another glass of milk.

OLIVER: If you've had one, then I'll take that. (*Takes glass and sits down*) I'm an old man and feel very weak. (*Looks up*) Would the British be after you, by any chance?

SAM (*Startled*): Oh, sir, have mercy. Do not give me away until Felicity has found the Hickory Nut Lane pattern. Let me explain. (*LIBBY rushes in.*)

LIBBY: Oh, dear, someone come and help. Chester has followed the dear old silhouette man and is pummeling him! (*OLIVER jumps up.*) Who are you?

OLIVER: I am Oliver Purcell.

LIBBY: Oh, no, you can't be! The silhouette man was just here, and I gave him—oh, no!

OLIVER (*Groaning in anguish*): Too late, too late!

SAM (*Looking from one to the other*): I'll go to see what is wrong. (*Exits right as* TOLERANCE, *followed by* DAME WHITING, FELICITY *and* SARAH, *rushes in from left.*)

TOLERANCE (*Screaming*): Where is he?

OLIVER: Felicity, tell this scullery maid who I am.

FELICITY: Libby, he is Oliver Purcell.

LIBBY: Oh, woe is me! I thought Oliver Purcell had come and gone. A few minutes ago, a man came up to the back road who looked just as you described Mr. Purcell. He bowed, and smiled when I called him Oliver Purcell. I said I had the silhouette ready and that he must take it at once to George Washington. I gave—I gave him the silhouette from the chocolate pot! (*She points to chocolate pot in dismay.* DAME WHITING *starts, then sinks down on settee.* LIBBY *rushes off.*)

OLIVER: After that girl, Felicity. (FELICITY *exits, and he turns to* DAME WHITING. SARAH *and* TOLERANCE *hover over her.*) This is all very disturbing, knowing how well you must guard your neutrality, Dame Whiting.

DAME WHITING (*Confused*): What is this talk of a silhouette and my chocolate pot? And what about this strange man Tolerance saw? Who was he?

OLIVER: A harmless fellow. (FELICITY *and* LIBBY *return.*)

FELICITY: Oh, woe is me, Oliver! We are discovered.

OLIVER: Too late, too late. (*He sinks down on low stool, his head in his hands.* FELICITY *sits, her hands over her face, as* LIBBY *speaks.*)

LIBBY (*Almost in tears*): It is my fault. I didn't ask him for the secret sign. I rushed in here, took the silhouette which Felicity had cut in code and hidden in the chocolate pot—

DAME WHITING (*Horrified*): My chocolate pot? (*Turns to stare at it*)

FELICITY: I did so presume as to hide a most valuable silhouette therein.

CHESTER (*Appearing at door, disheveled, pointing at* LIBBY): Hold that girl. She's a British spy. She gave a message to another spy on the back road. (*He walks forward and* SAM *appears at door behind him.*)

FELICITY: No, Chester, no. Libby thought the man was Oliver. The blame is mine for not letting you know, dear Dame Whiting, that I was working for the patriots' cause against the British.

OLIVER: Did he get away?

SAM: I was too late. Chester couldn't hold the man alone.

SARAH (*Loudly*): Chester, don't you understand what has happened? That was a most important message for the Continental cause that you took from the chocolate pot. Do you still have it?

OLIVER (*Jumping to his feet*): What did you say, Sarah, my child?

SARAH: Chester, you must have it. You must!

CHESTER (*Going through his pockets*): Unless I lost it in the scuffle—

FELICITY (*To* CHESTER): You took it from the pot? (CHESTER *nods.*) Then what did Libby take?

SARAH (*Miserably*): We put one of our own poor silhouettes into the chocolate pot. We only meant to tease you, dear Felicity, because you had not told us you could cut silhouettes. Chester thought you might be a spy when he found the folded silhouette in the pot.

LIBBY (*Excitedly, sobbing*): Oh, thank heaven! That impostor, the British spy, did not get the real silhouette!

CHESTER (*At last extricating the rumpled silhouette from pocket*): Ah! (FELICITY *grabs it and opens it, as* LIBBY *and* OLIVER *observe intently.*)

OLIVER: 'Tis safe, 'tis safe.

DAME WHITING: And all this going on in my house! We should not have deceived each other, Felicity, for I, too, am a patriot, but dared not proclaim it.

TOLERANCE: Indeed, we are all for George Washington's cause, and the cause of freedom from the British.

OLIVER (*Taking command*): Chester, you must come with me. As soon as that real spy reaches his camp, the British will come looking for us. There must be only Dame Whiting and her two young pupils here—and her scullery maid.

FELICITY: And a very old housekeeper, whose fingers can barely stir the kettle. Sam, I only wish I had the Hickory Nut Lane pattern for you. 'Twas ever in that basket, a yellowed piece of paper.

SARAH (*Shouting*): Chester, did you take that?

CHESTER (*Hanging his head*): I thought I was doing something for the cause, if Felicity proved to be on the British side. (*Pulls out rumpled paper from another pocket*)

FELICITY (*Taking it*): The Hickory Nut Lane pattern!

SAM: My quilt pattern?

OLIVER: Take it, my good fellow, and follow me. Come on, Chester.

CHESTER: Just as I am?

OLIVER: It is a fine disguise. Two poor country boys helping me out with my horses. We'll turn peddler on the way. Felicity, your cutting days are over. This house will be watched more closely now. We must go quickly. (OLIVER, CHESTER, *and* SAM *exit. The women stand and wave goodbye, then turn toward each other.*)

LIBBY (*Timidly*): It is true, then, Dame Whiting? You, too, are a patriot?

DAME WHITING (*Stiffly*): Women of breeding do not tell falsehoods.

LIBBY: Then may I stay on here, as your scullery maid?

FELICITY (*Softly*): Now that Chester's room is empty, she need no longer sleep in the vegetable room.

TOLERANCE: And perchance we may learn to read!

SARAH: And to dance!

DAME WHITING (*Sternly, but smiling*): It may be best for young patriots to learn to read. And to dance—the minuet, of course.

LIBBY (*With a deep curtsy, smiling*): The minuet, of course, dear Dame Whiting! (*She begins to hum and step to the music.* SARAH *and* TOLERANCE *join in.* FELICITY *smiles and joins the minuet.* DAME WHITING *rises and starts to dance, as the curtain falls.*)

THE END

The Trial of Peter Zenger

Freedom of the press is threatened

by Paul T. Nolan

Characters

NARRATOR
PETER ZENGER
ANNA ZENGER, *his wife*
MRS. ZENGER, *Peter's mother*
CATHIE ZENGER, *Peter's sister*
TWO WOMEN
FRANCIS HARISON, *the Governor's writer*
JAMES ALEXANDER
SHERIFF OF NEW YORK
TWO CONSTABLES
RICHARD BRADLEY, *Attorney General*
ANDREW HAMILTON, *defense attorney*
CHIEF JUSTICE JAMES DELANCEY
JUSTICE FREDERICK PHILIPSE
MEMBERS OF THE JURY

SCENE 1

BEFORE RISE: NARRATOR *enters and speaks to audience.*

NARRATOR: I'm a newspaper man. I publish a small local paper called the *Weekly Chronicle,* and it's a good business to be in. My father got me started, and I've been in it all my life. I can print exactly what I please in my paper—take up the local issues or even national ones—no one censors what I print. No one tells me what I can or can't say. (*Gestures to audience*) That wasn't always the case for newspapers. As a matter of fact, our traditional right to a free press began way back in 1734, all because of the courage of a man named Peter Zenger, who ran a little one-man print shop in New York. (NARRATOR *exits.*)

* * *

TIME: *1734.*

SETTING: *Peter Zenger's printing shop, in Colonial New York. There is a table down left, with sheets of newsprint on it, and there are two chairs beside the table.*

AT RISE: *Stage is dimly lighted. Spotlight comes up on* PETER ZENGER, *holding up sheet of newsprint and reading it critically.* ANNA ZENGER *enters.*

ANNA (*Calling*): Peter! Peter Zenger! Where are you?

PETER: Here I am, Anna.

ANNA (*Joining him at table*): Is it finished, Peter?

PETER (*Nodding*): It is ready to be printed. (*Showing* ANNA *newsprint*) This is the first issue of our *Journal.* We are making history, Anna.

ANNA: I am glad for you. You are a good printer, Peter—I have always said so.

PETER (*Pointing to newsprint*): See my name? (*Reading*) "Printed by John Peter Zenger." It's a good thing to see one's name on one's own work.

ANNA (*Looking at newsprint*): It *is* a good thing. I see that your *Journal* says that Governor Cosby is an idiot and a Nero. I don't think that such opinions will please Governor Cosby. This is very strong language, Peter—very strong.

PETER: There are times when only strong language will do.

ANNA (*Uneasily*): I didn't know that you used such language, Peter.

PETER: I didn't write that, Anna. You know that. I just print the *Journal.* Perhaps *I* would not say things that way if I were the writer, but it is the truth. And it is a good thing to publish the truth, Anna.

ANNA (*Looking carefully at newsprint*): I do not see anyone else's name in the *Journal.* One would think that you had written it all.

PETER: Mr. Alexander writes most of the paper. You know that. Everyone knows that.

ANNA (*Stubbornly*): Mr. James Alexander? I do not see his name. I see only strange names like Cato, Philo-Patrias, Thomas

Stand-by. No such people live in New York.

PETER: Anna, you know that if Mr. Alexander were to sign his real name, the Governor could arrest him. He uses a pen name, but everyone knows he is the real author.

ANNA: Ah, but you use your real name. Why don't you use a pen name, Peter?

PETER: Anna, this paper is our chance to have our own little business. I want people to know that I have printed it. (*Impatiently*) Don't you want me to be successful, Anna?

ANNA: Don't I work with you, Peter? Don't I set the type and pound the proofs and crank the press? Yes, and make the ink? (*Staunchly*) I want you to be the best printer in all America.

PETER: I'm not complaining, Anna. You are a better printer than I am. But ever since we began talking about starting the *Journal,* you have seemed—forgive me for saying this—you have seemed to be against me.

ANNA: No, Peter, I have never been against *you.*

PETER: Then against the paper. (ANNA *turns away.*) Anna, someone must stand up and tell Governor Cosby that we do not wish to be robbed, cheated and insulted! We came to this new world so that we might work and be free men. Now this governor comes, like a cattle buyer looking for hides, to strip us of everything. (*Takes sheet of newsprint from* ANNA. *She turns.*) Listen to this and tell me if Mr. Alexander has not written the truth. (*Reads*) "A Governor turns rogue, does a thousand things for which a small rogue would have deserved a halter; and because it is difficult to obtain relief against him, therefore it is prudent to keep in with him and join in the roguery. A Governor does all he can to chain you, and it being difficult to stop him, it becomes prudent to help him put on the chains and rivet them fast!" That is the truth, Anna. Look at what he has done to our courts. Our Royal Governor is a jailer, and he is making all of us his prisoners. (*Earnestly*) Is it not the truth, Anna? If I am wrong, tell me.

ANNA: It is the truth, Peter. (*Agitated*) But it is also the truth that it is only your name signed to the paper. The Governor can arrest you and send you to jail for printing this!

PETER (*Patiently*): Mr. Alexander has told me a hundred times the chance I am taking. I know that I may be sent to jail.

ANNA: And still you will print this paper?

PETER: Yes, Anna. Truth and freedom are worth the chance.

CATHIE ZENGER (*Calling from offstage*): Peter! Anna!

MRS. ZENGER (*Calling from offstage*): John Peter! (*Entering with* CATHIE) Peter! Anna! I have just heard the most awful thing in the marketplace.

PETER (*Alert*): Yes, Mama? What have you heard? Is it something I can print in the *Journal?*

CATHIE: Then it is true, John Peter. You *are* publishing a newspaper!

MRS. ZENGER: Oh, Peter, people say that Governor Cosby will not like it.

CATHIE: Don't you know the Governor is opposed, John Peter?

PETER: I don't know, little sister. I don't know what the Governor opposes. Our Governor Cosby likes so few things in our colony that it is difficult to say whether or not he will like my *Journal.*

MRS. ZENGER: Peter, it is a dangerous thing to offend men in high office.

PETER: It is also a dangerous thing for men in high office to offend the people. I am doing Governor Cosby a service by letting the *Journal* tell him so.

CATHIE: Peter, don't cause trouble. You are not a great soldier. You are simply a small businessman. You cannot fight the great people. Please, Peter, don't cause trouble.

PETER: I will try *not* to cause trouble.

MRS. ZENGER: That is a good son. Then you will not print this paper?

PETER: No, Mama, it is because I don't want trouble that the *Journal* must be published. And I will be a good son if this paper makes our New York a better village in which to live. That is my only desire.

MRS. ZENGER: Anna, you are his wife. He will listen to you. Tell him not to do this foolish thing.

ANNA: I can't do that, Mama. I am helping him. New York needs such a paper.

MRS. ZENGER: There is already one paper, Mr. Bradford's *Gazette*. Surely in a village as small as New York we do not need two papers.

ANNA: The *Gazette* is not a paper for the people. It is just the voice of the Governor. The *Journal* will publish for the people. And it will publish the truth.

MRS. ZENGER (*Shaking her head*): There will be trouble, Anna. Great trouble.

PETER: Try not to worry, Mama. This is something that I must do. And we have known trouble before, have we not? (*Spotlight goes out.* PETER, ANNA, CATHIE *and* MRS. ZENGER *exit. There is a pause to indicate passage of time, and then spotlight comes up down right on* TWO WOMEN, *who are carrying shopping baskets.*)

1ST WOMAN: Another of Zenger's *Journals* was published today.

2ND WOMAN: I didn't think the Governor would let him continue. Each week the paper grows bolder. . . .

1ST WOMAN: And Governor Cosby grows angrier. The paper will not last much longer. It is said that the *Journal* is even causing the Governor trouble with the lords in London.

2ND WOMAN: His wife's relatives will protect him here. They do not want him back in London.

1ST WOMAN: Lewis Morris has gone to London to protest his tampering with the courts.

2ND WOMAN: It would be better for Peter Zenger if Mr. Morris had stayed here. Peter will need all the help he can get when the Governor moves against him. Last week, he had Harison burn a copy of the *Journal* at the public hanging place.

1ST WOMAN: I feel sorry for Anna.

2ND WOMAN: And for Peter's mother.

1ST WOMAN: And for Peter.

2ND WOMAN: Poor little Peter. What can one small man do against such powerful enemies? (*Spotlight goes out.* TWO WOMEN *exit. There is a pause to indicate passage of time. Then spotlight comes up down left on* JAMES ALEXANDER *and* PETER ZENGER. *They are standing at printing press, talking.* ALEXANDER *holds sheaf of papers.*)

ALEXANDER (*Handing papers to* PETER): And, Peter, remember to be careful when you set the type. Some of these sentences will be completely misunderstood if the type is scrambled.

PETER: I shall be careful, Mr. Alexander. These are good words. (*Reading*) "The liberty of the press is a subject of the greatest importance, and in which every individual is as much concerned as he is in any other part of liberty." (*Looking up*) Mr. Alexander, do you think many people care about the liberty of the press? I know they say they do, but even my old friends are a little frightened to speak to me in public anymore.

ALEXANDER: Perhaps not many know that they are concerned—
yet. But they will. They will. (*Strongly*) All men want to be
free, and no man can be free unless he knows the facts. (*Pauses*)
Peter, this article is going to cause you trouble. Maybe, great
trouble.

PETER: I suppose it might. (*Slowly*) I suppose it might. (FRANCIS
HARISON, *the Governor's writer, enters suddenly at left.*)

HARISON: Aha! I see that I have caught the two principal plotters
together. (*Swaggers up to the men*)

ALEXANDER: Plotters, Harison? Have you a charge to make against
me and my friend, Mr. Zenger?

HARISON (*In smug tone*): No. Not yet. No charge. But I know
what I know.

ALEXANDER (*Sharply*): What would a spaniel dog like you know,
except to run and fetch for your master, and sit up and beg?
Oh, yes, and to bark at your betters. That's all that you know.

HARISON (*Angrily*): You go too far, sir!

ALEXANDER: I would go much farther to avoid the sight of you.

HARISON: There's no need to say more. I know what you think of
me, sir. I read the *Journal!*

ALEXANDER: Then you read a better paper than the one you
write for.

HARISON: What—do you mean you read the *Gazette,* sir?

ALEXANDER: I do. I read it for penance. But it is much better to
wrap the fish in. (PETER *turns to hide smile.*)

HARISON: Since you read our paper, did you like what the *Gazette*
said about the enemies of our good Governor Cosby being
"seditious rogues"?

ALEXANDER: I was pleased the author could spell the words.

HARISON: I wrote that!

ALEXANDER: Then I am even more surprised. I did not know you
could spell your own name, Harison.

HARISON (*Turning his back on* ALEXANDER; *to* PETER): And you,
Master Zenger, what do you think of my proposal that the name
Zenger be used as a synonym for *liar?*

PETER (*Calmly*): I think you know even less about the Dutch
language than the English. *Zenger* does not mean *liar,*
Mr. Harison.

HARISON: No, it means *fool!* (*Furiously*) I am here to warn you,

Zenger, to stop these attacks on the Governor! And this is the last warning you are going to get. Good day to both of you! (*He turns and stamps offstage, as* ANNA *enters.*)

ANNA: The Governor's dog has a loud bark.

ALEXANDER: And sharp teeth, too. Peter, perhaps we had better stop. Mr. Morris seems to be doing little good in England. We cannot fight on alone much longer. (*Sadly*) Why should you go to jail for no purpose? Perhaps the *Journal* should stop.

PETER: If you say the *Journal* is to stop, it will stop, Mr. Alexander. I cannot do the writing without you, I know.

ALEXANDER: It's up to you, Peter. I will continue to work for justice in what ways I can. But it is you, Peter, whom the Governor has warned. It is you who will receive the full force of his attack. Harison was sent here to warn you.

PETER: Anna, what do *you* think?

ANNA: I was not anxious for you to start the *Journal,* Peter.

PETER: I know, Anna, and maybe you were right.

ANNA: It is like picking up a stray dog on the streets. One does not need to do it, but once a person has adopted the stray, he has a responsibility. The *Journal* is like that stray dog, and I would not want to give it up now.

PETER (*Smiling*): Thank you, Anna, thank you! (*To* ALEXANDER) It is not easy for me to print this paper in the face of such powerful opposition. I am not a brave man—I want only to do my work, eat my bread, and be with my family. But if I were to stop printing the *Journal* now, because I am frightened, I would be no man at all.

ANNA: You are a brave man, Peter. It takes great courage to make a stand, in spite of your fear.

ALEXANDER: And the time is coming when you will need all your courage. It may come sooner than we know. I have heard rumors. . . . (*Spotlight dims.* ANNA *and* ALEXANDER *exit.* PETER *remains onstage, at table, where he begins to work busily on papers. Spotlight goes out, then comes up down right on* SHERIFF *and* TWO CONSTABLES.)

SHERIFF: If he's not alone, we will wait.

1ST CONSTABLE: Why wait? No one can stop us. We are on the Governor's business.

2ND CONSTABLE: We are not afraid of being stopped. But this

business must remain private. You were told that. Don't you ever listen?

1ST CONSTABLE: I did listen. I just don't understand. Why should a public arrest be kept quiet?

SHERIFF: Both of you be quiet! Don't say a word. Now, follow me, and do what I say. (SHERIFF *starts to cross stage, followed by* TWO CONSTABLES. *Spotlight crosses to* PETER, *working at table, and comes up full.* PETER *looks up, startled, as* SHERIFF *points to him.*) You there. Are you John Peter Zenger, the printer?

PETER: Why, Sheriff, you know I am. A hundred times you have seen me in the streets of New York.

SHERIFF: Just answer the question yea or nay. This is official business.

PETER: Yea, I am John Peter Zenger.

SHERIFF: Then, John Peter Zenger, I have a warrant for your arrest. (*Takes paper from coat and reads it*) "It is ordered that the Sheriff for the City of New York"—I am that man—"do forthwith take and apprehend John Peter Zenger"—you are that man—"for printing and publishing several seditious libels." That means lies!

PETER: The *Journal* prints no lies.

SHERIFF: Do not interrupt!

PETER (*Loudly*): The *Journal* prints no lies.

SHERIFF (*Seriously*): It makes no difference if what you have printed is the truth. It is enough that you have printed materials that are offensive to the Governor. (*Firmly*) The greater the truth, the greater the libel. That is the law. (*Pauses*) Now, where was I? Oh, yes. (*Continues reading*) ". . . dispersed through his journal or newspaper, entitled *The New York Weekly Journal;* as having in them many things tending to raise factions and tumults among the people of this Province, inflaming their minds with contempt for His Majesty's government, and greatly disturbing the peace thereof." Do you understand?

PETER: I understand, but I would like to consult a lawyer.

SHERIFF: You do not need a lawyer until you are charged. Now, I charge you. (*Reading*) "The Sheriff is to take the said John Peter Zenger and commit him to the prison or common jail of the said city and county." Now you are charged, and now you will come with us.

PETER: May I now seek the services of a lawyer?

SHERIFF: The warrant reads "forthwith." We have no time for you to find a lawyer.

PETER: May I not even bid my wife goodbye?

SHERIFF: No. You may speak to no one.

PETER: May I write a letter? A short one?

SHERIFF (*Impatiently*): No, and no more questions. All right, Constables, he will come with us. (*Two* CONSTABLES *move up to* PETER *and each takes one of his arms. They lead him toward right, followed by* SHERIFF.)

ANNA (*Calling from offstage*): Peter! Peter! (PETER *turns his head and looks back as* CONSTABLES *lead him off right.* SHERIFF *follows them off. A moment later,* ANNA *enters left.*) PETER! (*She looks around, puzzled, then goes to table slowly, speaking to herself.*) Peter? Has it happened? Has it finally happened? (*She stands alone at table as spotlight goes out. Curtain.*)

*   *   *   *   *

SCENE 2

BEFORE RISE: *Spotlight comes up on* TWO WOMEN, *carrying shopping baskets. They slowly cross stage, talking.*

1ST WOMAN: So, finally, Peter is getting his trial today.

2ND WOMAN: If you can call it a trial. He doesn't stand much chance.

1ST WOMAN: It is better than being in jail without a trial.

2ND WOMAN: They just dragged him off at night. Wouldn't even let him tell Anna where he was going, I've heard.

1ST WOMAN: For seven days, he was not permitted to talk to anyone. It was terrible for Anna.

2ND WOMAN: And a lot of good it did for Mr. Alexander to see him! Justice Delancey set Peter's bail so high it would have taken him ten years to raise the money.

1ST WOMAN: Anna has been so brave! During these nine long months that Peter has been in jail, she has kept publishing the *Journal.*

2ND WOMAN: If the Governor thought that keeping Peter in jail would silence the *Journal,* he must now be disappointed.

1ST WOMAN: But if Peter is sent to jail for a long time, can she go on?

2ND WOMAN: And Peter *will* go to jail. Governor Cosby's two hired judges are going to try the case.

1ST WOMAN: Even the Court Clerk is the Governor's man.

2ND WOMAN: Yes—that Harison! He is a dog.

1ST WOMAN: And what does Peter have? Just an old Philadelphia lawyer—Andrew Hamilton. He must be seventy years old.

2ND WOMAN: What could they do? The Governor will not allow Mr. Alexander to argue cases in New York now.

1ST WOMAN: But an old man—how can he help Peter?

2ND WOMAN: Andrew Hamilton was once a fine lawyer. I have heard of him.

1ST WOMAN: Once! Once! Once! All he is now is an old Philadelphia lawyer.

2ND WOMAN (*Shaking her head*): Poor Peter.

1ST WOMAN (*Also shaking head*): Poor Anna.

2ND WOMAN: Poor New York. (*They exit and spotlight goes out.*)

* * *

TIME: *1735.*

SETTING: *Courtroom. Upstage center is the Judge's bench, and in front of it, at one side, is a small table for Clerk of the Court. Down left is a table for Attorney General, and down right, a table for defense attorney. To right and at angle is the jury box —two rows of six chairs each.*

AT RISE: PETER, ANNA, *and* JAMES ALEXANDER *are sitting at defense table, right.* SHERIFF, TWO CONSTABLES, *and Attorney General* RICHARD BRADLEY *are sitting at table left.* JURY MEMBERS *sit in jury box.* HARISON *sits at Clerk's table. Judges* JAMES DELANCEY *and* FREDERICK PHILIPSE *sit at bench, upstage center.* ANDREW HAMILTON *is addressing* JURY, *standing in front of jury box.*

HAMILTON: Gentlemen of the Jury. This is a case of libel. But some larger questions must be considered. It is natural; it is a privilege—I will go further—it is a *right,* which all free men claim, that they have a right publicly to complain against the abuses of power, and to warn their neighbors against the craft or open violence of men in authority.

RICHARD BRADLEY (*Rising*): Your Honors, I protest. Mr. Hamilton goes too far. I don't like his liberties. (*Sits*)

HAMILTON: Surely, Mr. Attorney General, you can have no objections to what I have said thus far. You do not favor craft and violence, do you?

BRADLEY: Your entire speech sounds dangerously close to treason, sir.

HAMILTON: Only if you apply what I have said to the present government. Now, I do not. All men agree that we are governed by the best of kings, our good King George. It is because I believe that it is the will of the Crown that all men, without respect to their station in life, be accorded common justice that I am here to argue for John Peter Zenger. The laws of England know no exceptions. Men of authority are not exempt from observing the rules of justice.

BRADLEY: Your Honors, again Mr. Hamilton has suggested that the Governor has abused his power! I must protest.

CHIEF JUSTICE DELANCEY: Indeed, Mr. Hamilton, it would appear that you are going too far. Don't you agree, Justice Philipse?

PHILIPSE: Oh, I do. I do. Indeed I do.

HAMILTON: Your Honors, this is a dangerous precedent you are setting. Let us say that I am walking through the streets of New York and chance to be reading my Bible aloud, as for instance Isaiah 9:16. "The leaders of this people cause them to err; and they that are led of them are destroyed." If I were overheard reading my Bible, would I be in danger of treason? Would the Attorney General then have me arrested for libel because he would understand me to mean it thus: "The leaders of this people (he means the Governor and Council) cause them (he means the people of New York) to err . . ."?

DELANCEY (*Angrily*): That is quite enough, Mr. Hamilton. I do not know how you run your courts in Philadelphia, but here in New York, we know well enough what is meant. We'll have no more of it.

HAMILTON: Your Honors, if I am not permitted to reason for my client, what am I permitted to do?

DELANCEY: You may present the case. Did Mr. Zenger print the scandalous, false libel, or did he not? That is the only question in this case.

HAMILTON: I do not even know what is meant by the words, "scandalous, false libel." Your Honors will not permit us to examine what words my client has written to determine if they are scandalous or false. Your Honors, if my client were accused of stealing a plopple—

PHILIPSE (*Interrupting*): A plopple! What is a plopple? I have never heard the word before.

HAMILTON: Exactly, Justice Philipse. You have asked the right question. When one is accused of a crime, it is necessary to know what that crime is. Before we can determine if Mr. Zenger has committed libel, we must know if a libel has been committed.

PHILIPSE: But I still don't know what a plopple is.

DELANCEY: The learned gentleman from Philadelphia made a trap for you and you fell into it. There is no such thing as a plopple.

PHILIPSE: Oh! Oh, I see. It was an example. (MEMBERS OF THE JURY *laugh*)

BRADLEY: Your Honors, Mr. Hamilton has gone very much out of the way to make himself and the people merry. But his examples are not to the purpose. All the jury has to decide is that Mr. Zenger printed and published scandalous libels that reflect on His Excellency and the principal men of this government. Since Zenger has confessed he did the printing, and there can be no doubt the matter is scandalous, there should be no doubt that the jury will find the defendant guilty and leave the sentencing of the criminal to the Court.

DELANCEY: I quite agree, Mr. Bradley. It seems quite clear to me that since Mr. Zenger has admitted that he did the printing, the jury can find no verdict but guilty.

HAMILTON: Your Honor, does the jury have the right to render what verdict it sees fit?

DELANCEY: I see no reason for the jury to have any doubt. . . . But yes, Mr. Hamilton, the jury has that right. Now are you ready to let the jury speak?

HAMILTON: Your Honor, I would like to speak to the jury for the last time.

DELANCEY: Very well. But limit yourself to the matter at hand.

HAMILTON: I shall, Your Honor. (*He turns to look at* ZENGER, *then goes to address the* JURY.) Gentlemen of the Jury, freemen of New York. John Peter Zenger here, whom many of you know, is a simple, hard-working and law-abiding man. During the long time that I have worked with him on this case, I have grown quite fond of him. He is a gentle man, and his good wife, Anna, is a gentle woman. (*Changes pace; speaking more quickly*) But, Gentlemen of the Jury, something more important than Peter Zenger is on trial here today. The harm done to this man means more than a personal hurt. It can mean a loss of liberty that will affect our country—our new, struggling, hopeful country. (*Intensely*) Gentlemen of the Jury, I ask you to think on these words: How will you live in this Province if no man may speak the truth for fear he will be arrested for libel?

BRADLEY (*Jumping to his feet*): Your Honors, Mr. Hamilton goes too far!

HAMILTON (*To* BRADLEY): I do not think so. (*To* JURY) Gentlemen of the Jury, experience should warn us that when our neighbor's house is on fire, ours is in danger.

BRADLEY: Your Honors, is Mr. Hamilton to speak forever? We have all grown weary with this talk. (*Sits*)

HAMILTON: Not as weary as my client has grown at being restrained from speaking. If weariness is an issue in this court, think of the weariness of a wife and mother waiting for the return of her husband.

BRADLEY: Your Honors, the Court, too, is very sorry for Mrs. Zenger—sorry that she did not warn her husband more strongly.

ANNA (*Rising*): I did not warn him at all. I encouraged him, and I would do it again.

DELANCEY: What is this? A woman speaking in this court without permission? Is this what all this talk of liberty is coming to? (*To* ANNA; *sharply*) Woman, you are not to speak in this court, do you understand?

ANNA: But, Justice Delancey, the Attorney General has said—

DELANCEY: I said that you are to sit down and be quiet! If you speak again, I'll have you removed from the courtroom. (ANNA *sits*.) Now, Mr. Hamilton, have you finished?

HAMILTON: I have but a sentence or two more, Your Honor.

DELANCEY (*Curtly*): Well, make them brief. The Court has other business besides that of a poor printer.

HAMILTON: (*To* JURY): It is, Gentlemen of the Jury, not the cause of one poor printer, nor of New York alone, that I plead. No. In this trial may be the beginning of a rule of law that will affect every free man in all of the colonies. The cause I plead is the cause of liberty. Today, if you decide for my client, you will give all men the right to speak and write the truth.

DELANCEY: Are you quite finished, Mr. Hamilton?

HAMILTON: I am now content, Your Honor, to leave justice to the jury. (*Sits at table, right.*)

DELANCEY: Well, I am not. You have so twisted the issues that I must speak. (*Turns to* JURY) Gentlemen of the Jury, Mr. Hamilton hopes, no doubt, to make you disregard my instructions. I will, therefore, first point out that Mr. Zenger has already confessed to the crime of which he stands accused. Your verdict should simply acknowledge that you heard that confession. As to whether the words that Mr. Zenger wrote were libel or not, that is a matter for the Court—not you—to decide. Justice Philipse will tell you that I have spoken the law.

PHILIPSE: Indeed you have—indeed you have. The very law.

DELANCEY: Mr. Hamilton has also appealed to your hearts. The Court is not without sympathy for this poor printer and his wife. In fact, if Mr. Zenger were to rise and admit his full guilt —and give the Court assurances he will not err again—the Court would, upon the verdict of the jury, tend to temper justice with a goodly amount of mercy. (*He pauses and looks at* PETER.) Well, Mr. Zenger?

HAMILTON: Your Honor, may I speak to my client in private?

DELANCEY: It is not usual, but in the interest of mercy, the Court will consent. We will have a brief recess.

HAMILTON: Thank you, Your Honor. (*He leads* PETER *down right; others hold their positions.*) Peter, do you understand what has happened?

PETER: I am not sure, Mr. Hamilton.

HAMILTON: The Court is willing to free you, with just a warning, perhaps, if you will agree to admit your guilt and publish no more articles in the *Journal*.

PETER: Do you think I should do this?

HAMILTON: I don't know, Peter. I don't know. If the jury finds you guilty, you may be sent to prison for many years. It will be hard, Peter, hard for you and hard for Anna.

PETER: Will the jury find me guilty?

HAMILTON: I can't tell. The Judge has told them they have no choice. They, too, are only men, afraid that maybe by voting for you, they will anger the Governor and bring his wrath down on them. What has been done to you has made many of them afraid.

PETER: I see.

HAMILTON: Then you understand what your choice is?

PETER: I understand, and I have made my decision.

HAMILTON: Well, don't tell me. Tell the Court. (*They return to the table.*)

DELANCEY: Well, Mr. Zenger, have you decided to accept the mercy of the Court?

PETER: May I speak to the whole Court, Your Honor?

DELANCEY: Yes, but make it brief.

PETER (*Rising*): Gentlemen of the Jury, members of the Court: Mr. Hamilton has explained to me that if I admit my guilt and promise to print no more, I may be allowed to breathe the free air again. It is a pleasing prospect. I have, during these long months in prison, grown to hate bars. I miss my wife, my children, my friends. I thank the Court for its offer of mercy. But I cannot say what is not true! (*Passionately*) I did not publish libels! I will not promise to avoid the truth in the future! (*Judges half rise, shocked.*) Mr. Hamilton has told me that the jury is likely to find against me. If it is so, gentlemen (*Nodding to* JURY), I understand. I will not blame you. But I will not judge myself guilty when I am innocent. I will not sell my right to be free and honest in order to remain a prisoner out of prison.

DELANCEY (*Angrily*): Have you quite finished, Mr. Zenger?

PETER: Yes, Your Honor, and I thank you for what you have tried to do for me.

DELANCEY: Then the jury will now be dismissed to ponder upon its verdict. I again direct you, gentlemen, that your verdict need not determine if a libel was committed, merely if Mr. Zenger published the material. And to that question, there can be but one answer. The jury is now dismissed. (JURY MEMBERS *huddle together talking rapidly among themselves.*) What is going on here? I said the jury was dismissed.

1ST JURYMAN: Your Honor, must we be dismissed?

DELANCEY: Of course! You must come to a verdict.

2ND JURYMAN: But we already have, Your Honor.

DELANCEY: And is it unanimous? Do you all agree?

3RD JURYMAN: We do, Your Honor.

DELANCEY: Very well, the Court will hear the verdict. (*To* HARISON) Master Clerk, will you poll the jury?

HARISON (*Rising; to* JURY): Gentlemen, will each of you tell me privately his vote—guilty or not guilty—and I will record it. (*Takes paper and pencil and crosses to jury box. Each* JURYMAN *speaks to* HARISON, *who marks paper. Then he writes a note on paper and takes it to* DELANCEY. *All watch anxiously.*)

DELANCEY (*Taking paper from* HARISON): Is this the verdict?

HARISON: Yes, Your Honor.

DELANCEY: Mr. Attorney General, would you come here, please? (BRADLEY *goes up to bench.*)

ANNA (*Rising*): What is the verdict?

DELANCEY: Quiet in this courtroom! (ANNA *sits.* DELANCEY *and* BRADLEY *confer for a moment.* BRADLEY *returns to his seat.*) The Attorney General has requested that the jury be polled publicly. It shall be done. Clerk, poll the jury, and each juryman will answer publicly. (HARISON *starts to rise as* 1ST JURYMAN *stands.*)

1ST JURYMAN (*Quickly*): I vote not guilty!

2ND JURYMAN (*Rising*): Not guilty!

3RD *and* 4TH JURYMEN (*Rising*): Not guilty.

OTHER JURYMEN (*Rising*): Not guilty.

DELANCEY (*Furiously*): You will wait until the Clerk calls your names!

1ST JURYMAN: We will wait, Your Honor, but it won't change our verdict.

DELANCEY (*Rising and looking at* BRADLEY): Very well. This Court has found John Peter Zenger not guilty. The jury is dismissed.

JURYMEN (*Ad lib*): Hurrah! Zenger is freed! Hurrah! (*Etc.*)

DELANCEY (*Banging gavel*): Quiet in this courtroom! It becomes more and more obvious that you men have no notion of court justice. Cheering in a courtroom! This behavior is as outrageous as your verdict.

HAMILTON: Your Honor, there is a precedent for the jury voicing its satisfaction. In a case in London. . . .

DELANCEY: And, Mr. Hamilton, I've had all the lectures on law I want from you. Court is adjourned! (*To* PHILIPSE) Well, Justice

Philipse, the trial is over. Now we must report the result to the Governor. (*He rises and turns upstage.*)

PHILIPSE (*Following him*): Oh, dear. Oh, dear. I'm afraid *our* trial has just begun. (DELANCEY *and* PHILIPSE *exit, followed by* BRADLEY, CONSTABLES *and* SHERIFF. HARISON *watches unhappily as* JURYMEN *gather around* PETER, *shaking his hand and clapping him on back.*)

JURYMEN (*Ad lib*): Congratulations, Peter! You're a free man now! (*Etc.* HARISON *turns and exits. One by one,* JURYMEN *exit, talking happily to each other.* PETER *turns to* ANNA, *embraces her, then shakes* ALEXANDER's *hand. Finally* PETER *goes up to* HAMILTON, *who is standing alone at table, right.*)

PETER: Mr. Hamilton, I will never be able to thank you enough. Not if I live to be a hundred.

HAMILTON (*Smiling wryly*): Don't, Peter. Don't live to be a hundred. I am sorry I did.

PETER: Please, Mr. Hamilton, I want to tell you how I feel—how much I owe you.

HAMILTON: No, Peter, let me tell you what I owe you. Let me tell you what all free men owe you. A century from now, two centuries from now, men will still speak of you and what your courage has done this day. Peter, you have won a great battle for freedom. Freedom of the press was born today.

PETER: Freedom of the press! Those are big words, Mr. Hamilton.

HAMILTON: And from today on, they are not only words. With your courage today, Peter, with your insistence that all men have the right to speak the truth, to hear the truth, to write the truth, and to read the truth, you have made Truth a respectable citizen of our land. In years to come, when journalists name the heroes of their profession, John Peter Zenger will lead all the rest. (*Curtain*)

THE END

The Boston Tea Party

The defiant act that led to freedom

by Lindsey Barbee

Characters

NANCY, *a young Colonial girl*
DOLLY ⎱
ABIGAIL ⎰ *her friends*
ELIZA ⎰
JOHN, *Dolly's older brother*
ROGER, *Nancy's brother*
PHILIP, *Roger's friend*

TIME: *December 16, 1773.*

SETTING: *Living room of Nancy's Boston home, with furnishings of the Revolutionary period. At the back of the room is a fireplace with a low mantel. Portrait of a stern-looking man hangs over mantel, and a bench stands before fire. At the left is a window with white curtains. A small table with silver tea service, cups and saucers on it stands at upper right. Exits are down left and right center.*

AT RISE: NANCY *is standing at the window;* DOLLY *is on the fireside bench;* ABIGAIL *sits up left, busy with her embroidery;* ELIZA, *with her knitting, sits down right. Suddenly,* NANCY *claps her hands and cheers happily.*

DOLLY: What's happened? (*Runs to* NANCY *and peers out window*) Why, I don't see a single thing or a single person.

NANCY: That's why I'm clapping, Dolly.

DOLLY: Nancy, you do say the queerest things.

NANCY: There isn't a sign of a Redcoat. (*Laughing*) Isn't that worth a clap?

DOLLY (*Shocked*): It isn't right to speak of the King's soldiers in such a tone of voice.

ABIGAIL (*Angrily*): How can you worry about what is "right" for the Tories, when the King has just levied this abominable new tax on tea?

DOLLY: But at least the tea itself is inexpensive.

ELIZA: The question is not how much the tea costs, but that it not be taxed.

NANCY: You're just right, Eliza; and if we can't have untaxed tea, we'll have no tea at all.

DOLLY: How you girls talk! Why, we all belong to the mother country—we're all English.

ELIZA: I prefer to say that we are all colonists.

ABIGAIL: And as Nancy has just said, it is a joy not to see a Redcoat strutting up and down.

NANCY: Sending those two regiments to an island in Boston Harbor gives us a chance to take a long breath.

ABIGAIL: I'll never forget that Sunday morning when they all marched into Boston with flags flying and drums beating.

DOLLY: That shocked the good old Puritans, didn't it?

NANCY: It did more than that. It made us very angry.

DOLLY: If people would try to understand that the English are trying to help us. . . .

ABIGAIL (*Angrily*): One more word of such talk, Dolly, and you are likely to be hit.

DOLLY: But I'm still true to England.

NANCY (*Thoughtfully*): Now just how do you expect us to take that?

ELIZA: Let's take it just as Patrick Henry took the news of the Stamp Act. (*Rises*) I'll be Patrick Henry as he spoke in the Virginia House of Burgesses. (*Dramatically*) "Caesar had his Brutus, Charles the Second his Cromwell, and George the Third—"

NANCY (*Excitedly*): Right there, some of the members called, "Treason! Treason!"

ABIGAIL: Let Dolly be those members. "Treason! Treason!" Say it, Dolly.

DOLLY: Treason! Treason!

ELIZA (*Still quoting Patrick Henry*): "And George the Third may

profit by their example! If this be treason, make the most of it."
(*Sits*)

ABIGAIL: Oh, but that was stirring! It makes me want to be a man.

NANCY (*Jumping up*): Women can do a lot, too.

ELIZA (*Pointing to portrait over mantel*): Nancy, you look as fierce
as the man in that picture staring down upon you.

NANCY: He's an ancestor of mine—a fighting ancestor.

DOLLY (*Smugly*): And he fought for England, didn't he?

NANCY: That's because there wasn't an America to fight for.

DOLLY (*Sighing*): He must be disappointed in you.

NANCY: No such thing. He would be proud of us.

ELIZA (*Interrupting*): This is such a nice, rambling old house,
Nancy. I'm so glad you asked us to stay the night while your
parents are away. Did your father build this house?

NANCY: Mercy, no. (*Laughs*) It belonged to smugglers before we
moved here.

ABIGAIL: Smugglers?

NANCY: Haven't I ever told you?

ABIGAIL: Never.

NANCY: Maybe you'd call them pirates. Anyway, they brought all
their stolen goods right from the harbor without anybody's
knowing about it.

DOLLY: Just how?

NANCY: Through a secret passage.

ELIZA: *Secret passage!* Oh, Nancy!

NANCY: Now, watch. (*She presses a button by the mantel and a
part of the wood paneling slides slowly to the side.*)

ELIZA: How wonderful!

ABIGAIL: And all the smuggled things were brought right into the
house from ships in the Harbor.

NANCY: Smuggled or stolen. (*She touches the button and replaces
the panel*) Better not leave it open.

ELIZA: I should say not. (*Sound of knocker is heard.* DOLLY *runs
to window.*)

DOLLY: Oh, it's my brother, John. He's bringing my things for
tonight.

NANCY: I'll let him in. (*Goes out left.*)

DOLLY: Where's Roger, I wonder?

ELIZA: Up in his room. Philip is with him.

ABIGAIL: Why don't they come down for tea?

ELIZA: They probably will. (NANCY *enters from left with* JOHN.)

JOHN: Here's your bag, Dolly. (DOLLY *takes bag, as* JOHN *waves.*) This is a salute, girls.

NANCY: John, please stay for tea. I'll get it. It won't take a minute. (*Takes teapot.*)

ABIGAIL (*Running after her*): I'll help. (*They go out at right.* JOHN *and* ELIZA *sit on fireside bench.* DOLLY, *her bag on the floor beside her, sits down right.*)

JOHN: Speaking of tea, three ships are in the harbor, and they're about to land their cargoes.

ELIZA: The colonists won't allow it.

JOHN: They can't help it. King's orders.

DOLLY: The girls have been saying dreadful things about the King.

JOHN: Let them say what they wish. They can't get away from the fact that the King is King. (NANCY *enters with teapot, followed by* ABIGAIL *with a plate of cakes.* NANCY *sits behind the tea table and pours tea as* ABIGAIL *hands a cup and saucer to each guest.*)

DOLLY: John says that there are three ships of tea in the harbor. (ABIGAIL *passes cakes.*)

NANCY (*Calmly*): That's too bad. (ABIGAIL *sits up left.*)

JOHN: Can't do much about it. (*He sips tea, chokes and splutters.*) Great heavens!

DOLLY (*Anxiously*): What's the matter?

JOHN: This so-called tea! What are you giving us, Nancy?

NANCY: Oh, *that!* Why, it's sage tea, John. We're not serving tea here anymore.

JOHN: This isn't fit to drink.

ABIGAIL (*Calmly*): Then I'll remove your cup, John.

JOHN (*Annoyed*): I'll remove it myself. (*Puts cup on table*) Sage is not fit to drink, I say.

NANCY: Neither is taxed tea. But, perhaps, you'll have another cake.

JOHN: I'll be going. (*Crosses to left*) Mother wants you to come back early tomorrow morning, Dolly. (*At door*) Goodbye. (*Goes out.* ABIGAIL *brings cups and saucers to the table.*)

NANCY (*Demurely*): I do believe he's angry. (ELIZA *rushes to window.*)

ELIZA: He's hurrying as if the Redcoats were after him. (NANCY *and* ABIGAIL *cross to window and look out.*)

DOLLY: They wouldn't be after *him*. (*At left, door opens, and* ROGER, *wearing feathered Indian headdress, puts his head into room.* DOLLY *notices him, and, terrified, shrieks, pointing to door.* ROGER *quickly withdraws, pulling door shut.*)

ABIGAIL (*Turning*): Dolly!

ELIZA: What is it?

DOLLY (*Pointing to door left*): There! *There!* An Indian!

NANCY: How silly! The door is closed.

DOLLY (*Frightened*): But it opened—it did. (*Door begins to open again.*)

ABIGAIL (*In a whisper, as she goes to stand back of table*): It *is* opening, Nancy. (*Door opens, but no one enters.*)

NANCY (*Calling*): Who's there? (ROGER *enters, in Indian headdress and with paint on his face. Girls cry out in fright.* NANCY *crosses room slowly.*)

ROGER: Me Big Chief Teapot.

NANCY: You're Big Brother Roger! (PHILIP *enters, also dressed as an Indian.*)

PHILIP: Me No Tax Tomahawk.

ELIZA: It's Philip!

NANCY: You crazy boys! Why are you pretending to be Indians? To frighten us?

PHILIP: We scared you, all right.

ABIGAIL: Who wouldn't be scared to look at anything so hideous.

ROGER: We're the real thing.

ELIZA (*Returning to fireside bench*): Are you going to a masquerade?

ROGER: Better than that. We're on our way to the harbor.

PHILIP (*Excitedly*): Three ships loaded with tea have come into the harbor.

ROGER: And every bit of that tea is to be dumped into the water.

PHILIP: We'll show them.

ROGER: Sam Adams and a lot of other men dressed up as Mohawk Indians are gathering in that empty house at the corner.

PHILIP: As soon as it's dark, they'll creep down the street, board the ships, and dump every single tea chest overboard.

ROGER (*Proudly*): And Phil and I are allowed to go along.

NANCY: Wonderful! Oh, I wish I were a man!

ELIZA (*Crossing to table*): Here's some sage tea, boys.

ROGER (*Laughing*): Don't say tea to *us*.

PHILIP: But the cakes look good. (*As they crowd around table,* DOLLY *moves away and, unseen by them, takes her bag, hurries quickly and quietly across room, and exits.*)

ABIGAIL: Fill your pockets with the cakes. We won't want them.

ELIZA: And it gives us a part in the fun.

NANCY: Is there any chance of being hurt, Roger?

ROGER: We wouldn't be allowed to go along if there were.

PHILIP: Lots of the sailors have landed, and there won't be many on board.

ROGER: And it won't take us long to open the chests.

ABIGAIL (*Suddenly*): Where's Dolly?

NANCY (*Looking around*): She was here a moment or so ago— right over there.

ELIZA: Her bag is gone. (ABIGAIL *rushes to door down left, opens it, and peers out.*)

ABIGAIL: Her cape is gone.

NANCY (*Excitedly*): Then she's giving the alarm.

ROGER: What do you mean?

NANCY: It's no secret that she's taking the side of the King.

ELIZA (*Upset*): And she'll be telling everybody about your plans.

PHILIP: Then we'd better hurry.

ABIGAIL (*Sadly*): There'll be plenty of the King's men looking for you—now.

NANCY: Listen to me! (*As they crowd around her*) Listen to me.

ELIZA: What is it, Nancy?

NANCY: Go out by way of the secret passage. Nobody will see you go or follow you *that* way.

ROGER (*Excitedly*): And the secret passage leads straight to the harbor.

NANCY: The other men are nearby, you say?

ROGER: At the corner.

NANCY: Then have them all come here and use the passage.

ROGER: We'll do it. (*Rushes to door down left.*)

NANCY: Not *that* way. (*Points to right*) *This*. Then you can go out at the back.

PHILIP: Good thinking, Nancy. We'll see you later. (*Follows*

ROGER *out at right. Girls are silent. Then* NANCY *claps her hands in excitement.*)

NANCY: Oh, what a great event! We'll call it the Boston Tea Party. (*Curtain*)

* * * *

SCENE 2

TIME: *A short time later.*

SETTING: *The same as Scene 1.*

AT RISE: NANCY *is on the fireside bench;* ABIGAIL *is at upper left;* ELIZA *is in the chair back of the table.*

NANCY (*Impatiently*): Time drags so when one happens to be waiting.

ABIGAIL: There has been no sound of disturbance.

ELIZA: And wasn't it exciting to see that crowd of Indians hurrying into the secret passage?

NANCY: The men liked the strangeness of it.

ABIGAIL: I only hope that there isn't a single, solitary package of tea left to tell the story.

ELIZA: Will they all come back through the passage?

ABIGAIL: Oh, I hope so!

NANCY: Roger and Philip will be along. We can be pretty sure of that.

ABIGAIL: I'll take a look. (*Crosses to window*) Look! The street is full of people.

NANCY (*Joining her*): Then everything must be over.

ELIZA: I wonder how Dolly feels now!

ABIGAIL: Wasn't it appropriate for her to be the one to call out, "Treason! Treason!"

NANCY: She'll be sorry. (*Sharply*) We'll see that she is. (*Suddenly sharp tap is heard from behind panel beside mantel.*)

ELIZA: There they are—Roger and Philip.

ABIGAIL: Be sure before you open the passage.

NANCY (*Crossing and calling*): Who is it?

ROGER (*From offstage*): We're back!

NANCY: Oh, it is the boys! (*Excitedly, she touches button, and rolls back the panel.* ROGER, *still dressed as an Indian, appears in opening.*)

ROGER: Give us some air, for we're about to suffocate in that old passage. (NANCY *opens window, as* ROGER *enters room.* PHILIP *follows him in.*)

PHILIP: Suffocate is just the word. Here, Roger—let me in on that air. (*Both boys cross to window.*)

ROGER: Now I'm all right.

PHILIP: So am I.

NANCY: Aren't the other men coming?

ROGER: No.

PHILIP: They're scattered here and there and everywhere.

ABIGAIL: *Do* tell us about it.

PHILIP: Let me stretch out a minute. (*Sits on fireside bench and stretches his legs before him*)

ROGER: And I'll take this chair if nobody wants it. (*Sits at upper left*)

ELIZA: We just can't wait another moment to hear everything. Move over, Philip. (*Sits by* PHILIP)

PHILIP (*Laughing*): There's not enough tea left in those ships for an afternoon party.

NANCY (*Dragging chair from right*): Tell us.

ABIGAIL: Let me have the arm of your chair, Nancy. (*Sits on arm of chair*)

ROGER: The whole thing started at the meeting when the Governor persisted in carrying out the King's orders.

PHILIP: And Samuel Adams said, "This meeting can do nothing more to save the country."

ELIZA (*Puzzled*): What a strange thing to say!

ROGER: But it was a secret signal, for right away somebody called, "Will tea mix with salt water?"

PHILIP: And somebody else shouted, "Boston harbor for a teapot tonight."

ROGER: So that's how everything happened.

PHILIP: All the men—the Sons of Liberty—disguised themselves as Indians—

ROGER (*With a happy sigh*): And took us along. They say 342 chests of tea went into the harbor tonight. I hope that this settles the King for all time.

PHILIP (*Curiously*): Settles the King?

ABIGAIL: He'll learn that he can't impose another tax upon us.

PHILIP: Listen, girls. (*Pauses*) Things are just beginning.

ROGER: Beginning is right.

PHILIP: We've heard a lot of talk tonight.

ROGER: And men seem to think that one thing leads to another.

NANCY: What do you mean?

ROGER: The Stamp Act—these other taxes—the regiments—and now, *this*.

NANCY: The Boston Tea Party, we call it.

PHILIP: Some say that we'll pay for it by harsher laws.

ROGER: And most everybody feels that it will end in war.

ABIGAIL: *War?* Oh, no.

PHILIP: I'll fight.

ROGER: And so shall I.

ELIZA: There *can't* be a war—there just *can't*.

NANCY: Remember that war would make us free—for we would win.

ROGER: It *will* make us free.

PHILIP: And it's coming—(*Pauses*) We colonists are determined to be free.

ROGER (*Laughing*): Why, someday, school children will read about what's happened tonight.

NANCY (*Very seriously*): The Boston Tea Party. (*Curtain*)

THE END

Martha Washington's Spy

A case of mistaken identity

by Earl J. Dias

Characters

GENERAL GEORGE WASHINGTON
MARTHA WASHINGTON
SILAS WEGG ⎫
CALEB JENKINS ⎬ *young soldiers*
BETSY, *a young girl*
BENJAMIN JAEKEL
SAM HOWARD

TIME: *A cold night in January, 1777.*
SETTING: *A sentry outpost at Valley Forge.*
AT RISE: SILAS *is pacing back and forth, a musket on his shoulder. He stops occasionally to stamp his feet and rub his arms. Footsteps are heard from off left.* SILAS *points his musket in direction of the sounds.*

SILAS: Halt! Who goes there?

CALEB (*Offstage*): It's Caleb Jenkins, Silas.

SILAS: Come out here where I can see you. (CALEB *enters from left.*)

CALEB: Nervous, Silas?

SILAS: Cold more than anything. (*He shivers.*) Br-r—I could do with a big mug of hot tea.

CALEB: All of us could, I'll wager.

SILAS: Why are you traipsin' about on a night like this? If I could, I'd be back in the barracks with the covers over my head to keep out the cold.

CALEB: Orders from General Washington himself. Ever since

Tom Weeks fell asleep at his post a week ago, the General has seen to it that someone inspects the sentry posts every night.

SILAS: As if anyone could sleep in this cold. And anyway, why all the care and caution? Who would want to come to this forsaken place?

CALEB: A spy, for one.

SILAS (*Sarcastically*): A spy! What old wives' tales have you been hearing?

CALEB: This is no old wives' tale. I heard the General say that the countryside is swarming with them.

SILAS (*Laughing*): With what? Old wives?

CALEB (*Blowing on his hands*): With spies.

SILAS: Spies, indeed! If the lobsterbacks want this miserable place, they're welcome to it, as far as I'm concerned.

CALEB: Oh, you can laugh—but the British want to know our strength here, how many men we have.

SILAS (*Bitterly, as he begins his pacing once more*): I can tell them that easily enough. We've fewer men today than we had yesterday; and tomorrow, we'll have fewer men than we have today. They're certainly deserting fast enough.

CALEB: You sound as though you'd like to join the deserters.

SILAS (*Stopping his pacing and speaking angrily*): Let me make one thing clear, Caleb Jenkins—I'll not desert. Wars aren't won by the fainthearted, and liberty isn't gained by cowards. (*Pauses*) I keep thinking about Sam Howard. He comes from a farm near here, and, before I came on duty tonight, he told me he's decided to leave the army. "I can freeze at home as well as here," he said. "And at home, at least, I can be of help to my wife and baby." He has probably left by now.

CALEB: I never would have expected such an action from Sam.

SILAS: Nor would I. He always seemed a strong and honest enough fellow and devoted to the cause.

CALEB (*Sighing*): As Scripture says, "The spirit is willing, but the flesh is weak." Well, I'll be off about my duties. I have four more posts to inspect—if I don't freeze as stiff as a tree before I get to them. Good night, Silas.

SILAS: Good night, Caleb. (CALEB *exits right.* SILAS *begins pacing again. There is a sudden noise offstage left, a sort of thump followed by an exclamation.* SILAS, *pointing his musket in the direction of the noise, advances cautiously toward exit. He exits. In a moment,* SILAS *returns holding* BETSY *by the collar. She wears man's coat, a muffler, and a cocked hat.* SILAS *stands back and points his musket at his captive, who huddles, shivering and afraid.*) Now, my sly fellow, just what is your business here?

BETSY (*In high, shrill voice*): Don't shoot, sir. (SILAS *advances toward captive, examines the face closely, and then whistles in surprise.*)

SILAS: Why! You're a girl!

BETSY: Y-yes. My name is Betsy.

SILAS (*Still aiming his musket at her*): Betsy, is it? So the British are using females now to do their nasty work!

BETSY (*With spirit*): What do you mean?

SILAS: My meaning should be clear. Here you are, creeping about the camp on a night as cold as King George's heart, and dressed as a man, too! It's as plain as a dish of beans that you're bent on mischief.

BETSY: That's not true.

SILAS: Well, it will do until a better explanation comes along— and I doubt if a better one will. At least, my duty is plain. (*He whistles loudly—two long whistles and one short one.*) There. That will bring somebody here who'll take you to General Washington.

BETSY (*Cringing*): Oh, no—please let me go! I swear to you that I'm not a spy!

SILAS (*Laughing*): You're a splendid actress, miss.

BETSY: Please believe me.

SILAS (*Impatiently*): Then just what are you doing here?

BETSY: I can't tell you. It's something I must keep to myself. But I'm not a spy! (CALEB *enters hurriedly.*)

CALEB: What's wrong, Silas? I heard your signal. (*Looking at* BETSY) And who is this?

SILAS: A female dressed as a man, Caleb.

CALEB (*Going to* BETSY *and examining her closely*): I told you the countryside was swarming with spies.

BETSY (*Spiritedly*): Oh, you two are blockheads!

SILAS: Blockheads, indeed! Listen to her, Caleb. "I'm not a spy," she says, "but I can't tell you what I'm doing here. It's something I must keep to myself." (*Disgustedly*) Take her to the General.

CALEB (*Grinning*): That won't be necessary. I'll bring the General to her. He's not far from here now—inspecting posts himself tonight. And his wife is with him.

SILAS: His wife?

CALEB: She's visiting him for a spell. Brought him some warm stockings for one thing. She's a pleasant enough lady—and about the only warmth I've seen around here for a month. (*Going to* BETSY *and chucking her under the chin*) My, you're a pretty lass. Too bad you're on the wrong side.

BETSY (*Pushing his hand away*): Mind your manners! (CALEB *exits. A noise is heard offstage.*)

SILAS: Halt! Who goes there? (BENJAMIN JAEKEL *enters.*)

BENJAMIN: I am Benjamin Jaekel, sir, a friend to the cause. (*He goes to center and looks at* BETSY.) Aha! There you are! Caught, are you? I hoped you would be.

BETSY (*Surprised*): Who are you?

SILAS: This place is as crowded tonight as a Philadelphia street. Just what is your business here?

BENJAMIN (*Bowing with a flourish*): Benjamin Jaekel, as I told you, sir. A friend of the cause and sworn enemy to the British. I own a farm a few miles from here.

SILAS: Then why aren't you at home in your warm kitchen?

BENJAMIN (*Bowing again*): I'm in the service of liberty, young sir. I came out of my barn tonight and saw this person here (*Nodding toward* BETSY) sneaking across my fields. At first, I thought she was a man. Then I noticed the way she walked, rather mincing-like. I said to myself, "Benjamin Jaekel, there is something peculiar and sinister about all this." Oh, I've heard talk a-plenty about spies in these parts. So I said to myself, "Benjamin Jaekel, follow that woman. She's up to no good. And if she's a spy, why, perhaps there'll be a small reward for unmasking her." (*He grins.*) I've heard that General Washington is a generous man.

SILAS (*Scratching his head*): Your story sounds reasonable.

BENJAMIN: Young sir, surely no one will doubt the word of Benjamin Jaekel. Honest Ben, they call me.

BETSY (*Angrily*): I tell you again. I am not a spy.

BENJAMIN (*Bowing to her*): Ah, young lady, never let it be said that honest Ben Jaekel ever argued with a woman (*He winks at* SILAS.) and a fetching one at that. But, at the risk of violating

the politeness for which I am famous, I must contradict you.
(*He places his hand over his heart.*) But it wounds me here to
do so.

BETSY (*Heatedly*): Nonsense!

SILAS (*With mock concern*): We have a spitfire on our hands, Mr.
Jaekel.

BENJAMIN: Ah, well, I'm sure that you and the rest of General
Washington's men will be a match for her. Your lines seem
well guarded enough. How many sentry posts do you have?

SILAS: That's a military secret.

BENJAMIN (*Bowing to him*): Of course. It was foolish of me to
ask. I apologize, young sir, for my lack of discretion.

BETSY (*Impatiently*): Do we have to stand here in the cold like
addle-headed idiots?

SILAS: Hold your tongue.

BENJAMIN (*Coughing politely*): Er—I believe, young sir, that
our pretty and mysterious companion has a point. This cold
tonight is as piercing as a dagger. (*He rubs his arms.*) Could
we not take our fetching spy to the proper authorities, where
(*Winking at* SILAS) I might be rewarded for recognizing her evil
errand?

SILAS: General Washington himself will be here at any moment.

BENJAMIN: Ah, what an opportunity! A chance to shake the hand
of a man whose name is a byword among lovers of liberty
everywhere. I am honored, honored.

BETSY: I wish he'd hurry, then.

SILAS: There'll be bad news for you when he does get here.

BENJAMIN: Right, young sir—bad news, indeed. What do you
do with spies, sir? Hang them or shoot them? (*He shakes his
head in mock sadness.*) Such a lovely neck to have a noose
around it. It wounds me here. (*Placing his hand over his
heart.*)

BETSY (*Sharply*): Save your unwanted sympathy for those who can
use it. I'm not a spy, and there won't be any hanging.

BENJAMIN (*Sadly*): Ah, poor child. You little know what you say.
(CALEB *enters, followed by* GENERAL WASHINGTON *and* MARTHA
WASHINGTON, *both bundled up in warm clothing.* SILAS *lowers
his musket and salutes.* WASHINGTON *returns salute.*)

WASHINGTON (*Looking at* BETSY): And who is this? Is this war
now being fought by women?

SILAS: She's a spy, sir. I apprehended her attempting to get through the lines.

BENJAMIN (*Coughing politely*): With my help, General. I followed this young woman for several miles when I saw that her appearance was somewhat unusual.

WASHINGTON (*Looking at* BENJAMIN): And who are you?

BENJAMIN (*Bowing*): Benjamin Jaekel, sir, at your service and at the service of all true patriots. A farmer, sir, a poor but honest tiller of the soil, who counts it the privilege of a lifetime to meet the great General Washington face to face.

WASHINGTON: Hm-m. (*To* BETSY) And what have you to say for yourself, young woman?

BETSY: I am not a spy, sir.

MARTHA (*Looking closely at* BETSY): Why, George, she's just a child!

BETSY (*Firmly*): I'm a woman, ma'am. I'm eighteen.

MARTHA: You certainly don't look like a spy.

CALEB: She says she isn't, but she's a pert thing.

WASHINGTON: If you're not a spy, what are you? And what are you doing here?

BETSY (*Defiantly*): I can't say, sir.

WASHINGTON (*A bit impatiently*): What do you mean, you can't say? Surely, if your presence here is entirely innocent, you can tell us about it. (*More gently*) I don't bite, child.

BETSY (*Beginning to cry*): I—I can't say.

MARTHA: Don't bully the child, George. Can't you see that she's upset and close to tears?

WASHINGTON: My dear Martha, I'm not attempting to bully her. But surely it's my duty to discover just what errand she is on.

BENJAMIN: And mark my words—it's an errand that bodes no good to the Colonies.

MARTHA (*Impatiently*): You men are all alike—jumping to conclusions before the issues are clear.

WASHINGTON: But, Martha, this young woman seems to be making no attempt to clarify the issues for us.

MARTHA (*Gently*): Why can't you tell us why you are here, child?

BETSY (*As her sobs subside*): Because—well, because someone would get into trouble if I did.

MARTHA: But can't you see that you're in even greater trouble yourself?

BETSY (*Uncertainly*): But I—

MARTHA: Isn't it something you can tell me—just as one woman to another?

WASHINGTON: Martha, really—there's nothing to do but to take her to headquarters and to question her until she reveals the truth.

BENJAMIN: Wise words, sir, wise words. She'll confess with the proper treatment, I'm sure.

MARTHA (*Angrily, to* BENJAMIN): No one has asked for your opinion!

BENJAMIN (*Bowing*): My deepest apologies, ma'am. (*Placing hand on heart*) I am wounded here—but no matter.

BETSY (*Angrily*): You're always being wounded! I think you're perfectly horrible!

WASHINGTON: Please—let's get to the business at hand. You had better come with us, young woman.

MARTHA: Wait, George. (*She places her arm around* BETSY's *shoulders.*) Surely, child, your secret cannot be so terrible that it is worth being regarded as a spy. (*Very gently*) I ask you again—isn't it something you can tell me?

BETSY: B-but if I tell you, you'll tell the General, and I know that he'll be very angry.

MARTHA (*Gently*): Not necessarily. Please believe me, the General is a reasonable and a kindly man. (*With a laugh*) I ought to know, after nearly twenty years of marriage to him. (*She looks affectionately at* WASHINGTON.)

WASHINGTON (*Smiling*): Thank you, Martha.

MARTHA (*Leading* BETSY *right*): Let's go over here, and you can whisper your secret to me.

BETSY: Oh, I wish I could. (*Uncertainly*) I want to—you seem so understanding, but— (*They pause, right.*)

MARTHA: Of course you want to. And I know that everything will be all right. Problems that seem earthshaking often turn out to be really very small. Come.

BETSY (*Yielding*): Well—

MARTHA: Please, it's for the best.

BETSY (*Obviously relieved*): I will! (*She starts whispering to* MARTHA, *who smiles and nods with increasing signs of approval as* BETSY *goes on.*)

SILAS (*Speaking to* WASHINGTON *at left, as* BETSY *and* MARTHA *talk at right*): This is a strange case, General.

WASHINGTON: It's a strange war. You seem frozen to the bone.

SILAS (*Shivering*): It's a cold night, sir.

WASHINGTON: Do you know anything of a soldier named Sam Howard? He's missing from his quarters.

SILAS (*Hesitating*): W-well, sir—

WASHINGTON: I see. He has deserted, and you don't want to give him away. Well, I suppose one must be loyal to one's friends, and heaven only knows there are enough deserters.

CALEB: Sam has gone back to his farm, sir. It's only a few miles from here.

WASHINGTON (*Shaking his head*): If only we can get through this bitter winter. It does things to a man, weakens the very moral fiber of him.

BENJAMIN: No true patriot would desert his cause.

WASHINGTON: That may be true, but, after all, men are only human beings, compounded of strength and weakness. The conditions here try even the stoutest hearts. (*Grimly*) But we will survive.

CALEB: Amen to that, sir. (MARTHA *and* BETSY *walk to center.*)

MARTHA: One thing is certain, George—this young woman— her name, by the way, is Betsy—is no spy.

WASHINGTON: Indeed—then what is she?

MARTHA: I'll tell you privately, George. There is no reason for her secret to be shared by the entire army.

WASHINGTON (*Dubiously*): But, surely—

MARTHA (*Irritated*): George, certainly you don't doubt the word of your own wife. I'll take my oath that this young woman is innocent of any sinister designs.

WASHINGTON (*Shrugging his shoulders*): Very well, Martha. Of course I do not doubt you. (*To* SILAS *and* CALEB) You men had better take this young woman—Betsy, isn't it? (BETSY *nods.*) —to my headquarters. Otherwise, she's certain to catch her death of cold. Give her something warm to drink. (*To* BETSY) Please stay there until I return. I shall want to talk with you.

BETSY (*Happily*): Yes, General.

WASHINGTON (*To* SILAS *and* CALEB): When you two men have taken care of this young woman, have something to drink yourselves, and then return here. (*To* SILAS) I'll man your post until you get back.

SILAS (*Saluting*): Thank you, sir. (SILAS, CALEB *and* BETSY *go toward right. Before they exit,* BETSY *turns and speaks.*)

BETSY: And thank you, ma'am. Thank you with all my heart. (MARTHA *nods and smiles as the three exit.*)

BENJAMIN: I could have sworn that girl was up to no good.

MARTHA (*Acidly*): I'm sure that you, like all of us, have made your share of mistakes in your time.

BENJAMIN (*Bowing*): Naturally.

WASHINGTON: When we return to our quarters, Mr. Jaekel, you might join us for a drink of something hot before you go back to your farm.

BENJAMIN: Ah, thank you, General. You are generous beyond measure, and the night is indeed cold. (SAM HOWARD *enters quietly and pauses hesitantly for a moment.*)

WASHINGTON: Who goes there? Come forth to be recognized. (SAM *goes center, visibly surprised at the sight of* WASHINGTON.) Your face is familiar. Who are you?

SAM (*Saluting*): Sam Howard, sir.

BENJAMIN: Aha, the deserter! The traitor to the noble cause of the Colonies!

WASHINGTON: Why are you prowling around the lines at this time of night? I heard you had gone back to your farm.

SAM: I started back, sir.

WASHINGTON: And what happened?

SAM: I found I couldn't do it, sir.

MARTHA: Good lad!

SAM: You see, sir, I have been worried about Betsy—that's my wife. She hasn't been well, and then there is the baby to care for. I decided I *had* to get home—that I could do more good there than I could here. So I left.

MARTHA: Your Betsy is here.

SAM (*Astounded*): Here? Betsy here?

MARTHA (*Smiling*): Indeed she is—and she came near to being taken as a spy.

SAM: But I don't understand. What is she doing so far from home?

WASHINGTON: You're not the only one who would like to solve that mystery.

MARTHA: You may as well know the story now, George. (*To* SAM) When Betsy received your last letter, Sam—

SAM (*Sighing, ruefully*): I said a lot of foolish things in that letter.

MARTHA: When Betsy received it, she could read between the lines. She had a suspicion you might be planning to desert the army because you were worried about her. So she walked a good eight or ten miles to see you tonight.

SAM: Poor Betsy—in all this cold.

MARTHA: She wanted to persuade you to stay. Betsy is all right. She says that things are now going well, that she is over her sickness, and that she can manage things on the farm. Her mother and father have come to stay with her.

SAM: But this is wonderful news! Now she won't be alone.

WASHINGTON (*Thoughtfully*): So that is why young Betsy attempted to break through the lines tonight. I see now why she was reluctant to discuss her mission.

SAM: And to think that I almost deserted. (*To* WASHINGTON) But do you know, sir, that after I had gone a few miles, my conscience began to plague me. That's why I turned back. I suddenly realized that freedom and liberty are worth fighting and being uncomfortable for. And I said to myself, "If all the army looked to their own comfort first, how could we win the war?"

WASHINGTON: How, indeed!

BENJAMIN (*Unctuously*): A very pleasing sentiment.

SAM (*Eying* BENJAMIN *closely*): General, who is this man?

BENJAMIN: Farmer Benjamin Jaekel, sir, at your service and devoted to the fight against tyranny.

SAM: Jaekel? (*Gazes intently at* BENJAMIN.) That wasn't your name a year ago.

BENJAMIN (*Nervously*): I was born Benjamin Jaekel, and I shall die the same. Explain yourself, young man.

SAM (*Excitedly*): General Washington, when we were stationed at Trenton, months ago, I saw this man at a tavern there. He made several attempts to bribe a group of us soldiers—offering money for information about troop movements. Some of us set on him, but he escaped. I'll take my oath this is the same man. His name was Langdon then.

BENJAMIN (*Nervously*): Young sir, you're mistaken—mistaken, indeed. Ben Jaekel is the name—honest Ben to all who know me. My farm is but a few miles from here.

SAM: So is mine. I know all the farms for miles around, and there's no Jaekel on any of them.

WASHINGTON: Well, honest Ben. What have you to say for yourself?

BENJAMIN: This is all a terrible error, General.

SAM (*To* BENJAMIN): Take off your hat.

BENJAMIN: Be reasonable, young sir. This joke, or this case of mistaken identity—call it what you will—has gone far enough. (*Righteously*) And to ask a man to remove his hat in this cold is an insult to his intelligence.

MARTHA: Why do you make such a request, Sam?

SAM: Because the Langdon I knew had a long scar on his scalp— a deep, red one.

WASHINGTON (*Sternly*): Remove your hat.

BENJAMIN (*Moving toward exit*): Sir, I will not be bullied! I— (*Together,* WASHINGTON *and* SAM *grab* BENJAMIN *and pull off his hat.*)

MARTHA (*Inspecting* BENJAMIN'S *head as the others hold him*): You're right, Sam. (*Excited*) Here's the scar, as big as life.

BENJAMIN: This is an outrage! The Continental Congress shall hear of this!

WASHINGTON (*Coldly*): It will—though not in a manner favorable to you, Mr. Langdon. (*To* SAM) Sam, take this fellow to my headquarters. I'll be there as soon as the sentry returns. (*Sternly*) I'll want a few words with you, too.

SAM (*Saluting*): Yes, sir. Come along, Langdon.

MARTHA: And there's someone there whom I'm sure you will enjoy seeing.

SAM: You mean Betsy, ma'am?

MARTHA (*Smiling*): Find out for yourself.

SAM (*Grasping* BENJAMIN *roughly by the arm*): Come on.

BENJAMIN: Heads will roll for this!

SAM (*Sharply*): Yours among them! (*They exit right,* BENJAMIN *still protesting.*)

WASHINGTON (*Sighing*): Well, my dear, you see now that anything can happen in the military life. The question now, I suppose, is what to do about Sam. After all, he did try to desert, so he should be court-martialed.

MARTHA: George, you wouldn't do such a thing to such a nice young man!

WASHINGTON (*Firmly*): Military regulations are severe.

MARTHA: Well, they may be, but *you're* not, thank heaven. And I know you wouldn't want to make that courageous young woman unhappier than she is.

WASHINGTON: Now, about that young woman—wives of enlisted men aren't supposed to visit their husbands here, you know.

MARTHA: But it's perfectly clear why she did. She's a brave child. (*Smiling and very softly*) And, George, I came to you, after all, because I missed you so.

WASHINGTON (*Somewhat appeased*): And it's good to have you— but this is no place for a woman.

MARTHA: But about Sam?

WASHINGTON: Well—

MARTHA: Please, George.

WASHINGTON (*Softening*): It's against regulations—

MARTHA: You won't have him court-martialed, will you? After all, he unmasked that horrible Langdon.

WASHINGTON: That's true. He did. (*He looks at her affectionately.*) Martha, you could charm a robin from a tree. No, I won't court-martial him.

MARTHA: Thank you. (*She kisses him lightly on the cheek.*)

WASHINGTON (*Chuckling*): You know, I believe I'll resign from the army.

MARTHA (*Surprised*): George, what are you saying?

WASHINGTON: And I'll recommend my wife as Commander-in-Chief. She seems to know more about human nature than I do.

MARTHA (*Smiling affectionately*): I was worried for a moment. No, George, you're the man for the position. Only sometimes an army can use a woman's touch.

WASHINGTON: Can it, indeed? Well, as your first duty, I command you to walk this post with me. (*He places an arm about her shoulders.*) Come, now—and with true military posture, mind you. (*They begin walking back and forth, in regular military fashion. Both laugh affectionately at each other, as the curtains close.*)

THE END

Summer Soldier

Pamphleteer Thomas Paine's inspiring words

by Jacqueline V. Smith

Characters

HAWKER
THREE MEN
THREE WOMEN
THOMAS PAINE
CORPORAL McKAY
SMITH
DUVAL   } *soldiers of the Continental Army*
COBB
WICKS
VANDERHOFF
AIDE-DE-CAMP
MEN AND WOMEN OF COUNTRYSIDE

SCENE 1

TIME: *January 10, 1776.*

SETTING: *A street in Philadelphia.*

AT RISE: HAWKER *enters, carrying armful of pamphlets, which he is trying to sell to* MEN *and* WOMEN *standing along street.*

HAWKER (*Calling out as he walks along*): Tom Paine's newest pamphlet! (*Holding a few in one hand*) Get your copy of *Common Sense* by Tom Paine—right off the press! Just three pence each. (*Walking along and handing out a few pamphlets and taking coins from buyers*) Read what Tom Paine says in his new pamphlet!

1ST MAN (*Handing* HAWKER *money*): I'll take two copies. (*Takes them*)

1ST WOMAN: I'll take one. (*Hands him coins in return*)

2ND WOMAN (*Following* HAWKER *and pulling his coat sleeve*):
Here now, let me have one. I always like to read what Tom
Paine writes. (*Takes pamphlet and hands him coins*)

2ND MAN (*As he leafs through pamphlet, to* 3RD WOMAN): This
is better than ever. (*Nodding his head in agreement*) How
King George will rage at this! (*Reading*) "To be always running three or four thousand miles to England with a tale or
a petition, waiting four or five months for an answer, which
when obtained requires five or six more to explain it, will in
a few years be looked upon as folly and childishness. There
was a time when it was proper, and there is a proper time for
it to cease."

3RD MAN (*With spirit*): That's absolutely true. And the time is
now!

2ND MAN (*Reading again*): "I am not induced by motives of
pride, party, or resentment to espouse the doctrine of separation and independence; I am clearly, positively, and consci-
entiously persuaded that 'tis the true interest of this continent
to do so; that everything short of that is mere patchwork. . . ."

3RD WOMAN: Tom Paine has put into words the sentiments of
all patriots.

ALL (*Ad lib*): Let's hear more of what he says. Read the next
part. He's absolutely right! (*Etc.*)

2ND MAN (*Reading*): "Nothing but independence . . . can keep
the peace of the continent."

1ST WOMAN (*Reading from her own copy of the pamphlet*): Listen to this. (*All crowd around her as she reads*) "A government
of our own is our natural right." (TOM PAINE *enters, unnoticed
by others and stands quietly at the side.*)

ALL (*Ad lib*): Absolutely right. We must have our independence.
The British shall not govern us. (*Etc.*)

2ND MAN: We must all fight in our own way to make this an independent nation.

HAWKER: All of my copies of *Common Sense* have been sold.
Everyone will be talking about it by sundown. This is a real
blow for freedom—the strongest statement Tom Paine has made
yet against unjust laws and taxes imposed by a distant power.

PAINE (*Stepping forward*): I had a deeper purpose when I wrote
this pamphlet.

1st MAN (*With surprise*): Why, it's Tom Paine himself.

ALL (*Ad lib*): This is your best pamphlet yet. We hope everyone reads it. We want to be free. Independence to our colonies. (*Etc.*)

TOM PAINE: Thank you all. There is one part of my pamphlet which really states my message, for you must remember that we fight not only for our independence, but in order to set an example for all humanity. Let me read it to you. (*Takes pamphlet from his pocket and reads*) "O ye that love mankind! Ye that dare oppose not only the tyranny, but the tyrant, stand forth! Every spot of the old world is overrun with oppression. Freedom hath been hunted round the globe. Asia and Africa have long expelled her—Europe regards her like a stranger, and England hath given her warning to depart. O! receive the fugitive and prepare in time an asylum for mankind." (*All cheer, talk excitedly among themselves, nod vigorously in agreement, as they exit. Curtain.*)

*   *   *   *

SCENE 2

TIME: *December, 1776.*

SETTING: *Campsite of Continental Army, late on a gloomy afternoon.*

AT RISE: *A drum lies down left, flat, on a low stand, and near it on a stool sits* TOM PAINE, *wearing a worn uniform, and writing with a quill pen on a paper which rests on drum. There is an inkwell on drumhead.* CORPORAL MCKAY, *a tall soldier, enters left, rubbing his arms and hands to keep warm. He looks dejected at first, but smiles when he sees* PAINE.

MCKAY (*Friendly*): Writing again, Tom. . . . The pen is mightier than the sword, eh?

PAINE (*Glancing up, friendly*): Each weapon has its proper use, Corporal McKay. I wield both.

MCKAY: Have any of your camp writings been published?

PAINE (*Pausing to blow on his fingers, to warm them*): One, recently. There should be copies here soon.

MCKAY: If you have one to lend me . . .

PAINE: *You* don't need the message, Corporal McKay. But you shall have a copy.

MCKAY: Thank you, Tom. (*He starts right, but stops as* VANDER-

HOFF, WICKS, *and* COBB, *three soldiers in ragged uniforms, enter. They are shivering and swing their arms to keep warm.*) Where are you bound for, men?

WICKS: To our tents (*Bitterly*) to pack up our bundle of rags and go home. (PAINE *looks on.*)

McKAY (*Alarmed*): You must not leave. So many of our men have deserted, our ranks are depleted.

WICKS (*Bitterly*): I enlisted for the regular three months. The term is up this week. My farm is in ruins, uncultivated. If only I can reach home for Christmas and scrape together a little food for my wife and children . . .

VANDERHOFF (*In a Dutch accent; wearily*): I came from The Netherlands—from Europe—to be free from wars. I have served two enlistments. Six months is enough for me. (*During next speech,* SMITH *and* DUVAL *enter right.*)

COBB (*In a southern accent*): Fighting in summer time is one thing, but I can't stand your fierce northern winters—certainly not in these rags. (*Rubbing his hands together vigorously*) I'm going home.

McKAY (*Desperately*): But your country needs you now more than ever! (*He notices the newcomers.*) You, Smith—

SMITH (*Quietly*): Summer or winter, I stay.

McKAY (*Putting his hand on* SMITH'S *shoulder, appreciatively; then turning to* DUVAL): What about you, Duval?

DUVAL (*In a French accent*): I have one more month to serve. Then, I do not know. I would fight on, gladly, but (*Shrugging*) the odds—they are against us, hopeless.

WICKS (*Heatedly*): We have been enduring privations, while others back home reap the profits! The country is divided and in despair. The British with their Hessians outnumber us overwhelmingly. How can we hope to prevail? (PAINE *rises, comes forward.*)

PAINE (*Speaking in a low-pitched voice, but with deep feeling*): New enlistments will strengthen our ranks. Perseverance and fortitude . . . the courage to fight on and on . . . will bring us victory, liberty, peace. Cowardice and submission—(*He stops at sight of an* AIDE-DE-CAMP, *who enters right and exchanges salutes with* McKAY.)

AIDE: Corporal, orders from General Washington. (*Holds out pamphlet*)

McKay: What is this?

Aide: We have just received copies of this pamphlet (*Hands it to* McKay)—it is an appeal, newly printed and being distributed and sold throughout the states. General Washington has ordered it to be read to every camp right away.

McKay (*Looking through pamphlet*): *The American Crisis,* by Tom Paine. (*To* Paine) Why, you wrote this, Tom.

Paine: Yes, it's one I think you may like and find useful here. (*He takes pen, ink, and paper from drumhead, puts pen and ink under the drum, and with paper in hand, goes right with* Aide.)

McKay: Smith, sound muster.

Smith: Yes, sir. (*He goes to drum.*)

Aide (*Low, confidentially, to* Paine): Mr. Paine, General Washington plans a surprise attack against the Hessians tomorrow night. But, for that, the fighting spirit of the soldiers must be aroused. If the appeal in your pamphlet fails, I fear we are lost. Washington is counting on it to stem the tide of desertions.

Paine (*Fiercely*): Liberty will not fail! (Smith *beats out long, loud drum roll. Soldiers line up center, facing forward. They stand at ease, some looking sullen and dejected. Drum roll stops.*)

McKay: By order of General Washington! (*He opens pamphlet and starts to read slowly, holding it up to catch fading afternoon light. As he reads, soldiers' faces gradually grow serious, ashamed, solemn, finally grim with determination. Soldiers shift about uneasily.* McKay *reads.*) "These are the times that try men's souls. (*Pause*) The summer soldier and the sunshine patriot will, in this crisis, shrink from the service of their country; but he that stands it *now,* deserves the love and thanks of man and woman. Tyranny, like hell, is not easily conquered, yet we have this consolation with us, that the harder the sacrifice, the more glorious the triumph. What we obtain too cheap, we esteem too lightly: it is dearness only that gives everything its value. Heaven knows how to put a proper price upon its goods; and it would be strange indeed, if so celestial an article as Freedom should not be highly rated. . . . (*Pause*) I call not upon a few, but upon all: not on this state or that state, but on every state: Up and help us! Lay your shoulders to the wheel, better have too much force than too little, when so great an object is at stake. . . . By perseverance and fortitude we have the prospect of a glorious issue; by cowardice and submission, the sad choice of a variety of evils—a ravaged country—a depopulated city—habitations without safety and slavery without hope. . . . Look on this picture and weep over it . . . and if there yet remains one thoughtless wretch who believes it not, let him suffer it . . . unlamented!" (*There is a pause.*)

WICKS (*Stepping forward*): I'll enlist again, right away. (*He salutes.*)

VANDERHOFF (*Coming forward*): Me, too.

COBB (*After a pause, stepping forward*): Put me down, sir. (*Salutes*)

DUVAL (*Stepping forward*): And me, too. I'll be proud to serve again. I'm no summer soldier! (*Smiling,* McKAY *nods to* PAINE, *then signals to* SMITH, *who begins a long drum roll. Soldiers stand proudly at attention.* MEN AND WOMEN OF COUNTRYSIDE *enter with baskets of food, muskets, etc.*)

AIDE (*To* McKAY): Men and women from nearby farms have read Tom Paine's pamphlet and come to help.

McKAY (*To* PAINE): Tom, we are all in your debt. Our fighting spirit is restored, thanks to you.

SMITH (*To* McKAY): Sir, what about a rousing song? (*Begins to sing "Yankee Doodle," keeping time with drum beats. Fife or flute may be played. Others join in, softly at first, then growing louder until song bursts forth. Curtain.*)

THE END

Molly Pitcher Meets the General

Two patriots of the American Revolution

by Marjory Hall

Characters

WILLIAM
JAMES   } *three ragged soldiers*
RICHARD
MOLLY PITCHER
GEORGE WASHINGTON
CHARLES } *two young officers*
FRANK
MAJOR SMITH, *Washington's aide*

SCENE 1

TIME: *Early June, 1778. Evening.*

SETTING: *The interior of a hut. It is dark, the only light coming from the fireplace and a lantern.*

AT RISE: *Two ragged soldiers,* WILLIAM *and* JAMES, *sit quietly on bench, right, near fireplace.* WILLIAM's *shoes are on floor in front of him.* RICHARD, *another soldier, leans back against wall, his eyes closed. A mug and spoon are beside him.* MOLLY PITCHER, *her sleeves rolled up and an apron tied over her long skirt, stirs a soup pot hanging over fireplace. She turns, looks at* RICHARD *with a worried expression, and walks over to him.*

MOLLY: Here, lad, try some more. You'll feel better if you get something hot into you, you know. Come on, just to please Molly? (RICHARD *shakes his head and says nothing.* MOLLY *picks up mug and spoon and starts to feed him, by spoonfuls, which he swallows reluctantly.*)

JAMES: I could fancy some more soup myself, if you'd help *me* that way.

MOLLY (*Sharply*): There's not so much in the kettle that you can have third and fourth helpings.

WILLIAM: You want us to leave, I suppose?

MOLLY: No, no, I didn't mean that. You're welcome to sit there until the space is needed.

WILLIAM: Or until they come for us and tell us to start chasing that British general. I don't see why we should chase him at all.

MOLLY: To keep him from getting away, of course. Besides, they say that General Clinton has food and guns and a whole lot of other things that would come in mighty handy for our own boys. He's trying to skedaddle, so they tell me, after living like a king in Philadelphia all winter. I heard, too, that it has something to do with the fleet the French have sent to help us. That British general doesn't like that a bit.

WILLIAM: I've no use for generals, no matter which side they're on.

JAMES: I suppose you'd have the war all won by this time, if you were in charge.

WILLIAM (*Sneeringly*): I don't think the officers know any more about soldiering than I do. Take Washington, now. How'd *he* get to be a general?

JAMES: He's been a soldier for years. Didn't you know that? He fought the French and the Indians, and he made a good job of it, too.

WILLIAM: He probably owned a good horse, that's all. I heard tell he's a high and mighty Virginian, and probably rich, too.

JAMES: High and mighty? Why, they say at Valley Forge he wandered around by himself talking to the soldiers, away from his aides. My cousin told me Washington walked right up and sat down at his campfire one night just to talk to the men. (*Proudly*) Now there's a real leader. Why, he could be around this camp right this minute and walk right in *here*.

WILLIAM (*Scoffingly*): Oh, sure! Maybe he could shine up our shoes for us, or stir the soup for this lady here.

JAMES: There's not much use talking to you, I can see that. (*He looks around cabin, then turns to* MOLLY.) When I looked in this morning, this place was full of rubbish. How'd you get it cleaned up so quick?

MOLLY (*Briskly*): Cleaning up comes naturally when you've been at it a lifetime.

WILLIAM: Not so long a lifetime, in your case. How old are you, missus, twenty?

MOLLY (*Smiling*): That's close enough.

WILLIAM: I wouldn't mind having a girl like you around to clean up and make good soup for me. Would you be interested?

MOLLY: Not in the least. (*Laughing*) Besides, my husband wouldn't like it.

JAMES (*Surprised*): Husband? So that's why you're here. I heard tell a lot of wives came up here in wagons last night. Where'd you come from?

MOLLY: New Jersey. And it's a good thing for you we did come, too. This place looked as if you could use a few brooms—and some food.

RICHARD (*Weakly*): We just got here ourselves, ma'am. There's been no chance for us to do any brooming yet.

MOLLY (*To* RICHARD): I'm glad to hear you talk, soldier. And you look better, too, and stronger. I told you the soup would help. Would you like some more?

WILLIAM (*Roughly*): Well, I like that! You just told me that there wasn't enough for another helping.

JAMES (*Firmly but quietly*): Can't you see he needs it to get his strength back? (MOLLY *smiles at* JAMES *and nods.*)

MOLLY (*Turning back to* RICHARD): Let me have your mug, soldier! (*She picks up* RICHARD's *mug and begins to ladle more soup into it, as* GEORGE WASHINGTON *enters quietly from right and crosses over to sit on empty bench, left, in dim light, his back mostly to the audience. He wears a cloak with collar upturned, and others do not recognize him.* MOLLY *gives him a brief glance, then turns back to kettle and continues to ladle soup into* RICHARD's *mug. She turns to* WILLIAM, *and hands him* RICHARD's *mug.*) Here. Take this over to him. (*She points to* RICHARD. WILLIAM *gets up and reluctantly takes mug from her.*)

WILLIAM: Do you want me to feed him, too?

MOLLY: He can manage for himself now, I reckon. (*Turning to* RICHARD) Can't you, soldier? (*As* WILLIAM *walks over to* RICHARD *and gives him mug,* MOLLY *picks up another mug and fills it, picks up spoon, then hands mug and spoon to* WASHINGTON. *He nods thanks, and begins to eat.*)

WILLIAM: Say, missus, how far away is this place you come from?

MOLLY: Thirty–forty miles, I guess. It seems longer, riding in a farm wagon on a road that feels as if it's made out of tree trunks.

WILLIAM (*Bitterly*): You should try *walking* that far. (*He sits down, rubs his hands over his stockinged feet, then starts to put his shoes on, groaning as he does so.*)

MOLLY: Where'd you come from? All the way from Valley Forge?

WILLIAM: No. I thank my stars for that, anyway. I just joined up two weeks ago, and that's three or four weeks too long to be in this dratted army.

MOLLY (*To* JAMES): You, too?

JAMES: Me, too. What about your husband, if you really have one? Did he ride over in that wagon with you?

MOLLY: Indeed not! He's been in the army since last November —seven and a half months he's been gone from me. Yesterday was the first time I'd seen him since he left Carlisle. That's where we live.

RICHARD: Was your husband at Valley Forge?

MOLLY: He was. It must have been as terrible as they say, because he won't speak of it. "Over and done with," he says, "over and done with." And that's all I get out of him, so I know it must have been bad.

RICHARD (*Shuddering*): Bad! You could never know, ma'am, how it was.

MOLLY: You were there, too?

RICHARD: Yes, I was there. And I understand about your husband, ma'am, because I can't speak of it either. My younger brother died there, just from being cold and hungry, and that's the truth. What do I tell my mother, when I get back to Massachusetts—if I ever do get back there? He died, and I didn't, and she'll think I could have shared my food with him and taken care of him somehow. Lots of others died, too, or froze their toes off. I was lucky—I just got sick.

MOLLY: But you're all right now.

RICHARD (*Sighing*): Yes, I guess I'm all right now, but I don't get along so well on this marching. (*Shakes his head*) Maybe tomorrow, or whenever we move on again, it won't be so bad. (*He *stands up, hands* MOLLY *mug, sways a little.* JAMES *tries to help him, but he pushes him aside.*) I'm right enough. It was your soup that did it, ma'am—gave me my strength back. Your husband is a lucky man. (*He walks out slowly.*)

JAMES (*Looking after him*): That one won't make many more miles, if you ask me.

WASHINGTON (*Speaking for the first time, so that others turn quickly at sound of his voice*): He might. Men do more than they can, sometimes.

JAMES: Yes, they do. I suppose we'll all be like that after a while, although it was that snow and cold at Valley Forge that did him in. Were you there too, soldier?

WASHINGTON: Yes, the whole time. I was fortunate. I had shoes and food. There were many that lacked both. (*To* MOLLY) What's your husband's name, ma'am?

MOLLY: Hays. John Hays. He's just been made a lieutenant!

WASHINGTON: And I'm sure he is worthy.

WILLIAM (*Scoffing*): It doesn't follow. A man buys his commission, and then sits by the fire and lets others do his work for him.

JAMES (*Angrily*): That isn't true. They told me the highest-ranking officers gave the men their food and even the shoes off their feet and the clothes off their backs. Most of the time they never ate any better than the men did. You sure have a grudge about officers. What did any one of 'em ever do to you?

WILLIAM: You just don't look at the facts head-on. (*To* WASHINGTON) Does he?

WASHINGTON: There are men who are bad officers, and men who are good ones. No one was really ready for this war, you know. The best we could do was take the men who had some knowledge of fighting and put them in charge.

WILLIAM: The officers ride their horses and let us walk, you know. Do you fancy that, James? Yesterday it was hot. Wouldn't you have been glad to sit quietly on a horse and let him do the walking for you?

JAMES (*Firmly*): The officers ride those same horses ahead of the men right into the fighting, too, you know. (*Impatiently*) There's no use arguing with you, William. Come on, we might as well go find the others and get some sleep. We have a lot more walking to do tomorrow, I expect. (*To* MOLLY) Thanks for the soup, ma'am. It sure was good.

MOLLY (*Kindly*): Good night to you. And may God be with you. (JAMES *and* WILLIAM *walk out, and she stirs the pot again. Over her shoulder, to* WASHINGTON) A bit more soup, soldier?

WASHINGTON: Won't it be needed for others?

MOLLY: If one man comes in, I could give him only half a mug, and that would only aggravate him, I reckon. I didn't let on to the others we were down to the bottom of the kettle, because that weak one needed all he could get into him. That was plain to see. Here, give me your mug. (*She takes his mug and ladles the last of the soup into it.*) Now I'll start to clean up while you finish up. There'll be more in the morning. I brought everything my father could spare from his farm and hid it under the false bottom in the wagon, just in case there were any thieving Redcoats on the road. I had enough to fill that kettle for today and tomorrow anyway. When do you think you'll move on, soldier?

WASHINGTON: As soon as we can. Two days, maybe. It depends on what news the scouts bring back. Maybe tomorrow, but I hope not. The men have done well, but we must take care of them, give them as much rest as possible before—(*He pauses.*)

MOLLY (*Quietly*): Before the battle, which will be a big one. Is that what you didn't finish saying? I think I knew anyway. (*She sighs.*) A big battle that means lots of killing and wounding. My husband told me something fearful is just ahead; he's sure of it.

WASHINGTON: We always hope not.

MOLLY: You sound like a doctor, worrying about the men. Are you?

WASHINGTON: No. You don't have to be a doctor to know that men have limits to their endurance.

MOLLY: My husband knows a lot about doctoring. He's a barber, you see. A barber-surgeon. He pulls teeth and treats many ills. He's well thought of back in Carlisle.

WASHINGTON: He does important work. And such men are badly needed in the army. Has your husband been barbering and doctoring in the army, Mistress Hays?

MOLLY (*Sighing*): Alas, no. He is a gunner. (*Shaking her head sadly*) My John never even liked to shoot squirrels or rabbits for food, and now he's shooting men.

WASHINGTON (*Sympathetically*): Even the gentlest of men are fighting for the cause of freedom and independence these days. That's the way of a true patriot. What must be done, he will do. You are lucky to have such a husband.

MOLLY: Oh, I *know*.

WASHINGTON: And he is lucky in his wife. (*Rises*) Your soup was most welcome, Mistress Hays. I believe it was the best I have tasted since long before Valley Forge—almost since I can remember. (*Sighs*) Somehow the weeks and months are all run together in a nightmare of hope and hunger and despair. (*He turns to go.*)

MOLLY (*Sharply*): Since you are the only man here and you say you enjoyed my soup, would you help me with the kettle before you go?

WASHINGTON: Oh, I beg your pardon. I didn't think. (*He walks back to hearth.*)

MOLLY (*Holding one side of kettle*): Men! Well, here's the kettle and it must be lifted down and put there (*Points to bench or floor*) so I can scour it later. (WASHINGTON *lifts kettle down from crane and sets it on bench or floor.*)

WASHINGTON: There. Now, is there anything else I can do for you before I go?

MOLLY: Thank you, no. And I'm sorry I snapped at you. (*She puts her hands to her back, wearily.*) This has been a long day and tiring as well as worrisome. I hope you understand.

WASHINGTON: Of course, I understand, Mistress Hays, and I'm sorry I didn't think to do it myself. What is your given name, may I ask?

MOLLY: Molly. I am Mary Ludwig Hays, but always called Molly. And what is your name then, soldier?

WASHINGTON (*Walking toward door, then turning back*): My first name is George. (*He goes out, then puts his head in doorway, smiling broadly.*) Since you told me both of your names, I should in all fairness do the same. My name is George Washington. (*He exits.* MOLLY *claps her hands to her mouth, looks after* WASHINGTON *in amazement, as he exits and the curtain falls.*)

*   *   *   *   *

Scene 2

TIME: *Two or three weeks later.*

SETTING: *A clearing in a wooded area. There are bushes all around and a log on the ground at right.*

AT RISE: WILLIAM *and* JAMES *sit on ground, leaning against log. They look exhausted and mop their faces continually.* WILLIAM *is wrapping a handkerchief around his leg.*

JAMES: What a day! So hot, so confounded hot. But not as bad as yesterday. Never was such a day as that. Never.

WILLIAM: If you say that again, I'll shoot you, I swear it.

JAMES: With what? You have no ammunition left, any more than I have. I'll bet there isn't a bullet left in the whole army.

WILLIAM: Then I'll use a club.

JAMES: With all that extra energy you have? I doubt it!

WILLIAM: Oh, keep quiet. (*There is a long silence.*) Well, we won, didn't we? Though I guess we almost didn't. I heard tell that General Charles Lee went the wrong way, or something that made General Washington terribly angry. But we won just the same—chased those Redcoats out and took their whole wagon train away from them.

JAMES: Chased them! (*Laughing*) They didn't run, they just melted away in those heavy red coats, if you ask me.

WILLIAM: So did a lot of our own men, and our clothes were much better for 94 degrees in the shade. But no matter how you're dressed, this is no weather to be rushing around with guns and dragging cannons up hills. I hope what they call our independence is going to be worth all this.

JAMES (*Wryly*): It won't be to all those who died of the heat. I'd rather be killed by a bullet any day than die that way. I'll tell you something. I was never so happy to see anything in my whole life as the pitcher of water that woman carried around to the soldiers.

WILLIAM: They called her Molly—Molly Pitcher. That's a funny name.

JAMES: It was fitting, though the men didn't even look at her. Everyone was so exhausted and thirsty.

WILLIAM: It was almost dark when she got to us, anyway. But the water was just as welcome as the soup that woman gave us back in Pennsylvania. Remember that?

JAMES: I'll never forget it. She saved our lives. (JAMES *gets up and walks about, looking at bushes and off.*) The spring must be close by. Come on, let's get some more of that water.

WILLIAM (*Getting up*): I think we'd better move from here, anyway. We didn't find the guns the officers sent us for, and if they see us, they're sure to give us something else to do. (*Pauses briefly and looks off right, listening*) I hear hoofbeats coming. (*He walks to exit right, peers out, then turns back immediately.*) There are tents out here, and horses and officers coming this way. Come on, James. Let's go. (*They exit hurriedly left.* CHARLES, *a young officer, better dressed than soldiers, but dirty and hot, walks into clearing from right. He looks around, then beckons toward right.* FRANK *enters.*)

CHARLES: This will do well enough. Tell the General's aide to bring the woman here, then go for the General. He wants to get this over with as quickly as possible. He has a lot of other things on his mind. I hope he's still on his feet. He slept under a tree wrapped up in his own cloak last night. What a man!

FRANK: What's all this about, anyway?

CHARLES: Some woman took her husband's place at his gun yesterday.

FRANK: Oh, I heard about it. What happened to the husband?

CHARLES: Shot, I guess. Or perhaps the heat got him, like so many of the rest. I don't know. Anyway, some of Lafayette's boys took up a collection. Seems somehow she knew how to swab the gun, and stuck at it for a couple of hours. The Frenchies are all for honoring brave females! General Washington heard about it, and he decided he'd better give her some recognition, too, I guess. After all, it's *his* war!

FRANK: But, why here?

CHARLES: It's close to headquarters, that's all. Now you'd better make haste and fetch the woman. (FRANK *exits right.* CHARLES *starts to sit down on the log, then jumps to attention, as* WASHINGTON *enters right.*)

WASHINGTON: This is hardly what you'd call a parade ground, but it will serve. Where's the woman?

CHARLES: On her way, sir.

WASHINGTON: What's her name?

CHARLES: Mrs. Pitcher, sir.

WASHINGTON: Do we know her husband's condition?

CHARLES: Can't find a Pitcher on the rolls, sir, to inquire, but—

WASHINGTON: But of course that doesn't mean much. Our records leave a little something to be desired.

CHARLES: I'm sorry, sir, but—

WASHINGTON (*Kindly*): I'm not blaming *you*, man. Not unless *you* made the decision to have us fight this war before we were ready for it. Someone did, but I presume it wasn't you.

CHARLES (*Uneasily*): No, sir. (*Looking off*) Here comes someone, sir. It's Major Smith, and I suppose that's Mrs. Pitcher with him. (MOLLY *and* MAJOR SMITH *enter.* MAJOR SMITH *and* WASHINGTON *exchange salutes, then* MAJOR SMITH *steps to one side.* MOLLY *is wearing a soldier's jacket, much too big for her, and a soldier's hat, also too big. She looks frightened and tired. When she sees* WASHINGTON, *she looks quickly at the ground, then makes a quick, awkward curtsy.*)

WASHINGTON: Mistress Pitcher (*He looks at* MOLLY *closely.*)— Pitcher? But surely you're—

MOLLY: Molly Hays, sir. Yes, sir.

WASHINGTON (*Smiling*): You didn't always call me sir, as I recall. And I wish you would not do so now. But why do they call you by the name of Pitcher—? Mrs. Pitcher, I was told that distinctly.

MOLLY: Oh, it's—well, it's just that I carried water to the men, sir—er, General—and somehow they began to call to me that way to get me to come with the pitcher of water. I don't know how, sir—it just happened.

WASHINGTON: How is your husband, the lieutenant?

MOLLY: He will be all right, General. Thank you, sir.

WASHINGTON: And does he know what you did yesterday?

MOLLY: Yes. Yes, sir, he knows. And he's provoked with me (*Smiling*)—although of course not really, sir.

WASHINGTON: Good. Then I'll let you go back to him, where you wish to be and where you belong. (*Takes paper from his pocket*) But first I want to give you this honorary commission as a sergeant in our army, as a token of our great appreciation of your courage in battle. A grateful country will never forget what you did yesterday, and this bit of paper is an inadequate way of expressing our thoughts on the matter—mine, our soldiers', our country's. And I believe it will not reward you as much as the expressions on the faces of the men to whom you gave water, when they needed it so badly.

MOLLY (*Overcome, speaking softly*): Thank you, sir.

WASHINGTON: You are indeed welcome. I believe you will shortly receive another token of admiration for your brave deed. The soldiers have collected a purse of money for you, which may mean more to you than this formal, but actually useless, paper. (*He hands document to her.*)

MOLLY: Not to me, sir! I will cherish this forever.

WASHINGTON: I hope you aren't disappointed that we had no throng for you, no great ceremony. We have little time for such things, not today or tomorrow, not for some time to come, I'm afraid. You do understand?

MOLLY: Yes, sir. Yes, General Washington, I mean.

WASHINGTON: I liked it better when you were making me move your kettle for you. (*Officers smile*) We were friends then.

MOLLY (*Shocked*): Oh sir, if I had ever known—if I had dreamed —I was so—

WASHINGTON: If you had known, we—well, never mind. Molly Hays, if you ever wish to have another kettle moved, I insist that you call on me. I will be forever at your service. (*He holds out his hand, which she takes, then curtsies again.*)

MOLLY: Thank you, sir. Thank you very much, General Washington. (*She goes to exit right, then turns to face* WASHINGTON *again, grins impishly, then gives him a salute, which he returns with dignity. They look at each other seriously for a moment, holding salutes, as curtain falls.*)

THE END

Naughty Susan

The Liberty Bell rings for freedom

by Mary O. Slingluff

Characters

SUSAN PAGE
ANN, *her sister*
MRS. PAGE, *her mother*
MR. PAGE, *her father*
GRANDMOTHER PAGE
HENRY, *a cousin*
THOMAS JEFFERSON

SCENE 1

TIME: *July 8, 1776.*
SETTING: *The living room of a Philadelphia Quaker family.*
AT RISE: SUSAN PAGE *and her sister,* ANN, *are seated on footstools sewing on samplers. They are quiet for a few minutes, then* SUSAN *jumps up from her stool and throws her sampler on the floor.* ANN *looks up in shocked astonishment.*

SUSAN (*Stamping on her sampler several times in an outburst of temper*): I hate samplers! Oh, how I hate them!
ANN (*Horrified*): Susan, how can thee say such a thing! And to be in such a dreadful temper, throwing thy sampler on the floor.
SUSAN (*Angrily*): I don't care! I don't want to be good.

NOTE: The Liberty Bell was rung on July 8, 1776, for the first public reading of the Declaration of Independence. Earlier it had been rung to proclaim the Boston Tea Party and in defiance of British tax and trade restrictions. The actual crack in the Liberty Bell occurred on July 8, 1835, while it was tolling for the death of Supreme Court Chief Justice John Marshall.

129

ANN (*Listening*): Here comes Mother! (SUSAN *hastily picks up her sampler, brushes dirt off it, and sits on her stool pretending to be sewing industriously when* MRS. PAGE *enters.*)

MRS. PAGE: Here are my good girls working hard. And how is thee getting along, Ann? (*Taking* ANN's *sampler from her*) Why, it is all finished!

ANN (*Proudly*): The last stitch, Mother!

MRS. PAGE: I am sure thee is one of the most industrious little Quaker maids in all Philadelphia. We will tell thy father this evening.

ANN: And will he write in the family diary that it is finished?

MRS. PAGE: Thee may stand beside him while he writes, "My daughter Ann completed work upon her sampler today, July eighth, 1776." Now thee must put on thy bonnet for as soon as I have looked at Susan's work, we shall go for a walk. (ANN *exits.* MRS. PAGE *takes* SUSAN's *sampler and examines it. Then angrily*) What! Nothing done at all today—yesterday's stitches carelessly and wrongly done. And, look, thy sampler is soiled! What did thee do to it? (SUSAN *hangs her head sullenly.*) Answer me, Susan!

SUSAN: I stamped upon it, Mother.

MRS. PAGE: And why did thee do that?

SUSAN: Because I hate samplers!

MRS. PAGE (*Shocked*): Surely thee does not mean that, Susan.

SUSAN: I do mean it! (GRANDMOTHER *enters. She uses a cane and holds out her hand for help. Meanwhile a muffled bell begins to ring offstage.*)

GRANDMOTHER: Please help me to a chair. (MRS. PAGE *helps her; she sits.*) Now that my eyes are failing, it seems that my ears are so much the keener. Does thee not hear a bell ringing long and loudly?

MRS. PAGE (*Listening*): Thee is right. The State House Bell is tolling wildly. What can it mean? Perhaps there is news from the Congress.

GRANDMOTHER: In all the years that I have lived in Philadelphia never has it rung thus except for great events. There must be news of importance today.

MRS. PAGE: Let us hurry to see what it is. (*Starting to help* GRANDMOTHER *from her chair*) I will get thy bonnet and shawl, for there is no time to lose. (*Calls offstage*) Come quickly, Ann.

GRANDMOTHER: No, go without me. I am too old to go among so many people as must be gathering to hear the news.

SUSAN (*Happily*): Shall we wear our best bonnets, Mother?

MRS. PAGE: Best bonnet, indeed! I cannot allow such a naughty little girl as thee to go at all. No. Susan, thy punishment must be to stay at home to work on thy sampler.

SUSAN: But thee said it was news of great importance—oh, please!

MRS. PAGE: For one who has behaved badly, the only thing of importance is repentance.

SUSAN (*With gesture of resignation*): Yes, Mother.

MRS. PAGE (*Patting* GRANDMOTHER): Ann and I will tell thee about it when we come home. (MRS. PAGE *exits*.)

GRANDMOTHER: Here we are left behind, Susan. I, because I am old and feeble, thee because thee has been naughty. Is thee greatly disappointed?

SUSAN: Greatly, although it is not because of important news that I wish to be there, but because of something quite different.

GRANDMOTHER: And what is that?

SUSAN: Many times I have helped Old John, the State House bell ringer, and, oh, it is such fun. He puts my hand on the rope with his and together we pull to make the great bell ring out the slow hours. I am sure that Mother—if she knew—would think it more of my naughtiness. (*As* SUSAN *speaks*, GRANDMOTHER *starts to nod; dozes.*) I can just hear her say, "Susan, how could thee? It is not proper for a little Quaker maid to ring the town bell." But the way it is ringing today—I must be there—I must! Grandmother, if I run away now to help Old John, will thee promise not to tell? Couldn't thee pretend to be asleep while I go? (*Waits for an answer, and when there is none, she tiptoes over to* GRANDMOTHER's *chair, watching her carefully for a moment*) She is asleep! She really is! I'm going to ring that bell until it cracks! (*Curtain*)

* * * * *

SCENE 2

TIME: *Later the same day.*

SETTING: *The same as Scene 1, except that the table is set for dinner.*

AT RISE: GRANDMOTHER *is still seated in her chair.* ANN *and* MRS. PAGE *are sitting beside the table.* MR. PAGE *is pacing the floor, looking at his pocket watch impatiently.*

MRS. PAGE (*Upset*): That naughty Susan! Where can she be, William?

MR. PAGE: Up to some kind of mischief, I haven't any doubt, but we cannot punish her on this great day.

GRANDMOTHER: She is as excited as we are about the first public reading of the Declaration of Independence, and has forgotten all about her dinner.

MR. PAGE: But if she is not here by the time we have finished eating, I will go out myself to look for her.

ANN (*Eagerly*): Perhaps thee will take me along, Father. This has been such an exciting day. Wasn't it a wonderful Declaration?

MR. PAGE: "Life, Liberty and the Pursuit of Happiness." (*Pause*) Those are glorious words spoken on a glorious day.

ANN: "The Pursuit of Happiness"—that is what Susan wants always.

MRS. PAGE: Or the pursuit of naughtiness. Is thee sure thee did not see Susan in the crowd at the State House, Ann?

ANN: No, Mother, but I remember now where she might have gone—to ring the bell in the State House belfry.

MRS. PAGE: Susan to ring the bell! How could a little girl ring the great bell of Philadelphia?

GRANDMOTHER: Many times Old John, the bell ringer, has let her pull at the bell rope with him. She says nothing makes her happier.

MR. PAGE: If it were Susan's small hand on the rope when the bell cracked for Liberty, I should be the proudest father in all this city. (*Listening*) I hear thy Cousin Henry's voice in the hall. Perhaps he has found Susan. (HENRY *enters.*)

HENRY (*Breathlessly*): Cousin William, I ran all the way to tell thee. Susan is coming up the street now—and Mr. Thomas Jefferson is with her!

ALL (*Excitedly*): Mr. Thomas Jefferson!

MR. PAGE: Sit down, boy, get thy breath, and tell us what this is all about.

HENRY: No, I must hurry home to my dinner. They will be here in a minute, and Susan will tell her own story. (*Exits*)

MRS. PAGE (*Sternly*): Henry has certainly forgotten his manners today. (*Breaking off*) William, I hear someone at the door now. (THOMAS JEFFERSON *enters, holding* SUSAN's *hand.*)

SUSAN (*Excitedly*): Father, Mother, I brought Mr. Jefferson home with me.

MR. PAGE: Mr. Jefferson, this is an honor indeed. (*Holds out his hand.*)

JEFFERSON: The honor is mine—and also that of escorting your daughter. I am proud to have made her acquaintance. (*They shake hands.*)

MR. PAGE (*Gesturing*): This is my wife, my mother, and my daughter, Ann. (*They acknowledge greetings.* ANN *and* MRS. PAGE *curtsy.* JEFFERSON *bows.*) Has Susan been up to more mischief, Mr. Jefferson?

JEFFERSON: Mischief to Susan's thinking, but not to mine. I will make my story brief, sir. After the reading of the Declaration of Independence was over, we went to inspect the crack in the bell. There we found Susan weeping bitterly. She was afraid that she would be in great trouble and disgrace, since her hand was on the rope with Old John's when the bell cracked with rejoicing. (*Smiling*) She dared not come home for fear of punishment, so I came with her to explain the situation.

MR. PAGE: No, Susan, there will be no punishment—only praise.

SUSAN (*Doubtfully*): No punishment—not even for the sampler, Mother? I didn't work on it at all.

MRS. PAGE (*Sighing*): Thee will escape punishment this time.

JEFFERSON (*Kindly*): You do not care for sampler work, Susan? Ringing bells is more to your taste, perhaps?

SUSAN: Oh, I like bell-ringing much more!

JEFFERSON: But I am very fond of a well-made sampler. Will you make one for me to hang on the wall of my home in Virginia?

SUSAN (*Suddenly enthusiastic*): Yes, Mr. Jefferson. I will make you the most beautiful sampler in the world. But what words shall I put on it?

ANN (*Shyly*): I know. Thee can take the words from the Declaration Mr. Jefferson wrote and say, "Life, Liberty, and the Pursuit of Happiness."

SUSAN: Did *you* write it, Mr. Jefferson?

JEFFERSON: Yes, Susan. (*Laughing*) I wrote it for all naughty little girls like you throughout the colonies. So you write this for me on your sampler, "I, Susan, helped to crack the bell of Liberty in the Pursuit of Happiness."

SUSAN (*Eagerly*): I will, Mr. Jefferson, I will! Every stitch will be perfect and I will never, never be naughty again. I promise thee that, Mother.

MRS. PAGE: Thee is an easy promiser, Susan.

SUSAN: "I, Susan, helped to crack the bell of Liberty in the Pursuit of Happiness on July the Eighth, Seventeen Seventy-Six." Oh, I don't know which is more glorious—liberty or the pursuit of happiness.

JEFFERSON: You cannot have one without the other. Think a moment, Susan, and you will understand what I mean.

SUSAN (*Slowly*): I think this is it. Without happiness we cannot enjoy liberty, and without liberty we are not free to look for things that make us happy. (*Curtain*)

THE END

A Guide for George Washington

Crossing the Delaware—a verse drama

by Lindsey Barbee

Characters

GEORGE WASHINGTON
JOHN WINCHESTER
CAPTAIN
MRS. WINCHESTER
ELIZABETH WINCHESTER (STRANGER)
MARIA, *the maid*

SCENE 1

SETTING: *A slight rise on the banks of the Delaware, Christmas night, 1776.*

AT RISE: GEORGE WASHINGTON *and* JOHN WINCHESTER, *wearing heavy cloaks, stand shivering in the cold, dark night. The* CAPTAIN, *a lantern swinging in his hand, enters, climbs the hill laboriously, and approaches the commanding figure of* WASHINGTON *and the stalwart, young* JOHN WINCHESTER, *who grasps his arm excitedly.*

JOHN:

What think you, Captain, of the risk tonight—
The river and the way the wind has turned—
The ice—what chance have we to venture?
How long before we dare a crossing? (CAPTAIN *makes impatient gesture.*) Wait!
You must know that tonight we win or lose.

This play is suitable for either spotlight stage production with minimal costumes and scenery, or for round-the-table classroom reading, which requires no memorization, scenery, or costuming.

CAPTAIN:

    Have patience, John, have patience till I speak.
    The fire of youth is oft at war with reason
    And knows not prudence nor the wiser course
    That bids one watch and wait and counsel. (*Turns*)
    My General, we must not cross tonight.

WASHINGTON:

    You are quite sure?

CAPTAIN:

                    Quite sure, for even now
    The river clogs with ice, the air is sharp,
    The very wind is hostile to our venture.

WASHINGTON:

    But still, in some strange way, it comes to me
    That we must cross—tonight—if we would win.

CAPTAIN:

    My General, it is not courage fails us
    Nor keen desire; the elements themselves
    Make it impossible.

WASHINGTON:

                  Impossible?
    We know not such a word.

CAPTAIN:

                    Nay, but the truth
    Has come to us in hard and bitter ways.
    At Trenton and at Bordentown there stand
    The Hessian and the British troops. Your plan
    To send a force across the Delaware,
    To sever any union of the two
    Has come to naught. We cannot cope with storms.

WASHINGTON:

    There also was a third phase to my plan.
    Have you forgotten? I, with my own men,
    Had thought to cross the Delaware—to creep
    Upon the Hessian troop at Trenton.

CAPTAIN:

                      True,
    You were to lead the main attack; but now
    The icy storms have played a tragic part
    In thwarting our designs. (*Pauses*) We cannot cross.

WASHINGTON:

But still I say—we cross ere dawn.

CAPTAIN:

My General!

WASHINGTON:

We cross ere dawn—for now at heart I feel
It is the Hand of God that points the way.

CAPTAIN:

The river is not open for our men.

WASHINGTON:

Then we must make it so. It can be done.

CAPTAIN:

Then be *your* wish *my* wish. (WASHINGTON *grasps his hand.*)
It can be done.

JOHN:

Perhaps it is our very chance. Tonight
Is Christmas night. The Britishers forget
There is a war. The Hessian troops are gay
And careless. Oh, it is our chance to win!

WASHINGTON:

Hold fast that faith, my boy, for only faith
Can work the miracle we sorely need.
The British hold the towns. Their leader waits
The freezing of the Delaware before
He pushes on to Philadelphia.
Our loyal colonists have heavy hearts.
The enemy seems slowly closing in.
It is a crisis. For without the spur
Of victory we hold a losing cause.

CAPTAIN:

When do we cross?

WASHINGTON:

At three o'clock. 'Tis then
They will be taken unaware. By four
We should effect a landing.

CAPTAIN:

Save for storms—
For ice—for wind. Somehow, my General,
I fear the elements. And should we land—

WASHINGTON:
And land we shall.

CAPTAIN:

How can we know the way?
The point of vantage? And the crucial time
To strike?

JOHN:

Through me. I beg of you, send me.
For Trenton is my home—I know each inch
Of ground. I can be stealthy, too, and wise;
And I can lead you to the Hessian camp.
Oh, grant me this to do!

CAPTAIN (*Aside to* WASHINGTON):

The boy is young.
He has not yet been tested.

JOHN:

Grant me this.
It is my opportunity to serve.

CAPTAIN:
But there are older, wiser men who know
The devious ways of strategy.

JOHN:

Send me.
I will succeed. It is my chance—my chance.

WASHINGTON:
Your chance. Why not, my lad? 'Tis such as you
That must infuse new zeal into our hearts. (*Pauses*)
Accept the trust I give you. Be our guide
When we shall reach the shore.

JOHN:

I shall be there.

WASHINGTON:
Above—nine miles—the ferry—

JOHN:

Yes, I know.
And even now the time is short. Farewell.
Across the river—four o'clock—we meet. (JOHN *rushes off.*
After a moment of silence, WASHINGTON *puts his hand on*
CAPTAIN'*s shoulder.*)

WASHINGTON:

> You doubt the wisdom of my choice, good friend,
> But in a time of weakness and of doubt
> We need the fearless spirit of adventure,
> The faith that brooks no failure—and the youth
> That never falters, never faints and never fears.

CAPTAIN:

> To you is given the vision, General.
> I trust your word as always.

WASHINGTON:

> Then, my friend,
> We work together on this Christmas night. (*Pauses*)
> Christmas night! The time of peace, goodwill.
> How can we plan for war—perhaps, for death?
> How is the holy season marred—and yet—
> Tonight we work toward peace, our lives we
> Consecrate to liberty, to justice and to right.

CAPTAIN:

> The ice—the snow—if there could only be
> A sign that they would hinder not.

WASHINGTON:

> A sign?
> Perhaps this Christmas night the sign will come.

CAPTAIN:

> A sign will come? I do not understand.

WASHINGTON:

> Did you not wish that there would be a sign?
> I only say—perhaps the sign will come.

CAPTAIN:

> Signs herald miracles, 'tis said.

WASHINGTON:

> Why not?
> It is the very night for miracles. (*Pauses*)
> The air is very still. The wind has ceased.
> Beyond us is the banner—and its folds
> Are drooping. But a little time ago
> The wind blew toward us. Had we crossed just then
> We should have battled hard but now you see
> There is no wind.

CAPTAIN (*In a whisper*):

My General—you mean—

WASHINGTON:

That if another wind should rise and blow
Our banner outward, we should know the sign
As one that bids us godspeed on our mission.
We'll watch and wait and pray the sign will come.

CAPTAIN:

The air is still and cold. There is no sound—
The very silence is oppressive. See!
The banner hangs as lifeless as before.

WASHINGTON:

Look close. The banner moves. Can you not see
That something is astir? That something blows—
And blows it outward—*outward?* 'Tis the sign.

CAPTAIN:

The sign, my General. My faith returns.

WASHINGTON:

And now, tonight, we cross the Delaware! (*Curtain*)

*   *   *   *   *

SCENE 2

SETTING: *A room in the Winchester home.*

AT RISE: ELIZABETH WINCHESTER *stands at curtained window, looking out into the night.* MRS. WINCHESTER *enters right, wearing a long, full cape which covers her formal gown.* ELIZABETH *turns toward her.*

MRS. WINCHESTER:

What foolishness is this, Elizabeth?
Have you forgotten that our Loyalist friends
Are celebrating Christmas with a ball?

ELIZABETH:

I've not forgotten, Mother.

MRS. WINCHESTER:

Then I ask

Why you have failed to be in readiness.

ELIZABETH:

Because I do not care to go; because
I have no interest in the gaieties
Of those who are our enemies.

MRS. WINCHESTER:

How dare
You speak so of the British when you know
Our hearts and hands are pledged to good King George.

ELIZABETH:

Not *my* heart, not *my* hand. I choose to pledge
To that dear land I love—America.

MRS. WINCHESTER:

You still are wayward, stubborn. 'Tis because
Your foolish brother—

ELIZABETH:

Hush! I shall not hear
One word against him. He has had the faith,
The courage to be true to what is right.

MRS. WINCHESTER:

And he has forfeited his heritage.

ELIZABETH:

That is your cruelty to him. You choose
The King and not your son. (*Suddenly*) I should not speak
So boldly to you, Mother.

MRS. WINCHESTER:

You must learn
That older heads are wiser—that the band
Of churlish wits who prate of liberty
Must now be kept subservient to the King.

ELIZABETH:

The patriot cause is mine.

MRS. WINCHESTER:

Why, even now
The British close upon the colonists. (*Impatiently*)
Why do I tarry thus? I shall expect
You later at the ball, Elizabeth.
The carriage will return.

ELIZABETH:

I shall not go.

MRS. WINCHESTER (*Firmly*):

I shall expect you. (*She exits right, and* MARIA, *the maid, enters, obviously frightened.*)

MARIA:

Oh, Miss Betty—I—

ELIZABETH:

What is it? What has happened?

MARIA:

Master John

Is waiting for you—there. (*Points to back, as* JOHN *enters*)

ELIZABETH:

Oh, John—dear John.

How can you be so reckless! All around
Are Tory soldiers.

JOHN:

Betty, I am here
Upon a secret mission—there is time
For just a word.

ELIZABETH:

Maria, stand outside—

Keep guard. (MARIA *exits*.)

Speak quickly, for I am afraid.

JOHN:

At three o'clock our General will cross
The Delaware.

ELIZABETH:

Impossible! The snow—

JOHN:

But on this Christmas night, the Hessian troops
Are off their guard. The British, too, forget
There is a war. They hold high carnival.
And if we force a crossing—victory
Is ours.

ELIZABETH (*Excitedly*):

And courage, too, will be renewed.

(MARIA, *the maid, enters from door at rear*.)

MARIA:

I saw two soldiers passing.

ELIZABETH (*To* JOHN):

Then, be gone—

No moment for farewell. (JOHN *hurries off*.) Maria, go
To watch—to listen—and to bring me word. (MARIA *exits*.
ELIZABETH *speaks to herself*.) The ferry—nine miles south—
at four o'clock—(*Pistol shots are heard from offstage*.
MARIA *rushes back in*.)

MARIA:

The Tory soldiers saw him and they fired—
They took him prisoner—

ELIZABETH:

Tonight—tonight—
When Washington will cross the Delaware! (*Curtain*)

* * * *

SCENE 3

SETTING: *A snow-covered bank of the Delaware River.*

AT RISE: *Against a snowy background with sparkling evergreen trees,* WASHINGTON *stands with his faithful* CAPTAIN *by his side.*

CAPTAIN:

There is no sign of Winchester. The men
Are restless—and they wish to march ahead
Toward Trenton. You will see, my General,
That Winchester has failed us, left us here
To make our way as best we can.

WASHINGTON:

Not failed,
Not faltered, Captain. I am sure of that—
But fallen into evil hands.

CAPTAIN:

If it is true
That he is intercepted, we must surmise
That our proposed attack is known, that we
Have little chance of pressing farther on.
The capture of a spy means watchful eyes
Upon our movements; and I fear that we
Must now expect to find the troops prepared
For quick resistance.

WASHINGTON:

Still my faith is strong
In ultimate success. And we shall march
To Trenton.

CAPTAIN:

And yet we do not know the route that leads
Directly to the Hessians.

WASHINGTON:

We shall make
Our own route. Providence will lead the way.

CAPTAIN:

Then I shall—(*He breaks off abruptly and gazes offstage.*)
Wait! Someone has ridden up—
'Tis Winchester—no, 'tis a stranger. See—
He makes his way to us.

> (STRANGER, *wearing a long cape and a cap pulled low on
> forehead, and high riding boots, enters.* CAPTAIN *turns to
> STRANGER suspiciously.*)

What is it, sir?

STRANGER:

My message is for General Washington.

WASHINGTON:

And I am Washington. What word have you
For me? Be brief, I beg, for time is short.

STRANGER:

I come to you from your own messenger,
John Winchester.

WASHINGTON:

And why has he transferred
His mantle to your shoulders?

STRANGER:

He has been
Imprisoned by the British. I have come
To lead you to the Hessians by the path
He chose—the shortest, truest path.

WASHINGTON:

And how
Then did you come to know his purpose?
Messengers do not reveal their secret tasks.

STRANGER:

Was it not better that he give his task to me
Than that you should be abandoned without guide?

WASHINGTON:

Who are you then that comes to take his place?

STRANGER:

John's friend and confidant—*your* loyal friend,
My General. I only ask that you

Believe my tale, trust John, and realize
That my great happiness is serving you.

CAPTAIN (*Aside to* WASHINGTON):
Somehow this story does not ring as true
As I would have it.

WASHINGTON:

Yet I trust this youth
And see in him the answer to our prayer
For guidance.

CAPTAIN:

Yet, if he should be a spy
From British forces—

STRANGER:

I am not a spy.
I come direct from your true messenger.
There is no time to tell you how and why.
The morning soon will break. Nine miles there are
To travel. And the British do not know
Of this, our undertaking. Take no time
To question, but believe me when I say
That I can guide you to the Hessian camp.
(*For a moment there is silence.*)

CAPTAIN:
I trust your word—but should you play us false—

STRANGER:
I shall not play you false.

WASHINGTON:

Then, lead us, lad! (*Curtain*)

*　*　*　*

SCENE 4

SETTING: *A small sparsely and plainly furnished room.*

AT RISE: WASHINGTON *sits at bare table, while* CAPTAIN *stands near him.*

CAPTAIN:
A thousand prisoners, my General—
And forty killed and wounded.

WASHINGTON:

And our loss?

CAPTAIN:
Two killed, three wounded.

WASHINGTON:
Every victory
Must have its toll of victims. But those who live—
How is their spirit now?

CAPTAIN:
Victory does much
To change the outlook and to cheer the heart.
This morning they could face the British force
In its entirety and never flinch.
Success means much, and now our patriot cause
Has passed its very crisis. 'Tis your faith
That brought us through the darkest, drearest days.

(JOHN *appears at the door. His head is bandaged, and his
arm is in a sling. He crosses to* WASHINGTON *and salutes.*)

JOHN:
I cannot find the words to plead my cause;
I cannot ask that you will ever trust
Another mission to me. I have failed—
Failed when I should have won. Is it too much
To ask for clemency?

WASHINGTON:
Are we not here?
Have we not won our victory? Success
Has crowned our venture.

JOHN:
But this same success
I had no part in gaining. May I speak,
If not to clear myself, to tell you why
I failed to meet you at the ferry?

WASHINGTON:
Speak, my boy.

JOHN:
In Trenton live my family, as you know.
They all are Tories save Elizabeth,
My sister who is very dear to me.
When I spoke for the patriot cause, she, too,
Declared the justice of our worthy cause—
A free and independent country. Now

My family has cast me off; and she
Has been forbidden to receive me, though
At times we have our stolen interviews.

CAPTAIN (*Impatiently*):

Come—come, the time is passing. We must know.

JOHN (*Motioning for silence*):

Tonight when I had seen the Hessian camp—
Had watched their carelessness—their revelry—
I knew that now the time was right to strike.
I passed my home. I saw my sister's maid—
She let me in to see Elizabeth.

CAPTAIN:

Treachery! You ran the risk of capture.

WASHINGTON:

Quiet, Captain, for this is no treachery.

JOHN:

I had but left the house. Two officers
Who happened to be passing shot at me
And kept me with them. It is only now
I have escaped their watchfulness.

WASHINGTON:

        And still
You played your part; you sent the messenger
Who guided us so skillfully, who knew
So well the path to follow. And before
We realized, he slipped away without
Our thanks. If you will tell his name, we shall
Express our gratitude.

JOHN:

       A messenger?

WASHINGTON:

Your messenger.

JOHN:

     I sent no messenger.

WASHINGTON:

Then who came to us claiming you sent him?

JOHN:

I am as puzzled as yourselves. I sent no one.

CAPTAIN:

And told no one your secret mission?

JOHN:

No.

CAPTAIN:

Think well and hard. For this same messenger
Knew all our plans, and knew that you, our guide,
Was wounded, could not come. You told no one?

JOHN:

I told no one—(*Suddenly*) save—save—

CAPTAIN:

Save whom?

JOHN:

Elizabeth. (ELIZABETH *appears at door, smiling.*)

ELIZABETH (*Curtsying*):

Your servant, General, answering to my name.
But much more proud to call myself your guide.
A leader of the loyal patriot band
That marched this morning into Trenton.

JOHN:

You?

ELIZABETH:

Why not? I knew your mission, knew that you
Were captured. Was it not my very chance
To aid the cause I love, uphold and cherish?
Your horse was waiting, and I hurried off,
A trifle late, dear General, but I did my best
And rode my fastest. And I had the joy
Of being for a little while a part
Of Washington's own army.

JOHN:

Dear sister,
It was you who did my work, who led the way.

ELIZABETH:

'Twas I indeed—and proud, so proud to do it. (*Crosses to*
WASHINGTON)
You will not blame John for such recklessness,
Such thoughtlessness in risking peril when
He should have thought alone of country's need.

WASHINGTON:

Since I now know you were the guide, you've proved
Your worth. I grant you any favor you would ask.

ELIZABETH:

    I thank you—for this Christmas gift to me.

    Our gift to you is our undying love

    And loyalty and service. (*Suddenly*) See how fair

    The day has grown—how dazzling the sun!

WASHINGTON:

    How happy are our hearts—for we forget

    The darkness and the peril we have seen.

ELIZABETH:

    Long shall we recall this Christmas night

    When Washington dared to cross the Delaware. (*Curtain*)

THE END

Horse Sense

An unbridled view of Paul Revere's ride

by Earl J. Dias

Characters

PAUL REVERE'S HORSE (*Brown Beauty*)
PAUL REVERE, *a man of 40*
MRS. DOROTHY QUINCY HANCOCK, *John Hancock's wife, in her 30s*
DEBORAH REVERE, *Revere's daughter, 17*
NED DEVON, *Revere's apprentice, 17*
MRS. LOCKSLEY, *a snappish woman of 50*
RACHEL WALKER REVERE, *Revere's second wife*

BEFORE RISE: PAUL REVERE'S HORSE, *Brown Beauty, parts the curtains and enters from behind the scenes. He is carrying a chair, which he places down right. He then comes to center, bows, and speaks to audience.*

PAUL REVERE'S HORSE: Hello. I suppose you're surprised to see a horse on these premises. But—and I say this in all modesty—I am a famous horse. Paul Revere's horse, to be exact. (*Nodding head*) Guess you've heard of me—right? I'll bet that you all know that wordy poem by Henry Wadsworth Longfellow. (*He strikes a pose and recites dramatically.*)

Listen, my children, and you shall hear
Of the midnight ride of Paul Revere,
On the eighteenth of April, in Seventy-five;
Hardly a man is now alive
Who remembers that famous day and year.

Well, there are some facts that Mr. Longfellow didn't remember, either. For example, you can search that poem from be-

150

ginning to end and never discover my name. There I was, playing an important role in warning the countryside that the British were coming, and my name isn't even a tiny footnote in the poem. It's exasperating, I can tell you. (*Pause*) And did you know that I hate to be ridden at night? (*Shivering*) Things are spooky at night. I get shivers up and down my mane. But Paul Revere—oh, he's a nice enough fellow, but rough on horses—Paul Revere always rode me at night, and I was with him for nigh onto twenty years. He was always riding somewhere; he had an itch to be in the stirrups. For instance, in 1773, without warning, he saddled me up and we raced to New York to inform the Sons of Liberty there about the Boston Tea Party. Oh, yes, Mr. Revere was one of the fellows who dumped the tea into Boston Harbor. He had his nose into everything. (*Pause*) Later, when the British General Gage planned to garrison British troops at Fort William and Mary, in Portsmouth, New Hampshire, who do you think rode to Portsmouth, to warn the patriots and John Sullivan? You guessed. Paul Revere and I. (*Pause*) And that's not all. On April 16, 1775, two days before the ride made famous by Longfellow, we galloped to warn the patriots to move their military supplies from Concord. It was on that journey that Mr. Revere arranged the details of the April eighteenth ride. His friend would hang one lantern in the Old North Church tower if the British were going by land and two lanterns if they were going by sea. (*Sighing*) Anyway, you can imagine how tired I was after all those rides. I was getting to be nothing but skin and bones, and I was bothered by shortness of breath, too. What I'd like to do today is to show you the *real* facts behind that April eighteenth ride. You'll see how much I was put upon. Now, please settle down. (*He goes to right.*) The curtain will rise in a moment on the work room of Paul Revere's house in Boston on the night of April 18, 1775. You'll see how it all happened. (*He sits.*) And I may make a few comments as the events unfold. (*Curtain opens.*)

* * *

TIME: *The night of April 18, 1775.*

SETTING: *The workshop in Paul Revere's house in Boston. There is a fireplace at right, in front of which is a settee. A door at upper center leads onto street. There is also a door at left. At*

upper left, there is a cabinet in which are a number of exam-
ples of Revere's work—silver bowls, trays, spoons, teapots, etc.
At center there is a long wooden table with a bench in front of
it that faces the audience. At left of the table is a rocking chair;
at right of the bench is a straight chair.

AT RISE: PAUL REVERE, *a stocky, capable-looking man of 40, is*
seated at bench in front of table. His oldest daughter, DEBORAH,
is standing behind him. DOROTHY QUINCY HANCOCK, *an attrac-*
tive woman in her thirties, is seated in rocking chair at left of
table. REVERE *has before him a silver teapot, on which he is*
engraving a letter with a pointed instrument. He works rapidly
and is obviously nervous.

REVERE (*Working quickly and speaking rapidly*): The "J" is done,
  Mrs. Hancock. (*Looks at his work quickly*) Now, with a few
  strokes, we'll have the "H." Then you'll have a teapot fit for
  a king.

MRS. HANCOCK: A king? I'll not mention the King to John.
  Whenever George III's name is mentioned, John's temper boils
  to white heat. He's always saying that he's had his fill of King
  George.

REVERE (*Continuing to work quickly*): So have we all. And John's
  feelings are well known to me. I spoke with him and Sam
  Adams yesterday about the danger that the British troops may
  march on us soon. (*The engraving tool falls suddenly from his
  hand and he picks it up.*) Drat!

MRS. HANCOCK: You seem unusually nervous tonight, Mr. Revere.
  As for the British, how soon will they march?

REVERE: Tonight, I fear. (*Smiling wryly*) So my nervousness
  shows, does it? Nervous or not, I have plans for the Redcoats.

DEBORAH (*Smiling*): Father always has plans for everything. Sometimes I think he's the busiest man in Boston.

REVERE (*Putting last touches on teapot*): There. That will do. A
  good piece of work, if I do say so myself.

HORSE (*Aside to audience*): You hear that? Modesty is not one of
  Mr. Revere's outstanding virtues.

MRS. HANCOCK (*Rising and going to bench where* REVERE *hands
  teapot to her*): It's lovely. This will be a wonderful present for
  John. It will cheer him mightily. The mercantile business has
  not been prospering lately.

REVERE: Why not leave the teapot here until tomorrow? I want to polish it a bit. I'll have young Ned, my apprentice, deliver it in the morning.

MRS. HANCOCK: That will suit me well. (*Looking worried*) Do you really think that the British will march soon?

REVERE: It's as certain as that the sun will rise tomorrow.

DEBORAH: There may be terrible times ahead.

REVERE: One must pay the cost of freedom. (NED DEVON, REVERE'S *apprentice, enters at left.*)

NED: I've fed Brown Beauty, Mr. Revere.

HORSE (*Aside*): Dry oats! Nobody ever thinks to wet the stuff with milk or water. They never butter my hay, either.

REVERE: Good. Are things quiet outside?

NED: Not a mouse stirring. Oh, except for Mrs. Locksley. And she seems to be on her way here. She must want to pick up the spoons she ordered.

REVERE: Drat! Mrs. Locksley—tonight of all nights!

MRS. HANCOCK: I know that she's a blazing Tory, but she's not a witch. Why are you so worried, Mr. Revere?

REVERE: I may as well tell you. John knows already. And so does Sam Adams. If the British plan to march through Middlesex tonight, I will ride to warn all the militia to make sure that they are prepared.

DEBORAH: Father!

MRS. HANCOCK: No wonder you're so jittery.

REVERE: My nerves will be jumping when Mrs. Locksley arrives. If she gets wind of what I'm up to, she'll spread the word among her Tory friends. And the British will be on me in no time at all. Ned, get Mrs. Locksley's spoons from the cabinet. We'll get rid of her as soon as possible. (NED *goes to cabinet for spoons.*)

MRS. HANCOCK: I wish you luck. If I know Mrs. Locksley, she'll stick to you like a burr. I had better be on my way now. John will be worried about me. He says the streets are not safe these days.

DEBORAH: I never thought I would see the day when one could not walk safely in Boston.

REVERE: These are perilous times, Deborah. (NED *places spoons on table.*)

MRS. HANCOCK (*Going to upper center*): Use care and caution,

Mr. Revere. And thank you for your work on the beautiful teapot.

REVERE: My pleasure. (MRS. HANCOCK *exits*.) Deborah, where is Mother?

DEBORAH: She is putting the children to bed—all seven of them.

REVERE: And heaven knows that's a time-consuming project.

DEBORAH: Father, how will you learn whether or not the British will attack tonight? And what will you do?

HORSE (*Aside*): Silly question! Mr. Revere's motto is, "When in doubt, saddle up poor Brown Beauty."

NED: I can tell you that, Deborah. I am to go to the end of the street and to keep my eye on the North Church tower. (*He takes out pocket watch and looks at it.*) I shall begin my vigil in about fifteen minutes. If one lantern appears in the belfry, that is the signal that the Redcoats will march by land; if two, they are going by sea. Then I shall report to Mr. Revere. (*Rubbing hands together*) It's exciting.

DEBORAH: And dangerous. Father, must you really be off on another ride? (REVERE *nods*.)

HORSE (*Aside*): That's the most sensible question I've heard tonight. (*There is a knock at door.*)

NED: That will be Mrs. Locksley.

REVERE: We must get her off the premises—and instantly.

DEBORAH: Easier said than done. (*There is another knock.*)

NED (*Face lighting up*): I have an idea!

REVERE (*Wryly*): Splendid. A good idea crops up seldom in a lifetime.

NED: It was inspired by something you just said. I think I know how to make Mrs. Locksley depart for home with the speed of an Arabian horse.

HORSE (*Aside; sarcastically*): Humph. What's so special about Arabian horses?

DEBORAH: That will be the miracle of the century.

NED: Just leave it to me. (*He rushes out, left.* REVERE *goes to upper center door, impatiently, and opens it.*)

REVERE: Oh, good evening, Mrs. Locksley. (MRS. LOCKSLEY, *a snappish woman, enters. She is carrying a cudgel.*)

MRS. LOCKSLEY: Not good at all, Mr. Revere. Mighty chilly for April—particularly when you make a body stand outside your door for so long. This Boston weather is enough to send us all to an early grave. Ah, I see that you have a fire tonight. Well, that's a blessing. I shall sit before it for a while and warm my feet. (*She goes to settee by fireplace and sits.*) I've come for my spoons.

REVERE (*Going to table*): I have them here for you. (*Nervously*) Don't you think that you had best leave soon? The streets are dangerous. (REVERE *picks up spoons, goes to* MRS. LOCKSLEY, *and hands them to her.*) Here you are. And I am sure that you'll want to get back with them at once.

MRS. LOCKSLEY (*Taking spoons*): Not so fast, Mr. Revere. I'm not one to buy a pig in a poke. Let me look at them—carefully. (*She takes a pair of spectacles from her pocket and puts them on.*) Now let's see. (*She examines the spoons carefully, squinting as she does so.*) Aha! Here's a spot on one of them. Look. (*She hands spoon to* REVERE.)

REVERE (*Exasperatedly examining spoon*): A tiny spot. (*He goes to table, opens the drawer, and takes out a polishing cloth.* MRS. LOCKSLEY *watches him with interest and notices that* REVERE's *hand is not steady.*)

MRS. LOCKSLEY: Jumpy tonight, are you not, Mr. Revere?

DEBORAH: Father has had a busy day. (REVERE *polishes the spoon with the cloth, then quickly returns spoon to* MRS. LOCKSLEY.)

REVERE: There. Good as new.

MRS. LOCKSLEY (*Looking carefully at spoon*): Hm-m. You might have cleaned it in the first place. Heaven knows this is costing me a pretty penny, and money doesn't grow on trees these days —what with all this revolutionary talk. God bless good King George, I say.

REVERE: I am sure that the King would appreciate your good wishes, Mrs. Locksley.

DEBORAH (*Giggling*): And the King needs blessing.

MRS. LOCKSLEY: You should watch your tongue, girl. I'll have no talk against His Majesty. It's bad enough to have to listen to firebrands like Sam Adams. He made a speech yesterday on Milk Street—attracted a large crowd of noisy good-for-nothings. He should be hanged for treason. (*Pointedly*) Some say our valiant British soldiers are going to put a stop soon to all this nefarious nonsense. (*Eying* REVERE *meaningfully*) Know anything about that, Mr. Revere?

DEBORAH: I like Mr. Adams. He's a jolly man.

MRS. LOCKSLEY: About as jolly as Satan himself. (*She rises, and* REVERE *looks hopefully at her.*)

REVERE: We shall say goodnight then, Mrs. Locksley.

MRS. LOCKSLEY: All in good time. I've toasted my toes, but now I'd like to rest a while before I venture forth. (*She goes to rocking chair and sits.*) I am partial to a rocker—relaxes a body. (*She begins to rock.*) Where is Mrs. Revere? I'd like to pay my respects to her.

REVERE: Rachel is with the children.

MRS. LOCKSLEY (*Sighing*): Ah, that woman is a saint. She showed courage and sacrifice when she married you after your first wife, Sarah, died. Not many women would want to wed a man who had eight children on his hands.

REVERE (*Trying to control his temper*): I've had no complaints.

DEBORAH (*Loyally*): Father would be a fine husband for any woman.

REVERE (*Again hopefully*): The hour grows late, Mrs. Locksley— and I repeat, the streets are not safe.

MRS. LOCKSLEY (*Suspiciously*): You keep harping on the lateness of the hour. (*Archly*) Am I keeping you from treasonous duties?

REVERE: I am thinking only of your welfare.

MRS. LOCKSLEY (*Banging her cudgel on floor*): Let anyone interfere with my coming and going, and I'll split his pate with this stick. If any one of the Sons of Liberty so much as makes a move in my direction, I'll send him to kingdom come.

HORSE (*Aside*): And don't think she wouldn't. She once cracked old Mr. Peckham's knee with a whack from that stick. Poor fellow has limped ever since. (RACHEL REVERE *enters at left.*)

RACHEL: The children are asleep, Paul. Oh, good evening, Mrs. Locksley.

MRS. LOCKSLEY: That's as may be. (*Rocking*) I came for my spoons, but I stayed in the hope of seeing you. We women have to knock some sense into the heads of the men of Boston. All this outcry against the throne—it's sinful, that's what it is.

RACHEL: But we colonists have suffered much from over-taxation and oppression.

MRS. LOCKSLEY (*Rocking furiously*): Nonsense! You've been listening to those lunatic Sons of Liberty.

DEBORAH (*Firmly*): Fine fellows all.

MRS. LOCKSLEY (*Snappishly*): Speak when you're spoken to, child. I suspect you've been giving ear to some of your father's ideas.

REVERE (*Irritated*): Really, Mrs. Locksley.

MRS. LOCKSLEY: Oh, I know you've had dealings with the hot-heads. But it's not too late to see the error of your ways. You're too good a silversmith to lose your trade because your head is foggy. There are some of us who won't continue to buy your wares, if—

RACHEL (*Determinedly*): Paul will follow the dictates of his conscience.

MRS. LOCKSLEY (*Rocking furiously*): Poppycock! It's his brain he ought to be using.

REVERE (*Pleadingly*): Mrs. Locksley, I am still worried about you. I do not like to think of a delicate lady like you abroad at this hour.

RACHEL: Yes, there is real danger.

DEBORAH: You never know what might happen.

MRS. LOCKSLEY (*Still rocking*): I fear nothing. And it's pleasant to sit here for a frank and cozy chat. (NED *re-enters suddenly at left. He looks frightened and is wild-eyed. His face is covered with unsightly spots.*)

NED: Oh, Mr. Revere! Mrs. Revere! I feel as though I have the ague—chills and fever! And when I looked into the mirror, not two minutes ago, I saw the most horrible sight.

MRS. LOCKSLEY: Your face is not so bad as that, Ned Devon. True, it won't win any beauty prizes, but it is normal.

NED: But it's not. (*He comes to rocking chair and thrusts his face close to* MRS. LOCKSLEY'S. DEBORAH *comes over to look at* NED'S *face and suppresses a giggle.* RACHEL *looks at* REVERE, *who smiles and nods.*) See!

MRS. LOCKSLEY: Have you gone mad, Ned Devon?

NED: Observe my face, Mrs. Locksley.

MRS. LOCKSLEY: I suppose I must humor the boy. (*She takes out spectacles, puts them on, and gazes at* NED. *Then she screams in horror.*) Spots! May heaven preserve us, the boy has the pox! It is a judgment on this house, Mr. Revere.

NED (*Putting his face closer to hers*): Can you see them plainly?

MRS. LOCKSLEY (*Leaping from chair and striking at him with her cudgel*): Get away from me! You are contagious! This house must be quarantined! (*She rushes toward upper center door.*)

REVERE (*Taking spoons from table*): Your spoons, Mrs. Locksley.

MRS. LOCKSLEY: Drat the spoons! I'll not eat with utensils that have been contaminated. And I'll not risk my own safety here any longer. (*She hurries out at upper center.*)

REVERE (*Laughing and shaking* NED's *hand*): Well done, lad.

DEBORAH: I didn't know that Mrs. Locksley could move so rapidly.

RACHEL: I suppose that this pretty kettle of fish was cooked up by you and Ned, Paul.

REVERE: It was Ned's idea.

NED: And a bit of soap and water will cure me miraculously. (*Taking watch from pocket and looking at it*) It is almost time. I must be off to watch the belfry tower.

REVERE: Saddle Brown Beauty before you leave, Ned. Then all will be in readiness for instant action.

NED: I will. (*He exits quickly at left.*)

HORSE: Mr. Revere doesn't know it, but his troubles are just beginning.

REVERE: The air is chill tonight. I must wear my cloak.

RACHEL: It is hanging in the kitchen, Paul. I sewed the button that was loose.

REVERE: Thank you, Rachel. (*Tenderly*) You think always of my comfort.

RACHEL (*Worried*): But I take no comfort in this venture tonight. You will be in grave danger.

REVERE (*Smiling*): No great danger—now that we are rid of Mrs. Locksley. And Brown Beauty is a trusty steed. He'll carry me safely on his strong back.

HORSE (*Aside*): Flattery will get you nowhere.

RACHEL: What if Mrs. Locksley should return with a doctor or the health authorities?

REVERE (*Chuckling*): Let her return. The doctor will examine Ned and find nothing wrong with him. He'll think that Mrs. Locksley is a lunatic.

DEBORAH: Brown Beauty seemed tired when I saw him this morning.

HORSE (*Aside*): There's a sensible girl.

REVERE: He has had ample time to rest. I'm sure he'll be as fresh as paint.

HORSE (*Aside*): Mr. Revere is due for a surprise.

REVERE: I'll fetch my cloak. (*He exits left.*)

DEBORAH: When Father makes up his mind, he is immovable.

RACHEL (*Smiling*): I suppose that is one of his charms.

DEBORAH: Have you ever seen anything so funny as Mrs. Locksley when she viewed the spots on Ned's face?

RACHEL: It was comical. But I fear that there will be little comedy in our lives now for a long time. (REVERE *enters at left, carrying his cloak, which he puts on the table.*)

REVERE: I looked in on the children. They're sleeping like lambs.

RACHEL: I wish they were lambs when they were awake. (NED *re-enters excitedly at upper center door and rushes to center.*)

NED: There are two lanterns, Mr. Revere! The British are to move by sea!

REVERE: Aha! Just as I suspected. (*Excitedly*) Get Brown Beauty from the stable, Ned, and bring him around to the front of the house. (NED *exits hurriedly left.*) The challenge has come at last. It was inevitable. (*He takes cloak from table and puts it on.* RACHEL *solicitously helps him to button it.*)

RACHEL: Keep your cloak buttoned to the neck. I do not want you to take a chill.

REVERE: No need to worry. Now that the hour has come, I never felt better in my life. Look. (*Holding out hand*) Not a tremor.

HORSE (*Aside*): That will change, I can tell you. Listen. (*The sound of a horse neighing is heard from offstage.*) That's me.

REVERE: What can ail Brown Beauty? (NED *rushes in at left.*)

NED (*Exasperatedly*): Brown Beauty will not budge from the stable. I cannot move him. He's as stubborn as a mule.

HORSE (*Aside; with sarcasm*): That's right. Insult me as well as abuse me.

REVERE: Drat the animal! What's wrong with him?

RACHEL: I have an idea. I'll fetch some lumps of sugar. Brown Beauty has a sweet tooth.

DEBORAH: But not a sweet temper tonight. (*Again the neighing is heard.*) I'll fetch the sugar, Mother. (DEBORAH *exits quickly left.*)

REVERE: Why does that horse elect to misbehave in an hour of crisis?

NED: He has seemed moody lately.

HORSE (*Aside*): And with good reason. (DEBORAH *returns at left, carrying several lumps of sugar.*)

DEBORAH (*Handing sugar to* NED): Take these lumps of sugar, Ned.

RACHEL: And pray that they do the trick.

HORSE (*Aside*): They won't!

REVERE: I'll go with you. I want to see for myself what's disturbing that blasted animal. (REVERE *and* NED *exit hurriedly left.*)

DEBORAH: Poor Father! He has had enough to bear tonight.

RACHEL: The dear man will be at his wits' end—and time is so important. (*More neighing is heard from offstage, followed by the sound of a thud.*)

DEBORAH: Gracious! I hope that no one is being hurt. (*There is more neighing and another thud. After a moment,* REVERE *and* NED *appear at left. Both look harassed.*)

RACHEL: No luck?

REVERE: That horse is a monster. He had the gall to eat the sugar —all of it. And then he stood there like the Rock of Gibraltar.

NED: We pulled and tugged, but he's as strong as—as—

DEBORAH: As strong as a horse.

REVERE: This is no time for joking. We must get that animal out of the stable—and at once.

RACHEL: But how?

REVERE: If I could only coax him outside, I could then leap onto his back and all would be well. Once I have the reins in my hand, I can control the beast.

HORSE (*Aside*): So I'm a beast, now, am I?

DEBORAH: I know something we could attempt. He likes music, as you know. Perhaps if I went out there and sang a soothing song, he would become calm, and we could induce him to leave his stall.

REVERE: I had not expected to spend this night in providing musical entertainment for a horse.

RACHEL (*Attempting to soothe him*): It might be worth a try, Paul. Deborah has a pleasing voice, and Brown Beauty has always seemed to like her.

NED: Strange situations demand strange solutions.

DEBORAH: Let me try—and I'll go alone. He might object if we all descended on him at once.

HORSE (*Aside*): How right she is! (DEBORAH *exits quickly at left.*)

REVERE: As the sailors say, any port in a storm. (*They listen intently. There is neighing and a thud. Then, after a moment,* DEBORAH's *voice is heard singing soothingly a few bars of "Drink to Me Only with Thine Eyes." There is silence.*)

RACHEL (*After a moment*): Good. All is quiet. Perhaps she has soothed him. (*All continue to listen intently. Then there is another thud and more neighing.*)

REVERE (*Gloomily*): She has not soothed him for long. (DEBORAH *enters at left, looking crestfallen.*)

DEBORAH: He liked the music—he listened to it and kept time with his head. But he will not move an inch from his stall.

REVERE: What are we to do? Our fortune must ride tonight, but even fortune needs a horse.

RACHEL (*Her face suddenly lighting up*): Needs a horse? Of course —why have I not thought of this before?

DEBORAH: Thought of what, Mother?

RACHEL: You know that Mr. Endicott next door has a beautiful mare. I have observed that Brown Beauty is mightily interested in her. Do you suppose. . . .

NED: Aha! You mean that if we bring the mare to the door of the stable, Brown Beauty may be enticed to come forth?

RACHEL: Exactly.

HORSE (*Aside*): Oh, no!

NED: I'll fetch the mare at once. Mr. Endicott will understand. He's a Son of Liberty. (*He rushes out at left*)

HORSE (*Aside*): You see how everything conspires against me? I have always had a weakness for a pretty face—it's my only fault—and Mr. Endicott's mare is a gorgeous creature. But how despicable—to play a trick like this on me! It's not fair to self-respecting horses, because even the best of us sometimes let our hearts rule our heads.

DEBORAH: If this ruse is not successful, Father, perhaps you can ride the mare instead.

REVERE: No—that would not be well. The mare has not the stamina for tonight's long journey. Only that stubborn Brown Beauty—drat his hide—has the strength and endurance for the enterprise.

HORSE (*Aside*): Thanks for the compliment—such as it is. Well, folks, to make a long story short, Ned came back from Mr. Endicott's triumphant, as you shall see. In fact, just five minutes after he had left, he had accomplished what he set out to do. Oh, he's a speedy young fellow, is Ned. Here he comes now. (NED *enters at upper center door. He looks elated.*)

NED: We have done it! I borrowed the mare, set her just outside the stable door, and held my breath. Brown Beauty perked up his ears, whinnied, romped from the stable, and began to rub noses with the mare. I led the mare to the front of the house, and Brown Beauty followed happily. He's now tied to the hitching post, ready for the journey.

REVERE: Rachel, we are all in your debt.

RACHEL (*Smiling*): You are indebted to Mr. Endicott's mare, I vow.

REVERE: However you will. But now I can be off on my mission. Thank you, Ned. (*He shakes* NED'*s hand.*) Goodbye, Deborah. (*He kisses her on the cheek.*) Farewell, Rachel. (*He clasps her in his arms.*)

RACHEL (*After he releases her*): Remember to keep your cloak buttoned tight, Paul.

REVERE: I will. I will. (*He rushes toward upper center door and waves. Others wave to him. Then all freeze in position.* HORSE *rises, comes to down center, and speaks to audience.*)

HORSE: Call me a romantic fool, if you will, but that's the way it was. As the philosopher says, the heart has reasons that the head knows not of. (*Pauses*) So there we have it—no matter what Mr. Longfellow may have told you. The true events of the night of April 18, 1775. I can tell you one thing—it was a hectic ride. And it was just as spooky as I expected; I'm always afraid of things that go bump in the night. Anyway, the farmers throughout the countryside were warned—and they stood up bravely to the British. (*Bows*) And now, with your permission, I'll ride into history with Paul Revere. (*As* HORSE *turns and crosses center, entering set, other characters spring into action, waving to* REVERE, *who exits up center.* HORSE *races after him, shouting.*) Wait for me! Mr. Revere! Wait for me! (*Quick curtain*)

THE END

"Woof" for the Red, White and Blue

Betsy Ross gets unexpected help

by Dorothy Brandt Marra

Characters

SARA JANE
MARY
MARY'S MOTHER
MESSENGER
BETSY ROSS

TIME: *Revolutionary times.*

SETTING: *A street in Philadelphia. Running diagonally from up center to down right is a picket fence with a gate. Behind fence is Betsy Ross's house.*

AT RISE: SARA JANE *and* MARY *are playing in the street.*

SARA JANE (*Drawing circle on ground*): I wish we had more players. Two aren't enough for a good game of Tom Tiddler.

MARY: I couldn't find anybody else.

SARA JANE: I'll be Tom Tiddler, and this is the treasure. (*She places stones inside circle and steps inside circle.* MARY *dances around circle, occasionally trying to grab the treasure. When she steps or reaches into the circle,* SARA JANE *tries to grab her.* MARY *is chanting as she plays.*)

MARY:
I'm on Tom Tiddler's ground
Picking up gold and silver.

(MARY'S MOTHER *enters left, waving her arms in distress.*)

MOTHER: Mary, Mary, are you playing that terrible British game again?

163

MARY: Oh, Mother, it doesn't mean anything. It's just for fun.

MOTHER: Mercy! And right in front of Mrs. Ross's house. She's inside sewing for Washington's army, and you're out here playing British games. Shame! Now you play something else. (*Exits left*)

SARA JANE: My mother feels the same way about the British, Mary. (MESSENGER *enters left, running and out of breath. He carries a package.*)

MESSENGER: Is this where Mrs. Ross lives?

MARY: Betsy Ross?

MESSENGER (*Checking name on package*): Yes, Betsy Ross. I have a package for her. (SARA JANE *goes through gate in fence, toward house.*)

SARA JANE: I'll get her. (*She knocks on door.* BETSY ROSS *opens it and comes out.*) Hello, Mrs. Ross. There's a messenger here for you.

BETSY ROSS: Thank you for fetching me, Sara Jane. (*She comes to gate. Loud barking is heard from house. She turns.*) Hush, you bad puppies! (*Turning to* MESSENGER) Is this package from General Washington?

MESSENGER (*Looking around carefully*): Sh-h-h! This is a secret mission.

MARY (*Clapping her hands to her face in excitement*): A secret mission!

SARA JANE: How exciting!

MESSENGER (*Handing package to* BETSY ROSS): Here is the package. General Washington said you'd know what to do with it. (*Exits left*)

BETSY ROSS: Thank you. (*She starts to go back inside her house.*)

SARA JANE: Oh, Mrs. Ross, aren't you going to tell us the secret?

MARY: Please, Mrs. Ross! We won't tell anyone!

BETSY ROSS (*Hesitating, looking at them*): Well, girls, I really shouldn't, but your fathers are with General Washington, and I know you wouldn't tell a secret. (*She comes back and starts to open package.*) Here, help me.

SARA JANE (*Helping to unwrap package*): It's fabric. Are you making a new coat for General Washington? (BETSY ROSS *unfolds a large square of red cloth.*)

MARY: Red! You won't sew a red coat for our general, will you? That's the color the British wear.

BETSY ROSS: I'm not making a coat at all. I'm sewing a flag for our new country.

MARY (*Excited*): Really and truly?

SARA JANE (*Clapping her hands*): How wonderful! (BETSY ROSS *hands red fabric to* SARA JANE, *then unfolds a large square of white, which she hands to* MARY. *Finally, she takes out a square of blue, and looks inside wrapping.*)

BETSY ROSS: Red, white, and blue material, but there's no pattern for the design of the flag. (*Shakes wrapping*) Where is the design?

SARA JANE: Maybe the messenger lost it.

BETSY ROSS (*Giving girls a gentle push*): Quickly, run after him. I must have the pattern. (SARA JANE *and* MARY *hand her fabric and run off left.*)

SARA JANE *and* MARY (*Calling as they exit*): Messenger! Wait! (BETSY ROSS *shakes out wrapping, then cloth pieces. As she searches, loud sound of barking is heard from house.*)

BETSY ROSS (*Calling toward house*): Hush, you bad puppies! Hush! (*To herself*) Now, what could have happened to that pattern? I don't know what to sew for the flag.

SARA JANE *and* MARY (*Entering left, out of breath*): He's gone.

MARY: There was not a trace of him anywhere.

BETSY ROSS (*Upset*): What am I going to do? I must have the flag finished by tomorrow evening.

SARA JANE: Send a letter to General Washington and tell him you didn't get the pattern.

MARY: We can take it over to the Meeting House for you. A package of letters goes to General Washington every day.

BETSY ROSS: I suppose that would be best. Wait, and I'll get the letter ready. (*She takes fabric and goes into her house. Girls caper around in excitement.*)

SARA JANE: Just imagine! We know a real secret about General Washington.

MARY (*Looking around and nodding*): And we won't tell anyone! Not even my mother! (*They shriek with laughter.* BETSY ROSS *comes out holding a paper in her hand.*)

BETSY ROSS (*Reading aloud from paper*): "Dear General Washington, The material you sent for the flag has reached me safely, but the design for the flag was not in the package. Please send the design to me with all good speed so that the flag will be ready when you arrive." (*To* SARA JANE *and* MARY) If you two will run as fast as you can to the Meeting House, my letter may reach General Washington tonight. (MESSENGER *runs in left, out of breath.*)

MESSENGER: A new message for you, Mrs. Ross.

BETSY ROSS: What is it?

MESSENGER: General Washington will be here at sunrise tomorrow to get the flag.

BETSY ROSS (*In a panic*): Tomorrow morning? But where is the pattern? He didn't send the design.

MESSENGER: I know nothing about a pattern. But General Washington will be here for the flag in the morning. (*Exits left*)

BETSY ROSS (*Holding her head in distress*): This is terrible! I must try to think of something to sew for the flag. (*She rushes into her house.*)

SARA JANE: Poor Mrs. Ross.

MARY: I wish we could help her.

BETSY ROSS (*Loudly, from house*): Oh, no! Puppies, what have you done? Bad puppies! (*She rushes from the house to the street, trailing remains of the material: long strips of white and red and a square of blue. In her other hand she clutches ragged scraps of white.*) Look what my puppies have done to the fabric!

SARA JANE: They ripped up the flag material!

MARY: They chewed it to shreds!

BETSY ROSS: What shall I do? There isn't time to get any more, and besides, there wouldn't be a scrap of material in these colors in the whole city of Philadelphia.

SARA JANE: Let me see. (*Takes a red stripe and gives the other end to* MARY. *Then she takes a white stripe while* MARY *holds the other end, so the colors are next to each other, as in the flag.*) I guess you will have to use what you have.

MARY: It looks pretty. Use a red stripe, then a white one.

BETSY ROSS (*Stepping back to look*): Why, it does have a certain elegance to it, at that. But look, some of the stripes are shorter than others.

SARA JANE: Put a blue piece up in the corner.

BETSY ROSS (*Holding up blue square and looking at it*): It's awfully plain.

MARY (*Taking one of the scraps of white and holding it against the blue*): There, the white will dress it up.

SARA JANE: That scrap looks like a star! (*Suddenly*) Why don't you make thirteen stars, one for each state in our new country?

BETSY ROSS: That's a wonderful idea. And thirteen stripes, too, red and white, I should say.

MARY: Make the Pennsylvania star the biggest.

SARA JANE: Yes, do, Mrs. Ross. Make our star the biggest.

BETSY ROSS (*Shaking her head slowly*): And how do you think the other states would feel about that? We are all equal in our struggle for freedom.

SARA JANE: Well, never mind. Make all the stars the same size.

MARY: It will be a lovely flag. In fact, the most beautiful flag in the world. (*As she speaks, dogs bark inside.*)

BETSY ROSS: Yes, I think you're right. (*They hold up blue square with white star against it and the red and white stripes.*) And maybe I'll even give my puppies an extra bone tonight! (*Curtain*)

THE END

To Test the Truth

Will the real George Washington please stand up?

by Tekla A. Grinins

Characters

NARRATOR
LARRY BORE, *host of "To Test the Truth"*
FOUR PANELISTS
THREE GEORGE WASHINGTONS
THREE ABRAHAM LINCOLNS
EIGHT VOICES
COLONISTS ⎫
UNIONISTS ⎬ *singing groups*

BEFORE RISE: NARRATOR *enters in front of curtain.*

NARRATOR: Good morning, ladies and gentlemen, boys and girls. We are happy to have you with us as we present our version of a great TV show, "To Test the Truth." We are honored to have as our extra-special guests two famous Americans who were born in the month of February. Here to explain how the show works is the host of "To Test the Truth," Larry Bore. (*Curtain opens.*)

* * *

SETTING: *Stage is decorated with red, white and blue bunting. Large paintings of George Washington and Abraham Lincoln and a large Colonial flag hang on rear wall. There is a table for host, up center, with chair behind it. A long table, at right,*

is for panelists, and there are four chairs behind it. At left is a
table for challengers, with three chairs behind it. Large sign
reading TO TEST THE TRUTH *hangs on rear wall.*

AT RISE: LARRY BORE *enters, waving to audience as he moves to*
center stage. COLONISTS, UNIONISTS, *and* VOICES *are sitting in*
chairs on sides of stage.

BORE: Good morning, everyone! So happy to see you all here. Let
me explain what's going to happen on our show today. We will
have four panelists who will try to guess which of the three
guests is really telling the truth about himself. Can you believe
what everyone tells you? Today we will test the truth and find
out. There will be only one famous leader. The other two are
impostors. It is up to our panel to determine who is the actual
hero of our country. Let me now introduce our four panelists.
(PANELISTS *enter, shake hands with* BORE, *and seat themselves,*
right. BORE *may introduce panelists using actors' real names, if*
desired.) Now we are ready to meet the team of challengers.
(*Recording of "The Stars and Stripes" is heard from off, as*
THREE WASHINGTONS, *dressed in Colonial costumes, march on-*
stage and stand, holding cards with numbers 1, 2, and 3. Music
stops.) Number 1, what is your name?

1ST WASHINGTON: My name is George Washington.

BORE: Number 2, what is your name?

2ND WASHINGTON: My name is George Washington.

BORE: Number 3, what is your name?

3RD WASHINGTON: My name is George Washington.

BORE: Let's listen now to George Washington's story. (1ST, 2ND,
3RD *and* 4TH VOICES *rise and face audience.*)

1ST VOICE: I, George Washington, was born on February 22, 1732,
in Virginia. My father, who was well-to-do, died when I was
two years old. It was my brother, Lawrence, who raised me.

2ND VOICE: I studied how to survey land. I served as a British
soldier in the French and Indian War. At that time there was
no country called the United States. There were thirteen colonies ruled by the mother country, England.

3RD VOICE: When the Colonists began a revolution against England, I was asked to be the general of the American army. We
had a difficult time in 1776, but after several years our army
won.

4TH VOICE: When the United States was created under its Constitution, I became its first president on April 30, 1789. Signed, George Washington. (*Recording of "The Stars and Stripes" is heard from off, as* THREE WASHINGTONS *march to seats at left and sit. Music stops.* BORE *sits at desk, center.*)

BORE: It is now up to our panelists "To Test the Truth." Let's begin with Panelist Number 1.

1ST PANELIST: George Washington Number 1, I'd like to ask you about the Revolutionary War. Was it an easy war to win?

1ST WASHINGTON: No, it was not easy. Our army was small. We had very little money with which to pay the soldiers. They needed clothing and weapons. Very often they were ragged and hungry.

1ST PANELIST: George Washington Number 2, where did you get the money to pay the soldiers?

2ND WASHINGTON: I had a friend at Chase Manhattan.

1ST PANELIST: George Washington Number 3, where did *you* get the money for the troops?

3RD WASHINGTON: It was very difficult to raise the money. Since I was lucky enough to have money from my plantation, I spent much of my own funds. Later in the war, help came from France. (*Buzzer sounds.*)

BORE: The time's up for our first panelist. Let's continue the questioning with Panelist Number 2.

2ND PANELIST: George Washington Number 3, tell us more about the Revolutionary War. Why did the colonies want to break away from England?

3RD WASHINGTON: When England sent troops to Boston to collect taxes, it was an act of tyranny that could not be tolerated.

2ND PANELIST: George Washington Number 1, who was Betsy Ross?

1ST WASHINGTON: She was my teacher.

2ND PANELIST: George Washington Number 2, who do *you* think Betsy Ross was?

2ND WASHINGTON: She sewed our country's first flag. I asked her to put thirteen white stars on a field of blue. There were seven red stripes and six white stripes. You can see it right over there. (*Points to flag on wall. Buzzer sounds.*)

BORE: That's all for our second panelist. Panelist Number 3 will continue the questioning.

3RD PANELIST: George Washington Number 1, why are you called "The Father of Our Country"?

1ST WASHINGTON: Well, I was the first general of the United States Army. I was also elected the first President of the United States.

3RD PANELIST: George Washington Number 2, where was the first capital of the United States?

2ND WASHINGTON: In Washington, D.C. I took the President's Oath of Office on the steps of the Capitol Building. That's the same place where all the Presidents have promised to uphold the Constitution of this country. It was a beautiful day.

3RD PANELIST: George Washington Number 3, where did *you* become President of the United States?

3RD WASHINGTON: It was in New York City, in the Wall Street area. If you are ever downtown in New York, you will see a statue of me on the steps of the Sub-Treasury Building. (*Buzzer sounds.*)

BORE: That's it for Panelist Number 3. Our fourth panelist will now continue the questioning.

4TH PANELIST: George Washington Number 2, tell us about your family.

2ND WASHINGTON: I married a rich widow, Mrs. Martha Custis, and adopted her two children, Jack and Patsy. In 1799, I gave away my granddaughter, Nelly Custis, when she was married by candlelight at Mount Vernon.

4TH PANELIST: George Washington Number 1, can you tell us about the mint you helped to establish?

1ST WASHINGTON: Yes, I had a chewing gum factory that made spearmint gum.

4TH PANELIST: George Washington Number 3, can *you* tell us more about the mint?

3RD WASHINGTON: Yes, I can. It was a place for making money. Our new country needed a central money system. My picture is on the dollar bill and also on the quarter. (*Bell rings loudly three times.*)

BORE: Our time is up for questions, and the panelists will have to vote. Is it Number 1, Number 2, or Number 3? (PANELISTS *mark ballots and place them in holders on table as they speak.*)

1ST PANELIST: I vote for George Washington Number 3. He knew the colonists received help from France. George Washington

Number 2 said he got his money from the Chase Manhattan Bank. That is not true. (3RD WASHINGTON *puts card marked with X in holder on table.*)

2ND PANELIST: I vote for George Washington Number 2. He told us all about Betsy Ross and how she made our first flag. George Washington Number 1 said she was his teacher. That's not true. (2ND WASHINGTON *puts card marked with X in holder.*)

3RD PANELIST: I vote for George Washington Number 3. He knew that the first capital of the United States was in New York City. I have seen his statue on Wall Street. George Washington Number 2 told a lie, and we all know that George Washington cannot tell a lie. Washington, D.C., did not become the capital until Thomas Jefferson was elected President in 1800. (3RD WASHINGTON *puts X card in holder.*)

4TH PANELIST: I vote for George Washington Number 2. He told us all about his two stepchildren and granddaughter. He seems to be a good man as well as a good leader. (2ND WASHINGTON *puts X card in holder.*)

BORE: The votes are in. There are two votes for George Washington Number 2, and two votes for George Washington Number 3. There is only one true leader. Will the real George Washington please stand up! (3RD WASHINGTON *stands.* BORE *shakes his hand.*) In honor of your appearance on our stage, the Colonists are going to sing a song which you have often heard. In fact, the English soldiers sang it to make fun of you. (COLONISTS *sing "Yankee Doodle." Entire cast may join in. "The Stars and Stripes" is heard from offstage, as* THREE WASHINGTONS *march off. Music stops.*) Now it is time to meet our second set of challengers. (*"The Stars and Stripes" is heard from offstage, as* THREE LINCOLNS *march onstage, wearing black suits and beards, and carrying identifying numbers. Music stops.*) Number 1, what is your name?

1ST LINCOLN: My name is Abraham Lincoln.

BORE: Number 2, what is your name?

2ND LINCOLN: My name is Abraham Lincoln.

BORE: Number 3, what is your name?

3RD LINCOLN: My name is Abraham Lincoln.

BORE: Before we begin questioning our challengers, let's listen to Abraham Lincoln. (5TH, 6TH, 7TH, *and* 8TH VOICES *rise and face audience.*)

5TH VOICE: I, Abraham Lincoln, was born in a log cabin in Kentucky, on February 12, 1809. I had one older sister, Sarah. My father was a farmer, and when I was seven years old, he decided to move to Indiana. It was there that my mother died when I was nine.

6TH VOICE: My father married again. We loved our stepmother. It was with her help that I learned to read and write and do arithmetic. I studied as much as I could but continued to help my father on the farm.

7TH VOICE: When I grew older, I became a lawyer. I was elected to the state legislature in Illinois.

8TH VOICE: On March 4, 1861, I became the sixteenth President of the United States. The war between the North and South began a month later. The next year, September 22, 1862, I signed the Emancipation Proclamation which freed all the slaves. The War Between the States ended in 1865 during my second term of office. I had helped to keep all of the states together. Signed, Abraham Lincoln. (*"The Stars and Stripes" is heard from offstage, as* THREE LINCOLNS *march to seats at left and sit. Music stops.*)

BORE: It is now up to our panelists "To Test the Truth." Let's begin the questioning with Panelist Number 1.

1ST PANELIST: Abraham Lincoln Number 2, what did you like to do when you were a boy?

2ND LINCOLN: I loved to read books. Even when I was helping my father on his farm, I always brought along a book.

1ST PANELIST: Abraham Lincoln Number 1, you've been called a rail-splitter. What is that?

1ST LINCOLN: Fences were needed for all the farms in Illinois. I split wood into rails for fences.

1ST PANELIST: Abraham Lincoln Number 3, did you watch much television?

3RD LINCOLN: Only a little. I didn't have time. (*Buzzer sounds.*)

BORE: Your time is up. Panelist Number 2, it's your turn to question the challengers.

2ND PANELIST: Abraham Lincoln Number 3, did you have a lot of money?

3RD LINCOLN: No, I was quite poor.

2ND PANELIST: Abraham Lincoln Number 1, did you ever drive a Lincoln Continental?

1st LINCOLN: No, but I did ride in a Ford.

2ND PANELIST: Abraham Lincoln Number 2, how did you decide to become a lawyer?

2ND LINCOLN: I liked to help other people. When they got into trouble, I wanted to find ways of helping them. (*Buzzer sounds.*)

BORE: Let's continue the questioning with Panelist Number 3.

3RD PANELIST: Abraham Lincoln Number 3, I understand you hated war, yet there was a war between the northern and southern states when you were President. Why?

3RD LINCOLN: It's true that I hated war, but slavery was worse. The North fought to keep all the states together and also to free the slaves in the South.

3RD PANELIST: Abraham Lincoln Number 2, did you have children?

2ND LINCOLN: Yes, I did. My oldest son was Robert. I also had two small boys, Willie and Tad. Willie died while I was serving as President.

3RD PANELIST: Abraham Lincoln Number 1, do the words, "Four score and seven years ago," remind you of anything?

1st LINCOLN: Yes, they do. That is how I began a speech at a cemetery in Gettysburg, Pennsylvania. (*Buzzer sounds.*)

BORE: It's time for our final panelist to question the challengers.

4TH PANELIST: Abraham Lincoln Number 3, how tall are you?

3RD LINCOLN: I am five feet two inches tall.

4TH PANELIST: Abraham Lincoln Number 2, how tall are *you?*

2ND LINCOLN: I am over six feet tall.

4TH PANELIST: Abraham Lincoln Number 1, do you know which of our money has your picture on it?

1st LINCOLN: My picture is on the penny and the five-dollar bill. (*Bell rings loudly three times.*)

BORE: It is time now to vote. Is it Number 1, Number 2, or Number 3? (PANELISTS *write on ballots and place them in holders on table as they speak.*)

1st PANELIST: I vote for Abraham Lincoln Number 1. He knew that as a rail-splitter he helped to build many fences in Illinois. Number 3 is certainly not Abraham Lincoln. There was no television in 1865. (1st LINCOLN *puts card with X on table in front of him.*)

2ND PANELIST: I vote for Abraham Lincoln Number 2. He said he liked to help other people when they got into trouble. Number 1 could never be Abraham Lincoln. There were no cars in those days. (2ND LINCOLN *places card with X in front of him.*)

3RD PANELIST: I vote for Abraham Lincoln Number 3. Even though he hated war, he was President when a war was fought to free all people. The other two also gave good answers to my questions, but I still choose Number 3.

4TH PANELIST: I vote for Abraham Lincoln Number 2. We know Lincoln was over six feet tall. Number 3 said he was just five feet two inches tall. (2ND LINCOLN *puts second X card in holder.*)

BORE: All the votes are in. There is one vote for Abraham Lincoln Number 1, two votes for Abraham Lincoln Number 2, and one vote for Abraham Lincoln Number 3. There is only one true leader. Will the real Abraham Lincoln please stand up? (2ND LINCOLN *stands.* BORE *shakes his hand.*) In honor of your appearance on our stage, the Unionists are going to sing a song written at the time you served as our great leader. (UNIONISTS *sing "The Battle Hymn of the Republic." Entire cast joins in on chorus.*) And now to honor all our great heroes, let's close our show by singing "America." (*All sing "America." After song, entire cast bows. Curtain.*)

THE END

The Petticoat Revolution

If women had been in command . . .

by Claire Boiko

Characters

TWO FOREMOTHERS
QUEEN GEORGETTE THE THIRD
LADY HOWE
LADY BURGOYNE
LADY GAGE
LADY CORNWALLIS
MESSENGER GIRL

SAMANTHA ADAMS ⎫
POLLY REVERE ⎪
BENITA FRANKLIN ⎬ *The Minute*
PATRICIA HENRY ⎪ *Maids*
MOLLY PITCHER ⎪
MARTHA WASHINGTON ⎭

SCENE 1

BEFORE RISE: *A tinkling minuet is heard.* TWO FOREMOTHERS *enter, curtsy deeply to each other and to the audience.*

1ST FOREMOTHER: Ladies and gentlemen, patriots and loyalists, we beg your indulgence.

2ND FOREMOTHER: Pray, do listen to your foremothers.

1ST FOREMOTHER: You have certainly heard enough of your forefathers!

2ND FOREMOTHER: Your forefathers have been heard far too long and far too often. They wrote your history books.

1ST FOREMOTHER: According to your forefathers, they planned the campaigns, waged the battles and won the war. Stuff and non-sense!

2ND FOREMOTHER: Why, everyone who has any culture and refine-ment at all knows it was your foremothers who planned the campaigns, waged the battles, and won the war.

1ST FOREMOTHER: To be sure. Therefore, we have returned to set matters straight. We will tell you the true facts of such historic moments as the Battle of Bunker Hill and the Boston Tea Party.

2ND FOREMOTHER: That we will! (*The tune "Rule, Britannia" is heard in the background.*)

1ST FOREMOTHER: It all began in the court of that most wicked, stubborn queen, Georgette the Third. (*They fan themselves, then exit left and right, as the curtains open.*)

* * *

TIME: *Period of the American Revolution.*

SETTING: *The throne room of* QUEEN GEORGETTE THE THIRD.

AT RISE: GEORGETTE *is seated on her throne. On stools and cush-ions around her feet sit* LADY HOWE, LADY BURGOYNE, LADY GAGE *and* LADY CORNWALLIS. GEORGETTE *is admiring her wig in a hand mirror. From time to time she eats chocolates from a large box.*

GEORGETTE: What do you think of my new wig, ladies? 'Tis the latest fashion, all puffed and powdered like a summer cloud.

ALL (*Applauding*): Charming! Charming! (*There is a fanfare off-stage.* MESSENGER GIRL *runs in from left, carrying a document in an envelope. She kneels before* QUEEN.)

MESSENGER GIRL: An urgent message from the colonies, Your Majesty.

GEORGETTE: Colonies, colonies? Which colonies? I have so many colonies.

MESSENGER GIRL: The American colonies, Your Majesty. (*She hands* GEORGETTE *the envelope.* GEORGETTE *holds up her lor-gnette to read it.*)

GEORGETTE: Oh, the American colonies. Those wretched people. Where are they anyway, Lady Howe? Near India somewhere?

LADY HOWE (*Waving vaguely*): Somewhere over the ocean. Do you remember them, Lady Burgoyne?

LADY BURGOYNE: How can I forget them? You must remember them, Your Majesty. They are those impossible people who keep objecting to our taxes.

GEORGETTE (*Nodding*): Oh, yes. What have they to say for themselves this time? (*She reads*) Ah-ha. (*Pause*) Oh-ho. (*Pause*) Dear, dear. How tiresome. Now they won't pay the stamp tax. (*Admiring herself in hand mirror.*)

LADY GAGE: They won't pay the stamp tax? Then I say tax something else. Something they cannot do without!

LADY CORNWALLIS: Very clever, Lady Gage. They use air. They cannot do without air. Let's tax them three shillings for every breath they take.

LADY HOWE: Oh, piffle, Lady Cornwallis. Do be practical. You know those Yankees. They'll simply find a way to stop breathing.

LADY CORNWALLIS: Ah . . . perhaps. But they will never stop drinking tea. Why not tax their tea?

GEORGETTE: Oh, that's such a lovely notion, Lady Cornwallis. Hm-m. I fancy that very much indeed. Tax the tea. (*Decisively*) I'll send a writ immediately.

ALL (*Applauding*): Tax the tea. (GEORGETTE *hastily scratches a note with a quill pen.*)

GEORGETTE: How do you spell "American"? (*She pronounces it "Ameddican."*)

ALL: A-M-E-D-D-I-C-A-N.

GEORGETTE (*Blowing on paper, then folding it*): There! I've written a writ. And believe me, it's the right writ to have written. They'll mind their manners now.

LADY GAGE: And if they don't mind their manners?

GEORGETTE: Well, then, I suppose we must have a war.

ALL (*Alarmed*): A war!

LADY HOWE (*Showing her slippers*): How will I ever march in silken slippers?

LADY GAGE: Ugh. Wars are so noisy. I loathe noise.

GEORGETTE: Now, now, ladies. It's a last resort. However, do stay close to the court. Now, let me see . . . there's something I'm supposed to do in case of war. Oh, I know. Hand me my dubbing sword, Lady Burgoyne. (LADY BURGOYNE *brings sword from beside table, which is next to throne.*) Kneel down, everybody. (*All kneel in front of* GEORGETTE, *heads bowed. With sword, she taps each lady lightly on the shoulder.*) You, you, you, and you. There, it's done.

LADY CORNWALLIS: What's done, Your Majesty?

GEORGETTE: I made you all generals. Now you can all wear those divine gold epaulettes on your shoulders. (*All applaud and cheer in a ladylike fashion. Curtain.*)

* * * * *

SCENE 2

BEFORE RISE: *"Yankee Doodle" is heard from offstage.* 1ST FORE-MOTHER *enters.*

1ST FOREMOTHER: Meanwhile, back in Boston, the Daughters of Liberty Fancy Sewing and Tatting Society was having a deep philosophical discussion. (*She exits.*)

* * *

SETTING: *A Colonial parlor.*

AT RISE: SAMANTHA ADAMS, MOLLY PITCHER, *and* PATRICIA HENRY *are seated at a round table, sewing and tatting. Teacups are on table in front of them.* BENITA FRANKLIN *is tying a tail on a kite while* MARTHA WASHINGTON *stands at fireplace at right, stirring a kettle with a long wooden spoon.*

ALL (*Ad lib*): French knots! Slip-knots! (*Etc.*)

SAMANTHA ADAMS (*Tapping a spoon against a cup*): Ladies! Ladies! We must bring this important question up for a vote. Now the question is: Shall we embroider the handkerchiefs with French knots or slip-knots?

ALL (*Ad lib*): French knots! Slip-knots! (*Etc.*)

MOLLY PITCHER (*Shouting over noise*): I move we adjourn for refreshments.

ALL: Aye! Aye!

SAMANTHA: Fie! You're out of order, the lot of you. You can't move until a motion is made. Isn't that right, Benita Franklin?

BENITA FRANKLIN: But my dear Samantha Adams, if nobody moves until a motion is made, how does a motion ever become moved? (*All applaud.*)

PATRICIA HENRY (*Waving her hand*): A motion. A motion. I'm making a motion!

BENITA: A commotion, that's what you've made, Patricia Henry. Now, as I always say . . . (*All groan.*)

SAMANTHA: Order! Order!

MOLLY: I order refreshments.

SAMANTHA: Well, you can't have them.

MOLLY: Why ever not?

SAMANTHA: Because Martha Washington hasn't finished making the candy yet.

MARTHA WASHINGTON (*Holding up wooden spoon*): I'm so sorry, ladies. The fudge hasn't reached the hard ball stage yet. (*There is the sound of rapid hoofbeats offstage.* POLLY REVERE *staggers in from left, holding a message. She hands it to* SAMANTHA ADAMS.)

POLLY REVERE: A message from the Crown. (*She sits in empty chair down left.*)

ALL (*Ad lib*): Oh! Read it! What does it say? (*Etc.*)

SAMANTHA (*Opening the seals*): "To Whom It May Concern in the Ameddican Colonies . . ." Humph. She's misspelled "American."

BENITA: She never could spell.

SAMANTHA: I can't read her writing. She's smudged chocolate all over the paper. Let me see . . . "I am scandalized by your refusal to pay my pitiful taxes. I must insist that you mind your manners and pay your taxes. You shall have but one chance more. . . ."

BENITA: One chance more! Go fly a kite!

SAMANTHA: Hush, Benita. (*Reads*) "Therefore I request your payment of a modest duty on the import of tea . . ." ·

ALL (*Ad lib*): Tax the tea? Outrageous! Ridiculous! (*Etc.*)

PATRICIA (*Waving her fist*): Never!

SAMANTHA: Do be quiet. (*Reads*) "If you do not obey this trifling demand, I shall be obliged to . . . to . . ." (*Looks up*) Oh, dear!

POLLY: What's she going to do this time—hit us with her fan?

SAMANTHA: She's going to—declare war!

ALL (*Aghast*): War!

BENITA: War, eh? Well, as I always say . . . (*All groan.*)

PATRICIA (*Waving her fist again*): To war! To war! Roll out the cannon!

MARTHA: Do be sensible, Patricia. We haven't any cannon. And even if we had, we shouldn't know how to shoot them.

SAMANTHA: That's a good point, Martha. Now, candidly. Do any of you know how to fight a war? (*They all look at each other, confused.*)

MOLLY: I believe you start with a musket. They tell me you point it away from yourself and toward the enemy.

POLLY: Yes. You pull a little thingamabob on the side. It makes a terrible roar, and all your teeth rattle.

MARTHA: It makes a dreadful smell, too. My husband George used to come in from hunting, full of the most objectionable powder stains.

ALL: Powder stains!

PATRICIA: Fie! If we cannot fight with cannon and musket, we will use our bare hands!

BENITA (*Examining her hands*): What! And break our fingernails? As I always say . . . (*All groan*) Why is it nobody wants to listen to what I always say?

POLLY: I just thought of something. We need Intelligence.

SAMANTHA: Oh, I'm sure we have plenty of intelligence, Polly. Why, Benita Franklin alone has more brains than the entire British army. (BENITA *grins broadly.*)

POLLY: No, I mean—a spy. (*All nod approval.*)

PATRICIA: Now you have spoken common sense. I'll be the spy.

MOLLY: But I wanted to be the spy. I can tiptoe like an Indian.

ALL (*Ad lib*): I want to be the spy. No, me! I know how! (*Etc.*)

SAMANTHA (*Rapping her teaspoon*): Order! Order! We can't all be spies. We need a spy with transportation. Now, who has a swift, powerful horse?

POLLY: I have a slow, spavined mule.

SAMANTHA: That will have to do. I hereby delegate Polly Revere to be our spy.

POLLY: Isn't this exciting! Should I wear a black mask and hood, do you think?

MOLLY: Pink would be more becoming.

POLLY: Yes, pink. Well, ladies, as they say in the service—to horse! Or rather, to mule! (*She salutes snappily.*)

ALL (*Saluting*): Farewell! Good luck, Polly! (POLLY *exits.*)

SAMANTHA: Now there's one more small thing, ladies. We need an army. Will anyone volunteer?

ALL (*Ad lib*): I will! Me! Me! (*Etc.*)

SAMANTHA: Oh, you are all so patriotic! What shall we call ourselves?

PATRICIA: Dames for Liberty!

BENITA: The Grand and Glorious Girl Grenadiers!

MARTHA (*Demurely*): Perhaps we should call ourselves something
simple like—The Minute Maids.

ALL (*Ad lib*): Yes! The Minute Maids! (*Etc.*)

SAMANTHA: Minute Maids, we shall be. Shall we go and drill
now?

ALL: Yes, yes!

MARTHA: Pray excuse me. But we seem to have forgotten something. We don't have a general.

PATRICIA: I volunteer to be general. Attention, troops.

SAMANTHA: You cannot be a general, Patricia. You don't know a
manual of arms from a broomstick.

PATRICIA: Unfair! You're unfair. I never get to do anything. (*She
begins to sulk.* BENITA *crosses to her and pats her shoulder
comfortingly.*)

SAMANTHA: Oh, dear. Perhaps I'd better appoint someone. Martha
Washington, surely George has an old book or two about an
officer's duties. You will be our general.

MARTHA (*Coyly*): I'll do my very best. Now, let me see. We
ought to choose a place to have our first battle.

MOLLY: I know a place. We picnic there in the spring. It's a
lovely spot for a battle. Bunker Hill.

SAMANTHA: Bunker Hill. That sounds nice. All in favor of
having a battle on Bunker Hill say aye.

ALL: Aye! (PATRICIA HENRY *pouts and does not vote.*)

SAMANTHA: The ayes have it. Patricia Henry, are you abstaining
again?

BENITA: Don't pout, Patricia. You can write our slogans.

PATRICIA: Slogans? Very well. I have one. (*She poses dramatically,
her hand across her heart.*) Give me liberty, or give me death!

SAMANTHA: Oh dear, that's treason, isn't it?

BENITA: We'll tone it down a little. How about this? (*She stands,
posing like* PATRICIA, *who has sat down, fuming again.*) "Give
me liberty—or give me fudge!"

MARTHA (*Beaming, as she holds up her wooden spoon*): The
candy is ready, ladies! (*All clap loudly. Curtain.*)

*   *   *   *   *

SCENE 3

BEFORE RISE: 2ND FOREMOTHER *enters.*

2ND FOREMOTHER: As time went on, the two opposing forces surged toward each other. It was inevitable that the Minute Maids and the Redcoats should one day meet in a mighty battle. (*She exits.*)

* * *

SETTING: *A bare stage, containing only a small sign reading* BUNKER HILL.

AT RISE: *Stirring chords are heard as The Minute Maids,* SAMANTHA, BENITA, MOLLY *and* PATRICIA, *armed with mops, brooms, and rolling pins, enter from down right, led by* MARTHA WASHINGTON, *wearing a cape with epaulettes. She carries a book which she consults frequently.* PATRICIA HENRY *carries a sword on each side, a large pistol on her belt and a dagger in her teeth. All carry knitting bags which hang from sashes around their waists.*

MOLLY: Phew! What a strenuous walk. Did anybody bring lemonade?

PATRICIA (*Taking dagger out of her teeth*): This is not a picnic. This is a war. How stands the battle, General Washington?

MARTHA: Oh, dear. It doesn't stand at all, I'm afraid. The enemy doesn't seem to have arrived. However, while we are waiting for them, it seems sensible to draw up a battle line. Does anyone have a piece of chalk?

MOLLY: I do. I keep it for chalking hems. Where shall I draw the battle line?

MARTHA: Oh, right down the middle of things, I should think. (MOLLY *draws a chalk line down center stage.*)

BENITA: That's fair enough. They can have the Bunker. We'll keep the Hill.

MARTHA: Now, we're supposed to arrange ourselves in flanks. Samantha, you and Patricia may be the left flank. Face the battle line. And Benita, you and Molly may be the right flank. I suppose I should take the center of things in case I should lead a charge. (*They arrange themselves left and right of* MARTHA, *facing the battle line.*)

SAMANTHA: Now what, General Washington?

MARTHA: Well, I think the most sensible thing to do is to sit down quietly and knit.

ALL (*Nodding agreement*): Good idea. (*They take out their knitting needles and begin to knit, placidly.* PATRICIA *knits with her dagger between her teeth. "Rule, Britannia" is heard from offstage. Led by* LADY HOWE, LADY BURGOYNE, LADY GAGE, *and* LADY CORNWALLIS *enter, single file, then stand together. They are dressed elaborately, with large epaulettes on their shoulders. The Minute Maids put away their knitting very deliberately and toe the battle line, holding their mops, brooms and rolling pins like muskets. The British ladies advance elegantly, fanning themselves until they stand toe-to-toe at the battle line. At this moment, mule hoofbeats are heard offstage.*)

POLLY (*From offstage*): The British are coming! The British are coming! (*She runs onstage from up right, sees British ladies, and calls sheepishly.*) The British have come! The British have come!

MARTHA (*Resignedly*): We know, Polly dear. (POLLY *joins left flank. All stand silently glaring at each other for a moment.*) Ahem. How do you do! You are the British, I presume.

BRITISH LADIES: We are.

MARTHA: May I introduce myself? I am General Martha Washington. Who is in charge of your forces, please?

BRITISH LADIES (*Together*): I am! I am! I am!

MARTHA: One at a time, if you please. Who is the commander?

BRITISH LADIES (*Together*): I am! I am! I am!

MARTHA: How extraordinary. Who gives the orders, then?

LADY HOWE: I do.

LADY BURGOYNE: Lady Howe, Her Majesty decided *I* should give the orders.

LADY CORNWALLIS: Oh, no. We drew straws. I drew the longest.

LADY GAGE: Fiddle-faddle. The shortest straw wins. Any dunce knows that. I give the orders.

LADY CORNWALLIS (*Angrily*): Did you call me a dunce, Lady Gage? Did you hear that, Lady Howe? She called me a dunce. I demand satisfaction.

LADY HOWE (*Fluttering her fan at* LADY GAGE): Do stop that, Lady Gage. We're here to fight the Colonials. (*To* MARTHA) Madam, I insist you lay down your arms and surrender!

PATRICIA (*Through her teeth*): Never!

LADY GAGE: What did she say?

PATRICIA (*Taking the dagger out and enunciating clearly*): Nev-er!

LADY GAGE: That's what I thought she said.

PATRICIA: We will fight with bare fists, if necessary. *En garde!* (*She strikes a fighting pose and jams her fist under* LADY GAGE'S *nose.* LADY GAGE *faints into the arms of* LADY CORNWALLIS *and* LADY BURGOYNE, *who fan her vigorously.* PATRICIA *strikes pose again, taking aim at* LADY HOWE, *who ducks.* PATRICIA'S *blow rebounds, and she hits her own chin, going down in arms of* BENITA *and* MOLLY.)

MARTHA: Smelling salts! Get the smelling salts.

LADY CORNWALLIS (*Handing smelling salts to* MARTHA): Here. But give them back. Lady Gage hasn't come round yet.

LADY HOWE: How dare she attack a Lady of the Royal Court?

MARTHA: Why, why—you started it with your talk of surrender.

LADY BURGOYNE: She did not!

BENITA: She certainly did!

LADY HOWE: I certainly did not, you—barbarians!

PATRICIA (*Sitting bolt upright*): Barbarians! Who's a barbarian? You—Tory bludgeon!

LADY GAGE (*Sitting up*): She called Lady Howe a Tory bludgeon. (*To* PATRICIA) Vixen!

MOLLY: Impudent baggage!

LADY GAGE: Sticks and stones do breaketh bones, but names do never harm me. Hyena!

POLLY: Viper!

LADY CORNWALLIS: Agitators! Traitors! Seditionists!

BENITA: Oh-ho! Tax mongers! Oppressors! Tyrants!

BRITISH LADIES (*Pointing their fans at* BENITA): Treason! Treason!

PATRICIA (*Striking a pose*): If this be treason, make the most of it! (LADY GAGE *crosses to* PATRICIA *and pulls her shawl from her shoulders.*)

LADY GAGE: By gad, Madam, I *will* make the most of it. (*She stamps on shawl.*)

PATRICIA (*Aghast*): My shawl! My grandmother's Madeira lace shawl!

LADY GAGE (*Picking up shawl; distressed*): Oh, la. I *am* sorry. I had no idea it was your grandmother's shawl.

LADY HOWE (*Sternly*): See here, Lady Gage. You must control your passions. We do not fight with grandmothers.

LADY BURGOYNE: I don't think she should keep the shawl. It's stolen booty.

LADY GAGE: I didn't steal it. It was caught in my ring.

LADY CORNWALLIS: You've ripped it to shreds, Lady Gage. (*Indignantly*) How could you? Shouldn't she be court-martialed, Lady Howe?

PATRICIA (*Embarrassed*): Oh, do stop. 'Tis only a small tear. Just give me back the shawl and forget the rest. (LADY GAGE *curtsies and folds shawl neatly, handing it to* PATRICIA.)

MARTHA: Ladies! Ladies! I'm dreadfully muddled. Will the war please come to order?

MOLLY: Must we have a war? They don't seem such a bad lot.

LADY HOWE: A truce! I declare a truce! (*She waves a white lace handkerchief.*)

MARTHA: A sensible idea. Come, everyone, do let us be seated. (*They all sit down in a circle on opposite sides of battle line.*)

BENITA: It seems to me that the issue is quite clear. Who is to control the destiny of the American colonies—we or they.

ALL (*Ad lib*): We! We! We, of course! (*Etc.*)

BENITA (*Pointing to Minute Maids*): Just a moment—we are "we." (*Pointing to British Ladies*) You are "they." To solve this dilemma, I propose a tea party.

ALL: A tea party?

MOLLY: I accept the invitation. I'm simply starving.

BENITA: I propose that each side bake a pastry. The best pastry shall win the colonies.

LADY HOWE: One moment. Who will judge this contest of pastries?

PATRICIA: I will! I will!

SAMANTHA: Do be quiet, Patricia. You're out of order again. I have an idea. You should invite judges who are neither British nor American. How about Madame Lafayette and Baroness von Steuben?

ALL (*Ad lib*): Hear! Hear! Good idea! (*Etc.*)

BENITA: Then it's agreed upon. I further propose that the Americans shall bake a Boston Cream Pie!

MINUTE MAIDS: Hear! Hear!

LADY HOWE: And I propose that the British shall bake a Pound Cake.

BRITISH LADIES: Hear! Hear! (*Curtains begin to close.*)

BENITA: Well, as I always say—that's just like the British. Always thinking of their treasury! (*Curtain closes. Minuet is heard playing off.* Two FOREMOTHERS *enter through curtain, center.*)

1ST FOREMOTHER: And so, the memorable Boston Tea Party was held in the grandest possible style.

2ND FOREMOTHER: At a signal, the order was given to one and all: "Don't fire the ovens until you see the whites of their eggs!"

1ST FOREMOTHER: Then what a beating and a stirring and a whipping there was!

2ND FOREMOTHER: The air was filled with the tang of burnt powder—baking powder.

1ST FOREMOTHER: There was a clash of metal against metal as spoon met spoon.

2ND FOREMOTHER: Shells bombarded the room. Egg shells, to be sure.

1ST FOREMOTHER: But at four o'clock promptly, all hostilities ceased.

2ND FOREMOTHER: Tea was served. Molly Pitcher poured, of course.

1ST FOREMOTHER: At last Baroness von Steuben and Madame Lafayette judged the pastries.

2ND FOREMOTHER: The Pound Cake fell, alas, and the British surrendered.

1ST FOREMOTHER: But the Boston Cream Pie won a glorious victory, even though Lady Howe declared the Colonials had a lot of crust.

2ND FOREMOTHER: And so, that stirring Tea Party, steeped in drama and vanilla extract, passed into history. But somehow, your forefathers glossed over all the pertinent facts and took the glory for themselves.

1ST FOREMOTHER: We mention the truth only so that when the next July Fourth is celebrated, you may shoot off a Roman candle or two in honor of your most obedient . . . . (*Curtsies with flourish*)

2ND FOREMOTHER (*Curtsying*): Most humble . . .

TWO FOREMOTHERS: Most revolutionary foremothers! (*They curtsy to audience, and to each other, then, fanning themselves, they exit center. Minuet playing off swells to finish.*)

THE END

The Whites of Their Eyes

A modern cast of patriots scores a victory

by Frank Willment

Characters

POLLY WENDEL, *director of "The Pageant of Freedom"*
BARNEY, *owner of a costume store*
MR. KRICK, *owner of the theater*

DUSTY
DON
SKIPPER
SPIKE
HARRY
SHORTY
TIM
JILL
CINDY   }   *cast of the Pageant*
MIDGE
APRIL
DOODLES
DORIS
CHRISTY
PAM
PENNY

TIME: *Evening, three days before opening night.*

SETTING: *The stage of Mr. Krick's theater.*

AT RISE: *The stage is bare, except for a few red and white streamers, which a few members of the pageant cast are putting up at rear, supervised by* APRIL. SHORTY *and* HARRY *are working on a record player, which is on table left.* SKIPPER *is talking on phone, which is also on table.* DOODLES, *right, is sewing an American flag, and the rest of the cast are at center, standing or sitting on the floor.*

JILL: Polly or no Polly, we'd better get this rehearsal started. There are only three days before opening night. We need lots of practice if we want "The Pageant of Freedom" to be a success.

SPIKE: I'll say we need practice! Some of us still don't know all our lines. (*Looking around stage*) The scenery isn't up, either.

APRIL (*Coming forward, holding roll of green crepe paper*): We may never get the scenery up. Who brought the green crepe paper? How can I make a patriotic display out of red, white, and *green* crepe paper?

DOODLES (*Dismissing her with a gesture*): Never mind that, April. I'm worried about the costumes. We don't have them yet.

CINDY: Where *are* the costumes? How can we put on "The Pageant of Freedom" without costumes? What's holding Polly up?

SKIPPER (*Hanging up phone and joining group at center*): I just talked to Polly's mother. Polly's bringing the costumes with her. She went over to Barney's Costume Shop to talk the deal over with Barney himself.

MIDGE: She should be here by now. We'll never be ready by Saturday night at this rate. Polly's the director, and she should be here.

DON: We're about twenty minutes late already!

POLLY (*Entering from left, waving a script*): Sorry to be late. Hi, everybody! (*She comes to center.*) Let's get rolling! Time's a-wastin'! (BARNEY, *his arms full of costume boxes, enters. He follows* POLLY *center and puts down his packages.*)

HARRY: It's about time you got here, Polly. (*All gather around* POLLY.)

APRIL: Did you get the costumes?

POLLY: You bet I did, April. Say, I want you all to meet Mr. Barney. He's the sole owner of Barney's Better Costume Shop, Incorporated. In these boxes we have everything we need for our pageant, from Pocahontas' feathers to General Grant's beard!

DOODLES: Well, let's try them on. Do you have my Betsy Ross

dress? (*She starts to open one of the boxes, when* BARNEY *stops her.*)

BARNEY: Hold on, hold on! Not so fast! First there's a little matter of fifty dollars.

DORIS: Fifty dollars? What for?

BARNEY (*Impatiently*): What for? What for? For renting the costumes, of course. That's what for. You think maybe I'm in this business for my health? I have a slogan. I made it up myself. It's "No Cash—No Costumes."

CHRISTY: But we gave Polly ten dollars for a down payment.

SHORTY: And we can give you the rest on opening night.

BARNEY (*Cynically*): Opening night may be closing night. I operate on a cash-and-carry basis. You pay cash or I carry out the costumes.

POLLY (*Pleading*): Where's all your patriotism? This is a patriotic play. We wrote it ourselves. It's called "The Pageant of Freedom." (*Dramatically*) Did you know that right on this stage we are going to show Washington crossing the Delaware, the Boston Tea Party and Paul Revere's ride?

JILL: Paul Revere can't warn the farmers without a costume.

BARNEY (*Unmoved*): Just pay the fifty dollars, and Paul Revere can warn the British in Barney's best.

PAM: Paul Revere didn't warn the British. He warned the Minutemen.

BARNEY: That's between you and Paul Revere. Tell him to warn anyone he wants, *after* I have my money.

POLLY: I appeal to your patriotic spirit. Think of our glorious past—"Don't Give Up the Ship!" "Remember the Alamo."

BARNEY: I remember better the last time I got stuck. Now, I have a motto, too. It's "In God We Trust—All Others Pay Cash."

POLLY (*Gesturing dramatically*): Think of the glories we will show on this stage in three short days! Patrick Henry, decked out in Barney's best, will cry out the immortal words—"Give me liberty or give me death!"

BARNEY (*Losing patience*): Look—give me my fifty bucks or the costumes go back!

TIM: Can't we at least try them on for size?

BARNEY: Don't worry, they'll fit. I guarantee it.

PENNY: Have faith in us, Mr. Barney. Washington couldn't pay the troops at Valley Forge, but they stayed through a long, hard winter.

BARNEY: Not in Barney's costumes, they didn't.

MIDGE: But our country was built by those heroes at Valley Forge.

BARNEY (*Wearily*): Listen, for the last time—No cash, no costumes!

POLLY (*With resignation*): All right, Mr. Barney. You can wait over there with your precious costumes. (*Points to left*) Maybe something will turn up. (BARNEY *picks up his boxes and puts them on floor left, then stands guard over them, his arms folded observing rehearsal.*) Let's get on with the rehearsal, kids. We'll start with the Paul Revere scene. Places, everyone. (HARRY *goes to record player left.* SHORTY *and* DUSTY *exit right.*) Paul Revere, you come on from the right. (SKIPPER *exits right.*) Minutemen, take your places. (*Other boys move down left with girls.*) Get the record player started, Harry. (*He turns on record of patriotic music.*) Ready, everyone? (*All nod or ad lib "yes," "O.K.," "ready," etc. Sound of hoofbeats is heard from offstage right.*)

DON: Perhaps it is tidings of the British!

SKIPPER (*From off right*): Whoa! (*Hoofbeats continue.*) Whoa! (*Hoofbeats continue.*) I said, "Whoa!" (SKIPPER *strides on stage and goes to* POLLY.) Polly, will you tell Shorty to stop the hoofbeats when I say, "Whoa"? How can Paul Revere enter when his horse is galloping away?

POLLY (*Calling off right*): Watch your cues, Shorty.

SHORTY (*Entering from right*): O.K., O.K., but Skipper is just trying to shorten my part. (*Exits*)

POLLY: Go out and come in again, Skipper. (SKIPPER *exits, and hoofbeat sounds are heard from offstage again.*)

SKIPPER (*Off right*): Whoa! (*Hoofbeats stop, and* SKIPPER *rushes in, shouting to group down left.*) To arms! To arms! The Redcoats are coming!

BARNEY (*Moving toward center*): Not in Barney's costumes, they aren't.

HARRY (*Ignoring him*): Get your rifles, men. We will march on Concord Bridge, *now!*

DUSTY (*Rushing in from right*): Don't fire until you see the whites of their eyes!

POLLY: Hold it! Hold it! Dusty, you don't come in yet. That line is in the next scene.

DUSTY: It sounded like my cue, Polly. I come out when somebody shouts "Now!"

POLLY: Not this *now,* Dusty, the next *now.*

DUSTY: Oh, the next *now.* Now I have it. (*Exits right*)

POLLY: All right, kids. That's straightened out. Back to work. (*They take their places again.*)

DOODLES: Do your duty, my brave boys. Our hearts are with you as you ride to battle.

TIM: And what will you do, Betsy Ross, while we are gone?

DOODLES: I will make flags for our new nation. (*She unfolds a modern American flag and holds it up.*)

POLLY: Hold it, Doodles! There were only thirteen colonies in Betsy Ross's time. You can't hold up a flag with fifty stars!

DOODLES: Well, where am I going to get one with thirteen stars?

PAM: Right now we have to get on with the rehearsal, or we'll be here all night!

POLLY: Places, everyone. Let's take it from the Betsy Ross speech.

DOODLES: I will make flags for our new nation (*Holds up modern flag*), but with thirteen stars instead of fifty like this one.

SPIKE: Farewell, Betsy, we will go meet the British *now!*

DUSTY (*Rushing on*): Don't fire until you see the whites of their eyes!

POLLY (*Impatiently*): Not now, Dusty. You came in too soon, again!

DUSTY: You said the next *now.*

POLLY: I didn't mean this *now* now. I meant the next *now.* Now, do you know which *now?*

DUSTY: I thought this *now* was the next *now.* No, I don't know which *now* is *now* and which *now* is not *now.*

POLLY: You'd better go backstage and study your lines, Dusty. (DUSTY *exits.*) Back to the play. Where were we?

SPIKE: I had just said: "Farewell, Betsy, we will go to meet the British—*right away!*"

SKIPPER: I must mount my trusty steed and warn the other Minutemen! Farewell! (*Hoofbeats are heard from offstage. Turning to* POLLY.) Polly, will you tell that mixed-up sound effects man to let me get on my horse before we hear it gallop away?

SHORTY (*Entering*): All right, all right. I'll hold up the hoofbeats until you get offstage. Don't be such a crab about it. (*Exits.*)

SKIPPER (*Taking his place again*): Farewell! (*He runs off right, and hoofbeats start.* SPIKE *lines up Minutemen, who pick up broomsticks from pile at left and carry them like rifles.* SPIKE *calls out orders, and they march around stage in a disorganized fashion, as the girls wave in farewell.*)

POLLY (*Observing them critically*): Not so bad. Not good, but not too bad. (SHORTY *and* SKIPPER *re-enter*) O.K. Now, we'll try the scene with Washington and his men at Valley Forge.

PENNY: Polly, I just thought of something. Why couldn't all the girls make candy and sell it during this scene?

POLLY: Sell candy during the Valley Forge scene?

PENNY: Yes, we could call it Valley Fudge.

DORIS: We could dress as colonial ladies and sell the candy in the aisles, and . . .

BARNEY (*Cutting in*): No, you couldn't. Not until Barney gets his fifty bucks. I want it *now!*

DUSTY (*Running in*): Don't fire until you see the whites of their eyes!

POLLY: Not yet, Dusty!

DUSTY: Somebody said "Now!"

POLLY: Wait until *I* say *now*. Don't worry about other *nows*. Come out and shout your line when I say *now*. O.K.?

DUSTY: When *you* say *now*. Now I know which *now*. (*He exits again.*)

POLLY: Everyone, take your places. (*Looking at script, as girls watch scene*) It's a bleak, cold winter at Valley Forge. A group of soldiers are huddling around a fire—huddle over there, boys. (*She points down left, and the boys form a semicircle around an imaginary fire.*) George Washington enters from the left.

DON (*Warming hands over imaginary fire*): It has been a long, hard winter indeed.

TIM: If only our noble leader has been able to get supplies.

HARRY (*Pointing off left*): Here comes General Washington through the woods. (*All rise and face left, standing at attention.*)

BOYS (*Saluting*): Hail, General Washington! (MR. KRICK, *a middle-aged man in topcoat and derby, enters.*)

KRICK: Where's Polly Wendel? I want to see Polly Wendel!

TIM: Who are you? You're not General Washington!

KRICK: Of course I'm not General Washington! I'm Oliver J. Krick, the owner of this theater, and I want to see Polly Wendel!

POLLY (*Coming to center to meet him*): Here I am, Mr. Krick. Don't get excited.

KRICK: Polly, where's the fifty dollars rent for this theater? You promised to pay me three days ago.

POLLY: Well, you see—

BARNEY: You owe *another* fifty dollars? (*To* KRICK) You'll have to wait your turn, buddy. (*Pointing behind him*) The line forms on the left.

JILL: What's this all about? I thought you had paid the theater rent, Polly.

POLLY: Well, I meant to, but—

MIDGE: Didn't we have enough money from the advance sale to pay the rent?

POLLY: We had to use that money for properties, advertising, and other things, Midge.

KRICK: Am I to understand that you can't pay? (*Angrily*) Out! Out! Everybody out!

POLLY: Whoa! Hold your horses, Mr. Krick! You'll get your money on opening night.

KRICK: There'll be no opening night if I don't get my money.

CINDY: Have a heart, Mr. Krick. "The Pageant of Freedom" is bound to be a big success.

KRICK: No money, no theater.

CHRISTY: No money, no theater, no costumes. Let's change the name to "The Pageant of Failure."

POLLY: Where's your American spirit, Mr. Krick? Suppose the men who owned the boats had refused to let Washington cross the Delaware until they had been paid for. Where would America be today?

KRICK: They weren't my boats.

APRIL: A lucky thing! If they had been your boats, Washington would have had to swim.

PAM: Think of Washington, Jefferson, Benjamin Franklin!

KRICK: I'd rather think of King Midas. He had the right idea!

POLLY (*In despair*): Well, we just can't pay you *now*.

DUSTY (*Rushing on stage*): Don't fire until you see the whites of their eyes!

POLLY: Oh, Dusty! You're wrong again!

DUSTY: But you said to come in when you said *now,* and I heard you say *now.*

POLLY: Listen, Dusty. When it's your turn I'll shout *now.*

DUSTY: O.K. I'll be backstage. Shout it good and loud so I'll know. (DUSTY *exits.*)

POLLY: Mr. Krick, won't you let us finish the rehearsal? If you'll wait with Mr. Barney, we can all talk things over when the rehearsal has ended.

KRICK: I'll give you exactly ten minutes to come up with something —and it had better be good. (*He walks left to stand with* BARNEY.)

DORIS (*Resigned*): Let's face it. The pageant is off. We can't possibly raise one hundred dollars quickly enough to pay for the costumes and rent.

JILL (*Upset*): But we can't call it off. We've sold 172 tickets, and Polly has spent the money. We have to give a show!

SKIPPER: Where? Out on the sidewalk? I don't think the mayor would give us a permit.

MIDGE: This looks like the end of the line. What do we do now?

PENNY: I had an uncle once who couldn't pay his debts.

PAM: What did he do?

PENNY: He went into bankruptcy.

CHRISTY: Well, we're bankrupt, and at our age, too!

APRIL: Now, look. Things can't be that bad! Remember the spirit of our forefathers. That's what we're putting on this whole pageant for—to show their determination and perseverance.

DOODLES: That's the way to talk—"Remember the Alamo," Davy Crockett and Jim Bowie and the rest. They didn't give up when things looked blackest!

DORIS (*Wryly*): And, if I remember my history, none of them got out of the Alamo alive, did they? (*All are silent for a moment. Suddenly the phone rings.*)

MIDGE: Answer the phone, Polly. It's probably another creditor wanting money.

POLLY: (*Answering phone*): Polly Wendel speaking. Do you want Mr. Krick? (*Pause*) You just want to speak to whoever answers

the phone? Who is this? (*Pause*) You are what? Hold on a sec—
(*Puts hand over receiver and speaks to others*) Hey, kids, it's a
quiz program. They want me to answer some fool question for
one hundred dollars. (*Suddenly*) *A hundred dollars!* (*Into
phone*) Did you say one hundred dollars? Of course I know the
answer. What's the question? (*Pause*) What did the Colonial
commander say at the Battle of Bunker Hill? How long do I
have? (*Pause*) Thirty seconds? (*To the others*) Here's our chance
to make the hundred dollars we need! I have to answer this
question in thirty seconds. What did the Colonial commander
say at the Battle of Bunker Hill? Quick!

HARRY: Don't give up the ship?

CINDY: No, silly. What would a ship be doing on Bunker Hill?

POLLY: Don't argue! It's something famous. Keep shouting things
at me. I'll know it when I hear it.

SHORTY: We have met the enemy and they are ours?

JILL: Lafayette, we are here?

SKIPPER: I have just begun to fight?

CHRISTY: Taxation without representation is tyranny?

DON: You may fire when ready, Gridley?

APRIL: Life, liberty and the pursuit of happiness?

TIM: A penny saved is a penny earned?

MIDGE: Fourscore and seven years ago?

POLLY: No, no, it's none of those!

DORIS: I could go home and look it up in my history book.

POLLY: Time is running out! I need the answer *now!* Now, do
you hear me? *Now!*

DUSTY (*Rushing onstage*): Don't fire until you see the whites of
their eyes!

POLLY: That's it! That's it!

DUSTY: What's it? (*Others watch* POLLY *anxiously and pay no attention to* DUSTY, *who shrugs and goes off again.*)

POLLY (*Into phone*): Don't fire until you see the whites of their
eyes! Am I right? (*Pause*) I am? I've won the hundred dollars?
Golly, that's great! Say, mister, when do I get the money? (*Pause*)
You'll put it in the mail tonight? Gee, thanks! Thanks a million!
I mean, thanks a hundred! You've just saved our lives, that's all!
(*Pause*) Send it to Polly Wendel at Krick's Theater. Goodbye,
and thanks again! (*She hangs up the phone, and cast crowds
around her.*)

SPIKE: Did we get it, Polly? Did we really win the hundred bucks?

POLLY: We sure did—thanks to Dusty! (*To* BARNEY *and* KRICK) Gentlemen, your money is in the mail!

BARNEY: That's good enough for me. (*Indicating boxes*) Here are your costumes, Polly.

KRICK: Sorry I got excited. But you know how it is—business is business. The theater is yours, Polly. Best of luck with the show. I'll see you on opening night. Goodbye, everybody.

BARNEY: I have to be going along, too. Goodbye, and good luck. (BARNEY *and* KRICK *leave as all call* "*Goodbye.*")

POLLY: Now that we have settled the minor details, let's start the rehearsal. Everybody take your places—right *now!*

DUSTY (*Rushing onstage again*): Don't fire until—

ALL: Oh, no! (*All laugh, as curtain falls.*)

THE END

The Printer in Queen Street

Young Ben Franklin of Boston

by Grace Alicia Mayr

Characters

NARRATOR
BENJAMIN FRANKLIN, *17*
JAMES FRANKLIN, *his brother, 26*
JOSIAH FRANKLIN, *their father*
JOHN COLLINS
NICHOLAS SCUDDER
DANIEL, *12*
GILLIAM ⎤
PIERS ⎬ *apprentices*
PATRICK ⎦

NARRATOR: It is Thursday, September 23, 1723. The cloud-shrouded sun barely peeks over the eastern horizon of Boston Harbor when Benjamin Franklin comes out of a printer's shop. He is a stocky, broad-backed seventeen-year-old, wearing a leather apron, and carrying a bundle of the *New England Courant* on his shoulder. Two apprentices, Gilliam and Piers, stand waiting outside the shop to deliver subscribers' copies of the *Courant*. This weekly newspaper, which the Reverend Cotton Mather of Old South Church calls "a notorious, scandalous paper," was established two years ago by master-printer James Franklin, Benjamin's older brother. Because of James Franklin's publication of articles criticizing the clergy and other town

This reading play may also be performed as a stage play by adding simple sets, costumes and properties as described in the text.

officials, and because of his refusal to divulge the identity of his daring contributors, in January of this year James was arrested for the second time and forbidden to publish. Since then, the *Courant* has been published over the name of Benjamin Franklin. Now as Benjamin shifts the newspapers from his shoulder, he sniffs and exhales the tangy, salt sea breeze.

BENJAMIN: I can fairly taste that fog coming in. Stand aside, Piers. I'm dropping your stack to the cobbles. There you are, for the northside. Gilliam, yours is that bundle, for the southside. The third stack is Patrick's for our waterfront subscribers. (*Pause*) Where *is* that boy?

GILLIAM: Patrick will be along soon, Ben. (*Laughing*) With his usual lively tale of adventures or misadventures, I wager.

PIERS: May we have the morning off after we finish deliveries, Ben?

BENJAMIN: You should go to church. It's Lecture Day.

PIERS: Oh, no, Ben!

GILLIAM: Other printers' apprentices have free time Thursday morning, and don't—

BENJAMIN (*Laughing*): I won't waste breath urging you to church. Stay out of fights and taverns, and get to the boardinghouse for dinner on time or watch out for James's heavy hand.

GILLIAM: I've felt the master's hand too often already.

PIERS: Who hasn't, eh, Ben?

BENJAMIN: To my sorrow, my brother outranks me in size and strength, and too often he forgets we are brothers. (*Sighs heavily*)

GILLIAM: He treats you ill, Ben. You, acting as publisher and all, should have proper respect from him.

BENJAMIN: My brother and I have had our differences in the past, but of late, I admit, matters grow worse between us. (*Thoughtfully*) One day he may go too far, and then—

GILLIAM: At least the master should see that you're fed a good dinner at the boardinghouse.

PIERS: 'Tis so, Ben. You shouldn't have to eat your dinner here and mind the shop mid-days.

BENJAMIN: It's an arrangement of my own choice, lads. For a while I ate those big heavy meals with the others until I made a bargain with James—a bargain he well liked.

GILLIAM (*Laughing*): And the master's not easy to please.

BENJAMIN: I offered to board myself for half what the boarding-house charged him for my dinner. James snapped up my offer.

PIERS: The master's no fool!

BENJAMIN: I taught myself to prepare nourishing food—boiled potatoes or rice, a hasty pudding, and I save half of what James gives me. I spend what I save on books.

PIERS (*In disbelief*): You spend half your dinner money on books!

BENJAMIN: They tell me I was reading the Bible at five and knew how to write at seven. I can't remember when I couldn't read. Reading makes a full man. I'm willing to read half my dinner.

PIERS: I'd rather be full of meat and a good big sweet afterward.

BENJAMIN: You can have your roast beef and cider, and slug through the afternoon with a full belly and a dull brain. Here alone, I eat my light repast—a biscuit or a slice of bread, a handful of raisins, and a glass of water. Then I have the rest of the time, till you return, to study.

GILLIAM: You're a rare bird, Ben. There never was and there never will be another like you.

BENJAMIN (*Laughing*): There are those who would rejoice at that. (*Suddenly*) Where is that Patrick? Sea-gazing, I'll wager. (*Calling loudly*) Patrick!

PATRICK (*As from a distance*): Coming, Ben. (*Normal tones*) I'm sorry, Ben, I was—

BENJAMIN: I know. You've been down on Long Wharf again, dreaming, watching the ships in from distant ports. You've been longing for those faraway ports, to smell their smells, to hear their sounds, to savor their taste. I know, Patrick. The wide sea beckons, bewitching us all.

PATRICK (*With surprise*): Ben, you've a hankering to follow the sea yourself!

BENJAMIN: Always had, Patrick, but my father wouldn't hear of it. One son—my brother Josiah—lost at sea was enough, he said, and I had to learn a useful trade ashore. (*Sighing*) But to be free!—to escape the hemmed-in narrowness of my life here! There must be more I can be doing—something some place where I can be free to work and create.

PATRICK: Aye, there may be for you, Ben, but I've got a good trade now, so I content myself with sea-gazing instead of sea-sailing.

BENJAMIN: Yours, no doubt, is the wiser part, Patrick. Contentment makes poor men rich.

GILLIAM: Have you no adventures this morning to tell us, Patrick?

PATRICK: That I do indeed. There's a sloop in from New York. It was sitting there like a fat duck in the water when three passengers debarked—a man and his wife, young and pretty, and a boy. The boy stood there on Long Wharf in his gold-buckled black shoes, surveying Boston Town as if he owned the whole of it. Salty as a pickle, he was. The man was wearing a three-cornered cocked hat, a fine black broadcloth coat, and gray breeches—he looked a gentleman, he did. He called to me, so I ran over, and guess what he said, right out of the blue?

BENJAMIN (*Amused*): You'll make a capital newsman, Patrick, but make it short.

GILLIAM: He asked you the way to the Governor's mansion.

PATRICK: No.

PIERS: He wanted help with his luggage.

PATRICK: No.

BENJAMIN: He was a fortune-teller and he prophesied you'd have your ears cuffed like this!

PATRICK: Hold on! You're wrong, Ben! He gave me a message for Mr. Franklin, the printer in Queen Street.

BENJAMIN (*Thoughtfully*): Whom does James know in New York?

GILLIAM: Maybe the man has a printing job for us.

PIERS: Or an article for next week's issue.

BENJAMIN: Did he also give you his name, Patrick?

PATRICK: No, but he also gave me this Dutch coin, and I'm going to buy myself a tart from the pastry cook in Pudding Lane.

BENJAMIN: You're never going to get to Pudding Lane or anywhere else if you don't tell me the message. I warn you, I'll shake it out of you.

PATRICK (*Hurriedly*): The man said, "Tell Mr. Franklin, the printer in Queen Street, that an old friend will be lodging at the Green Dragon in Union Street across from the sign of the Blue Ball, and would welcome his visit."

BENJAMIN (*Thoughtfully*): 'Tis someone who knows my father's house at the sign of the Blue Ball. I must tell James.

GILLIAM: Hist, Ben! (*In fast whisper*) The master stands behind

you in the doorway, now, fire-hot mad as a stuck pig. Come on,
Piers. Patrick, grab your papers.

JAMES (*Angrily*): You lads—do you think our subscribers will
come up and tap your shoulders? Get to work!

GILLIAM (*Urgently*): Hurry along, Piers.

PIERS: I'll see you later in Pudding Lane, Patrick. I've a taste for
a bit of pastry myself.

PATRICK: See to it that you have a bit to spend, then.

JAMES: At last, they're gone. And you, Benjamin Clodpate, are
you too grand to earn your keep? Do you think God would have
given you arms and legs if he had not designed you to use them?
Hustle along and get us some new subscribers.

BENJAMIN (*Angry*): You want me to go about the streets selling
subscriptions—me, the editor and publisher?

JAMES: Someone has to build up our circulation. It's you or I,
lad, and who is truly the master-printer in this shop? Ah, I've
got you there. Inside you go, lazybones, and pick up some copies
to distribute as samples.

*　　*　　*

NARRATOR: Like most Colonial shops, the Franklin print shop has
whitewashed plaster walls and a wide-beamed pine ceiling. A
high desk and a three-legged stool stand to the right of the door
in front of the window. The printing press, a large wooden
structure a foot or two taller than a man, stands in the center
of the room, dominating the shop. Recently printed sheets
hang drying like pieces of laundry. The shelves of the print shop
library and the compositor's type box are against the left wall.
A door at the rear of the shop leads to an alley. James has flung
himself upon the three-legged stool before his desk in the
window. Goose quill in hand, he obviously is working on his
books. Benjamin glowers as he stamps noisily, assembling additional copies of the *Courant* and stuffing them into the leather
pouch slung over his shoulder. The atmosphere is tense with
the animosity between the brothers. Finally, James throws down
his pen and jumps up from the stool.

JAMES: Bah! I'm beset with political enemies who won't let me
publish. My financial accounts show heavy loss. And now you
give me trouble. Stop thrashing around like a bull-ox. Be off
with you!

BENJAMIN (*Heatedly*): Stop ordering me about like a slave-apprentice!

JAMES: You're legally bound until you're twenty-one by indenture papers signed by yourself.

BENJAMIN: You destroyed those papers, for you knew no apprentice could legally publish a paper.

JAMES (*Smugly*): You are conveniently forgetting the second indentures you signed more recently. They're binding.

BENJAMIN: You forced me to sign those. You wouldn't dare let the town officials know there are secret papers! You'd be thrown into jail the minute I let that news out of the bag!

JAMES (*Incredulously*): You dare threaten me—the master—in my own shop!

BENJAMIN (*Coolly*): Indisputably, James, this is *your* shop. I can never forget that fact. It's clear that we cannot work together. I must find employment with another printer.

JAMES: Not in Boston, you won't. I've talked with all the printers. Not one of them will hire you.

BENJAMIN (*Very angrily*): This time, James, you have gone too far. Even Papa cannot reconcile me to this blow.

JAMES (*Sneeringly*): Go, run and tell Papa. Take the shortcut through the back alley, Tattletale.

BENJAMIN: I will.

JAMES (*Bitterly*): As long as you're going home, take Papa's copy of today's *Courant* to him.

BENJAMIN: I'll do that, too. Like you, Papa may have forgotten that my name is given as publisher, not yours.

JAMES (*Angrily*): Ben, I warn you—foot it fast out that door, or— (*Sighs heavily*) He's gone.

*   *   *

NARRATOR: Ben races through the back alley, taking the shortcut to the junction of Union and Hanover Streets, where his father Josiah Franklin has his soap and candle shop, at the sign of the Blue Ball. Thick fog has begun to roll in, as Ben ducks into his father's shop. Josiah Franklin is a man whose legacy to his children will include not only deep religious convictions, but also common sense, a taste for the simple things of life, and respect for hard work. He is of middle stature, well-set, and very strong for his sixty-eight years.

JOSIAH (*Pleasantly but firmly*): Ben, you have quarreled with James again. I can tell by the look on your face.

BENJAMIN (*Heatedly*): Papa, James has gone too far. He dares—

JOSIAH (*Breaking in*): Aye, James dares much. He dares much in the articles he publishes. I know also that James is often bad-tempered over financial difficulties and seems to take his satisfaction in mistreating you. I can arbitrate your differences to a degree, but you must serve out your apprenticeship, behaving faithfully to James in all things. It is the law!

BENJAMIN: Papa, is it the law that I should be bound by secret indenture papers? What a flim-flam business such a law is that protects one person and injures another!

JOSIAH (*Firmly*): James is your brother, Ben, and your master. You are bound to keep his secrets and protect his interests.

BENJAMIN: Papa, what about *my* interests? I'm blacklisted with all the printers in town! Fortunately there are other places in the world.

JOSIAH (*Kindly*): Ben, be patient. Bear with James. How proud I was when James was in prison and your editorial blazed in fiery defense of him and his right to publish what he saw fit!

BENJAMIN: Yes, Papa. In this matter I have no quarrel with James. Perhaps none of us is always correct in his views, but we must have the right to be heard. I'm with James to the end in this struggle for the right to a free press.

JOSIAH: Then help your brother.

BENJAMIN: Wherever I go, all my life, Papa, I promise to fight with all my strength and wit for freedom, not only freedom of the press but all the rightful freedoms of man. But now I must fight for myself.

JOSIAH: Benny, only four years are left to your apprenticeship.

BENJAMIN: Papa, I'm almost a man. Four years is too long to wait. (*Quickly*) I am eager to do something important—worthy and important. You don't understand. (*Sighing*) No one does. Here's today's *Courant,* Papa. Goodbye.

* * *

NARRATOR: Outside in Union Street Ben finds the fog has thickened. The sign hanging over the door of the tavern across the street is hardly discernible, as are the man and a boy who come out of the tavern to stand under the sign. The man is Nicholas

Scudder, bookseller, and the boy is Daniel, the twelve-year-old brother of Nicholas Scudder's wife.

NICHOLAS: 'Tis difficult in this fog to know which way to turn, Daniel.

DANIEL: What shop are we looking for?

NICHOLAS: John Checkley's bookshop at the sign of the Crown and the Blue Gate, near the corner of King Street. (*Raising voice*) Holla, you sir, there! May I beg a favor?

BENJAMIN (*As if at a distance*): At your service, sir. I'll cross over.

NICHOLAS: Sir, can you direct me to—why, Ben! What a stroke of luck!

BENJAMIN (*Puzzled*): You have the advantage of me, sir.

NICHOLAS: Look closely, Ben. Think back—you were two years apprenticed to your brother James and hungry for books, starved for knowledge. I was apprenticed to John Checkley, bookseller. Have you forgotten our little arrangement? You could borrow every book and any book at the sign of the Crown and the Blue Gate, provided you had it back next day before it was missed.

BENJAMIN (*Excitedly*): Nick! Give me your hand, good friend! I can't begin to count the books I borrowed and sat up all night to read. You were my bookish friend in those days.

NICHOLAS: May we always be friends, bookish and otherwise. (*Pause*) Ben, this is my wife's brother Daniel. Daniel, this is my friend, Ben Franklin, the printer I told you about.

BENJAMIN: This is a pleasure, Daniel.

DANIEL: Good day to you, Mr. Franklin.

BENJAMIN: Daniel is your wife's brother, Nick? You're a married man then. A lot has happened since last we met.

NICHOLAS: Aye, a lot. Shall we walk as we talk?

BENJAMIN: Where are you headed?

NICHOLAS: That's it. I'm not headed. I'm confused in this fog. I'd like to get to Checkley's bookshop.

BENJAMIN: We turn right, ahead there at Dock Square, then along toward Cornhill a bit.

NICHOLAS: Follow closely behind us, Dan.

BENJAMIN: Dan looks a likely lad. He won't lose us. Now, give me your news, Nick.

NICHOLAS: When I finished my apprenticeship, I could find no opening in a Boston bookshop, so I sailed to New York. Now, there's a thriving port—bigger than Boston, but with no book-shop at all, alas!

BENJAMIN: I've heard of a printer in New York by the name of William Bradford.

NICHOLAS: I know him. His son Andrew has a printing establish-ment in Philadelphia. William Bradford's print shop in Hanover Square, New York, was next to the goldsmith's shop where I finally found work keeping the accounts.

BENJAMIN: Not very congenial work for you, was it?

NICHOLAS (*Laughing*): On the contrary, most congenial, for the goldsmith had a daughter named Anne, and we were married in July of this year.

BENJAMIN: You're on a wedding trip!

NICHOLAS: Always the incurable romantic, aren't you, Ben? But, no, it's not a wedding trip. Anne and I are setting out to make our fortunes. Shortly after we married, Anne's father died. He left everything to Anne and Daniel, but he was heavily in debt. We decided to sell everything, pay off his debts, and open a bookshop in a city where there is a demand for books, a more literary town.

BENJAMIN: The competition in Boston will be very keen. I know of ten bookshops here now. (*Pause*) Let's cross over to King Street. Did you have some city in mind?

NICHOLAS: We're going north to Portsmouth, where both culture and commerce thrive.

BENJAMIN: Then why stop off in Boston?

NICHOLAS: The sloop that brought us here is owned by a Dutch-man who could take us no farther. He is loading cargo now for an immediate return to New York.

BENJAMIN: He'll not sail in this foul weather.

NICHOLAS: The Dutchman claims that within thirty-six hours the fog will have risen. He vows he'll sail Saturday morning on schedule.

BENJAMIN (*Laughing*): Our Boston weather is variable enough, 'tis true—as variable as men's fortunes. (*Bitterly*) Behold me, close to the wide-open sea, and a prisoner here in Boston, which already has too many printers.

NICHOLAS: In Portsmouth there is no printer.

BENJAMIN: No printer? What an opening for an ingenious fellow that would be—had the ingenious fellow some supply of capital.

NICHOLAS: In time I'll have the capital to set up a press, and Daniel here shall be the printer. We'll operate a family business, printing and selling books.

BENJAMIN: It'll be a long time till then, Nick. Dan looks to be about twelve, the age I was when apprenticed to James.

NICHOLAS: Exactly what I wanted to see you about. Will you take Daniel as an apprentice?

BENJAMIN (*Surprised*): I—take Daniel—as apprentice?

NICHOLAS: Aye, Ben. 'Tis what I would talk with you about. You got my message from that red-headed rascal I spoke to this morning on Long Wharf, didn't you?

BENJAMIN: You sent it to the printer in Queen Street.

NICHOLAS: To you—the editor of the *Courant*. Surely, for old time's sake you'll take Daniel.

BENJAMIN (*Sighing*): I cannot, Nick.

NICHOLAS (*Stiffly*): Cannot, or will not?

BENJAMIN: Cannot. The plain truth of the matter is that I'm still apprenticed to James myself.

NICHOLAS (*Incredulous*): How is that? In New York I read a February number of the *Courant,* with your name given as publisher. Mr. Bradford has a copy he lent me to read.

BENJAMIN (*Pleased*): So Mr. Bradford knows about the *Courant*!

NICHOLAS: You can't imagine how pleased I was to show him that it is printed over the name of my friend, Benjamin Franklin.

BENJAMIN (*Sadly*): That is only a subterfuge of James's to evade a prohibition to publish.

NICHOLAS: A ticklish business, I see. I'll delve no farther; trust me. Perhaps James could use another apprentice. I'd like Dan to be where you could watch over him, Ben. My wife and I will be moving on to Portsmouth as soon as I have secured more books and merchandise to stock our shop.

BENJAMIN (*Slowly*): Yes, Nick, I think James will be wanting an apprentice shortly, within the week perhaps. (*More cheerfully*) Ah, here we are. You've only to follow your noses, and there is Checkley's shop on the right.

DANIEL (*Hesitantly*): Mr. Franklin—

BENJAMIN: Yes, Daniel.

DANIEL: Is your brother James like you? Will he be a good master?

NICHOLAS (*Laughing*): Listen to the boy—so sure James will have him!

BENJAMIN: James will need someone soon, Nick. I warrant you that. Daniel, my brother James is a good printer, no slovenly, self-taught craftsman. You'll find no better master in the colonies.

NICHOLAS: Well spoken, Ben.

BENJAMIN: Nick, I respect and admire my brother. But we are brothers—too much alike or perhaps too little alike to work in the same shop. Yet I stand firm beside him in the belief that a strong newspaper should bring controversial issues to the public attention.

NICHOLAS: I, too, agree with James in this. I look forward to seeing him soon.

BENJAMIN: You'll probably find James with Checkley. On publication day, James and his contributors, the Couranteers, as they call themselves, meet to talk over the latest issue. (*Laughing*) The Reverend Cotton Mather has another name for them. He calls them the Hell Fire Club because they attack the established church and the royal government. 'Tis a dangerous business for James and his friends. Yet, if all printers were determined not to print anything till they were sure it would offend nobody, there would be very little printed. (*Pause*) Here we are—The Crown and the Blue Gate is just ahead. I'll leave you and go back to the shop.

NICHOLAS: Thank you, Ben. If you ever need help, I'll be glad to do what I can—any time. Come on, Dan. Look alive, boy. You're going to meet my old master, Checkley, and maybe get a look at your future master.

DANIEL (*Calling sadly after* BENJAMIN): Goodbye, Mr. Franklin. I wish I could be apprenticed to you.

*　　*　　*

NARRATOR: Benjamin smiles wryly and turns toward Queen Street, where he finds Patrick and Piers engaged in a minor struggle, puffing and grunting as each claims his share of a meat pie.

PATRICK: That's enough, Piers. Don't cut off my fingers!

PIERS: Hold the pastry still so I can measure the halves.

PATRICK: That half is bigger. It's mine. I paid for most of it.

PIERS: Whose pence was it bought us the swigs of cider? You promised me half the pie.

BENJAMIN: Patrick! Piers! I said, "Stay out of fights," and I meant fights with each other, also.

PATRICK: Piers has cut my pie into two pieces with his pocket knife, and he's got the bigger half.

PIERS: You be the judge, Ben. This isn't the bigger half, is it?

BENJAMIN: You want me to be the judge. I'd rather not. I'd rather you'd be generous about this and one of you give the bigger half to the other. In the long run, you'd both be richer.

PATRICK: You must be the judge, Ben.

PIERS: We'll abide by your decision.

BENJAMIN: Well, then, let's see. Mm-m-m-m, yes, this piece that Piers was claiming is the bigger by a hair's breadth.

PATRICK: See, I told you!

PIERS (*Grumpily*): Well, you can have it, if you insist, Patrick.

PATRICK: That's only fair, isn't it, Ben? Buying the pie was my idea in the first place.

BENJAMIN (*With mock firmness*): I think you lads are laboring under a misapprehension. The larger half now belongs to me as my fee for passing judgment. A workman is worth his hire.

PATRICK: But—but—

BENJAMIN: I'm sorry for you, lads. Your share, for the two of you now, is the smaller half. Cut it into two pieces and enjoy what is left of your pie. I shall enjoy my fee for dinner today.

PATRICK: After this, I'll settle my own differences.

BENJAMIN: Ah, such words of wisdom I have never heard from one so young!

PIERS (*Disgruntled*): Good thing it's almost dinner time. This little piece of pie is hardly worth the eating.

BENJAMIN: It's just possible that I may not care for this piece of pie for my dinner. In which case—now I'm only saying maybe —you can share it this afternoon. (*Seriously*) Right now, before you go to your own dinner, visit my friend Collins. Ask him to come to the shop during the noon hour. It's urgent I see him.

PIERS: You mean John Collins, the clerk at the Post Office?

BENJAMIN: He's the only John Collins I know. You've seen me with him often. Now be quick about it, and don't blab to my brother.

PIERS: I don't talk, I eat at meal time. Come on, Patrick.

PATRICK: Nary a word I'll speak of it, Ben.

*　　*　　*

NARRATOR: It's a thoughtful Ben Franklin who makes his way into the print shop in Queen Street. Once there, and alone, he is all action. In a short time, he has filled a wooden chest with books from the shelves of the shop library. Then, he deliberates over which of the two volumes he holds in his hands shall be added to a separate stack of books piled on the windowsill. He has just decided when John Collins enters hurriedly, casts a quick eye around the shop, then stops short as he observes Ben's actions.

JOHN: Patrick and Piers said you wanted to see—(*Worried*) Ben, what's wrong? Why are you packing your books in that chest? Ben, I know! You've had a final fight with James and you're quitting him.

BENJAMIN: It's not just the trouble with James. I'm leaving Boston. This may be the biggest mistake of my life, but there is nothing else I can do.

JOHN: Where are you going? When? I'm going with you. What do we do first?

BENJAMIN: First, listen to me. I go alone. Don't argue. You must not risk your future for me. I am obliged to leave. There is no future for me in Boston. Because you are my friend, let me go alone, John. It's safest.

JOHN (*Sadly*): Aye, safest. As usual, you're right, Ben. I can always join you later.

BENJAMIN: But I do have something you can do for me that I dare not do myself.

JOHN: Ask me anything, Ben.

BENJAMIN: I need money, and my purse is light. I want you to take these books piled on the windowsill and offer them to Nicholas Scudder at the Green Dragon tonight.

JOHN: Do you think he'll buy them, just like that?

BENJAMIN: Just like that—if you say the books are the property of his bookish friend, who needs his help.

JOHN (*Savoring the intrigue*): It's all very secret. I like that—"his bookish friend."

BENJAMIN: Very secret. With the money Nicholas Scudder pays you, go to Long Wharf. A sloop lies tied up there. Arrange passage for me to New York.

JOHN: A sloop . . . Long Wharf? New York? There must be several sloops docked at Long Wharf. How will I know which one? What's the captain's name?

BENJAMIN: This sloop is out of New York. The captain, a Dutch-man, expects to sail Saturday with cargo now being loaded aboard. Make up some suitable story about why I can't arrange passage myself.

JOHN: I'll think of something, Ben, something convincing. (*Pause*) I've got it—you dare not show your face because you're being chased by a designing woman who means to marry you.

BENJAMIN (*Happily*): Capital! Come to my house afterward. I'll need your help smuggling out my clothes to pack in this chest with my books. We'll have to take everything out on our backs.

JOHN: Tell me more about your plans.

BENJAMIN: Later. James and the others will soon be back from dinner. Please, John, tell no one any of this. I've little faith in three-cornered secrets. All winter and spring and summer I've dreamed of escaping my long servitude, and I know the risk I run. Who knows better than I the listings printed every week in the *Courant*—names and descriptions of runaway slaves and apprentices, with handsome rewards offered for their capture and return? John, America is big. If I can get far enough away, perhaps I can find myself, and in time find the place in the world that I feel I'm fated to fill.

JOHN: On my honor, Ben, my lips are sealed. Give me the books.

BENJAMIN: Until tonight.

JOHN: Everything's as good as done, Ben.

* * *

NARRATOR: Everything was as good as done. By Friday evening, the fog dispersed, blustered darkly away by a threatening storm. In the lonely, unlighted streets, no one noticed the two young men carrying a sea chest through the streets toward Long Wharf. With each step Benjamin Franklin was moving inexorably toward the fulfillment of his destiny. Who would have guessed then that this self-taught genius would help to build a new nation and become known throughout the world as the Ameri-can success symbol—a poor boy reared in humble circumstances who became the companion of princes and the friend of the greatest men of his time? Tonight, however, as he boards the Dutchman's sloop that is tugging restlessly at its ropes to be away, Ben knows only that he has one good friend in John Collins.

BENJAMIN: Goodbye, John. Go quickly now before the storm breaks. You mustn't be seen here with me, lest anyone blame you for my escape.

JOHN: Who would blame me for helping a friend escape an intolerable situation?

BENJAMIN: You could be charged as my accomplice.

JOHN: I'll go, but not until the storm drives me away.

BENJAMIN: The span of time between the lightning and the claps of thunder indicates that the storm is now very close. Such bolts of lightning—a mysterious power like fire in the sky! One day some benefactor of the human race will capture that fire and harness it for our use.

JOHN: There's another project for you, Ben.

BENJAMIN: It interests me, John. The person who tames this sky power will be remembered forever. Tonight my thoughts are sad and all of myself. When I'm gone, no one will remember I was ever here.

JOHN: I will, Ben, always. Look, I brought you something—cheese and a few apples. I wish it were more, but like yours, my purse is light.

BENJAMIN: Thank you. How I enjoy a roasted apple! I have something here in this sack for you. Open it, John. (*Pause*) Surprised? Keep them as a memento of our boyhood friendship.

JOHN (*Pleased*): Ben, the swim-paddles you made for your hands and feet to give you more speed in the water! I'll never forget the first time I saw you use them.

BENJAMIN: I remember how you laughed, John. But they worked. However, my progress through the water was more satisfactory and less fatiguing when I floated across the pond on my back, pulled along by a kite that was driven by a high wind. I tried that but once. It was excellent sport.

JOHN (*Sighing*): I'm going to miss you, Ben, you and your bold ideas.

BENJAMIN: I'll miss our long talks and debates, John. Thank you for the cheese and apples. Pray for me, John—prayers and provisions hinder no journey.

JOHN: Where will you go in New York?

BENJAMIN: To a printer there named William Bradford. I'll seek employment with him. Failing that, I'll go on to Philadelphia, a city whose name appeals mightily to me. Philadelphia—that's Greek, John, for the City of Brotherly Love.

JOHN: Will you write to me?

BENJAMIN: I'll write, but you must tell no one of my letters. Give me your hand. Go, my friend. Think of me often, but speak of me never.

* * *

NARRATOR: At dawn on Saturday, the storm has come and gone, and the sloop has sailed away before an easy pleasant wind. Three days later, Ben reached New York, where he went immediately to see William Bradford, the printer. But Bradford had no work to offer Ben. He advised him to go to Philadelphia, where his son Andrew had a printing establishment. Benjamin Franklin, who could never resist adventure—especially if it led to freedom—left New York, and walked across New Jersey to reach Philadelphia, the city that would in time claim him for its own. Almost immediately Benjamin was missed in Boston. The next issue of the *Courant,* still published under the name of Benjamin Franklin, carried this advertisement: "James Franklin, Printer in Queen Street, wants a likely lad for an apprentice." (*Pause*) James could search the whole land over and no likelier lad would he ever find than the one he had just lost. James's loss, however, was the world's gain. In the sixty-seven years that lay ahead for him, Benjamin Franklin made his fortune before he was forty. He devoted the second half of his life to helping shape the fortunes of his beloved country— supporting the American Colonies faithfully through the War of Independence. He assisted in the formulation of the Declaration of Independence, then represented the new government as the American Minister Plenipotentiary to the Court of France, and lastly, in 1787 at 81 years of age, served as delegate from Pennsylvania at the Federal Convention which drew up the Constitution for the new Republic of the United States of America. Before he died at 84, the whole world was to acclaim this printer-inventor-scientist-patriot-diplomat, for with boundless inventive genius and statesmanship, Benjamin Franklin had lived out his life, guided by his own precept: The noblest question in the world is, *What good may I do in it?*

THE END

The Constitution Is Born

The Founding Fathers make history

by Carol J. Brown

Characters

NARRATOR

GEORGE WASHINGTON, *President of the Constitutional Convention, delegate from Virginia*

WILLIAM JACKSON, *secretary of Convention*

WILLIAM PATERSON ⎱ *delegates from New Jersey*
WILLIAM LIVINGSTON ⎰

ALEXANDER HAMILTON, *delegate from New York*

EDMUND RANDOLPH ⎱
JAMES MADISON ⎬ *delegates from Virginia*
GEORGE MASON ⎰

RUFUS KING ⎱ *delegates from Massachusetts*
ELDRIDGE GERRY ⎰

GEORGE READ, *delegate from Delaware*

BENJAMIN FRANKLIN ⎱ *delegates from Pennsylvania*
JAMES WILSON ⎰

NARRATOR: One of the most momentous periods in American history began on May 14, 1787, when fifty-five delegates, representing all of the thirteen original colonies but Rhode Island, met in Independence Hall in Philadelphia as a Constitutional Convention. It was eleven years after the signing of the Declaration of Independence in 1776 and four years after the end of the American Revolutionary War in 1783. During that hot summer this remarkable body of statesmen deliberated, debated, and finally compromised to produce the Constitution of the United States of America, which became the fundamental law of our land. (*Pause*) The mission of the Convention was, in Alexander Hamilton's words, "to render the Constitution of the Federal government adequate to the exigencies of the union." The delegates also sought to protect the mutual interests of the states. George Washington, former Commander-in-Chief of the Continental Army and a delegate to the Constitutional Convention from Virginia, was chosen President of the Convention. . . .

WASHINGTON: Gentlemen, we are met for a grave and serious purpose, that of framing a constitution for our United States. The Articles of Confederation and Perpetual Union, ratified by the states during the war, have proved inadequate to meet our nation's needs. It is your choice that I be chosen president of this convention, and I am honored to be able once again to serve you. No man has felt the bad effects of our present confederation more than I. We may justly ascribe the prolongation of the war to the want of powers in Congress. Almost the whole of the difficulties and distress of my army had their origins there. (*Pause*) Let us have the secretary call the roll of the states.

JACKSON: New Hampshire . . . Connecticut . . . New York . . . New Jersey . . . Pennsylvania . . . Massachusetts . . . Delaware . . . Maryland . . . Virginia . . . North Carolina . . . South Carolina . . . Georgia. . . . (*As each name is called, a delegate replies, "Here."*) Rhode Island. (*Pauses*) I call Rhode Island. (*There is no reply.*)

WASHINGTON (*Surprised*): Is Rhode Island not here?

PATERSON: Mr. President.

WASHINGTON: Mr. Paterson of New Jersey.

PATERSON: Rhode Island is not here. Rhode Island prefers not to join the union at this time.

WASHINGTON (*Firmly*): But that must not be! We must all work together. We all have the same needs, the same ideas about laws, freedom, religion, and self-government. We must come together and make some agreement.

HAMILTON: Mr. President.

WASHINGTON: Mr. Hamilton of New York.

HAMILTON (*With spirit*): Mr. President, it is imperative that we have a strong central government.

RANDOLPH: But, Mr. President . . .

WASHINGTON: Mr. Randolph of Virginia.

RANDOLPH (*Firmly*): There are many here opposed to Mr. Hamilton's proposal of strong federalism. The rights of the individual states must be preserved.

HAMILTON (*Soothingly*): Mr. President, we are here for one purpose—to form a more perfect union. I am sure we shall work harmoniously to achieve this.

WASHINGTON: Then, gentlemen, let us proceed.

NARRATOR: Throughout the summer of 1787, the delegates to the Constitutional Convention met and worked and debated the articles of the new Constitution. Many divergent views had to be reconciled. . . .

GERRY: Mr. President.

WASHINGTON: Mr. Gerry of Massachusetts.

GERRY: It is the fear of the smaller states that they shall be overpowered by the larger states.

READ: Mr. President.

WASHINGTON: Mr. Read of Delaware.

READ (*Indignantly*): We want equal representation! And Mr. Paterson of New Jersey and Mr. King of Massachusetts agree. We must protect the smaller states.

PATERSON *and* KING (*Together*): Yes! Yes!

RANDOLPH: Mr. President.

WASHINGTON: Mr. Randolph of Virginia.

RANDOLPH: As delegate from Virginia, one of the larger states, I should like to present the Virginia Plan. It provides that Congress shall be comprised of two houses—an upper and a lower house to vote on all proposals affecting the nation.

GERRY (*Heatedly*): I object!

RANDOLPH (*Continuing*): Representation in these houses would be based, of course, on the population of the state.

READ (*Angrily*): Never! My state of Delaware should send as many delegates as Virginia!

PATERSON (*Heatedly*): And my state of New Jersey as many as New York!

LIVINGSTON, KING *and* GERRY (*Shouting*): Yes, yes!

HAMILTON, MASON, *and* MADISON (*Heatedly*): No, no!

WASHINGTON (*Trying to restore order*): Gentlemen, gentlemen. (*Pause*) Mr. Read, do you wish to address this Convention?

READ (*Forcefully*): I do, indeed! Under Mr. Randolph's plan, the small states would cease to exist. The large states would control the Congress.

RANDOLPH: But the representation should be based on population.

PATERSON: New Jersey objects!

LIVINGSTON: Mr. President.

WASHINGTON: Mr. Livingston of New Jersey.

LIVINGSTON: My fellow delegate, Mr. Paterson, has a proposal to make.

WASHINGTON: Let us hear your proposal, Mr. Paterson.

PATERSON: Mr. President, I propose instead of the Virginia Plan submitted by Mr. Randolph, that we have a Congress of one house, with equal representation from each state.

MASON: No, we want the Virginia Plan.

READ: No, the New Jersey plan!

WASHINGTON (*Trying to calm them*): Gentlemen, please let us remember that the fate of a nation is at stake. We are met to raise a standard of government. Let us raise a standard to which the wise and honest can repair.

NARRATOR: Days passed in sessions filled with bitter arguments: What would the form of representation be? The debates lasted for hours, with neither side agreeing to compromise. At last, Benjamin Franklin, a delegate from Pennsylvania and eighty-one years old, rose to his feet. He was quite frail and had not taken much part in the debates, but he was always in attendance at these heated and prolonged meetings.

FRANKLIN: Mr. President.

WASHINGTON: Dr. Benjamin Franklin of Pennsylvania.

FRANKLIN (*Slowly and calmly*): I confess that there are several parts of this Constitution which I do not at present approve, but . . . the older I grow, the more apt I am to doubt my own judgment, and to pay more respect to the judgment of others. . . . I agree to this Constitution with all its faults, if they are such; because I think a general government necessary for us. . . . I doubt too whether any other Convention we can obtain may be able to make a better Constitution. For when you assemble a number of men to have the advantage of their joint wisdom, you inevitably assemble with those men all their prejudices, their passions, their errors of opinion, their local interests, and their selfish views. (*Pauses*) Since we cannot agree on the Virginia Plan or the New Jersey Plan or any other of the plans proposed in the course of this Convention, let me propose a compromise. Let our Congress be composed of two houses; a Senate, or an upper house, with two representatives from each state; and a House of Representatives, or a lower house, with the number of members determined according to population.

LIVINGSTON: I do not approve of equal representation.

PATERSON (*Interrupting*): I do not see the need for two houses.

MADISON: Mr. President.

WASHINGTON: Mr. Madison of Virginia.

MADISON: Since we cannot agree to Mr. Randolph's Virginia Plan nor accept Mr. Paterson's New Jersey Plan, it seems to me that Dr. Franklin has given us the only alternative. I move that we accept the compromise proposed by Dr. Franklin.

WILSON: Mr. President, I second the motion.

WASHINGTON: All those in favor, say "Aye."

ALL (*Except* GERRY, MASON *and* RANDOLPH): Aye.

WASHINGTON: Those opposed, say No.

GERRY, MASON *and* RANDOLPH (*Loudly*): No.

WASHINGTON: The ayes have it.

KING: Mr. President.

WASHINGTON: Mr. King of Massachusetts.

KING: Is it to be inferred that those states possessing slaves shall include them as part of the population?

RANDOLPH (*Quickly*): Why, certainly!

GERRY (*Objecting*): Mr. Randolph, it seems to me that only free persons shall be counted.

WILSON: Mr. President.

WASHINGTON: Mr. Wilson of Pennsylvania.

WILSON: Mr. President, it is my feeling that all human beings shall be included. The national government is not an assemblage of States but is of individuals for certain political purposes.

ALL (*Ad lib*): I disagree. Only free persons. The whole population must be counted. (*Etc.*)

FRANKLIN: Gentlemen, let us compromise on this question also. Let us count only three-fifths of the slave population. In other words, for every five hundred slaves, only three hundred shall be counted in fixing the population.

READ (*Hurriedly*): Mr. President, I move that this convention accept Dr. Franklin's compromise.

KING: Second the motion.

WASHINGTON: You have heard the motion. All in favor say "aye."

ALL: Aye.

WASHINGTON: All opposed, no. (*There is silence.*) The ayes have carried on the second compromise. I declare this session closed.

NARRATOR: The debate on various parts of the Constitution continued. After several months, George Washington called the final session of the Convention to order on September 17, 1787.

WASHINGTON: Gentlemen, a government has been formed, and a Constitution has been written. In time it shall be voted upon by all the states. May it endure for ages. Let the words of the Preamble serve as a standard for human beings to strive for. . . .

JACKSON: "We, the people of the United States, in order to form a more perfect union, establish justice, insure domestic tranquility, provide for the common defense, promote the general welfare, and secure the blessings of liberty to ourselves and our posterity, do ordain and establish this Constitution for the United States of America."

WASHINGTON: Are the delegates ready to sign it?

RANDOLPH: Mr. President.

WASHINGTON: Mr. Randolph.

RANDOLPH: I cannot accept the compromises. I will not sign.

MASON: Mr. President.

WASHINGTON: Mr. Mason of Virginia.

MASON: I cannot agree to sign this document.

GERRY: Nor I, Mr. President.

WASHINGTON: I am grieved, Mr. Gerry, that we do not all have the same ideas.

NARRATOR: Again it was Dr. Franklin, beloved sage of two continents, who finally turned the tide toward agreement and the signing of the Constitution on that history-making day. . . .

FRANKLIN: Mr. President.

WASHINGTON: Dr. Franklin.

FRANKLIN: From such an assembly can a perfect production be expected? It therefore astonishes me, sir, to find this system approaching so near to perfection as it does; and I think it will astonish our enemies, who are waiting with confidence to hear that our councils are confounded like those of the builders of Babel. . . . The opinions I have had of its errors, I sacrifice to the public good. . . . Much of the strength and efficiency of any government in procuring and securing happiness to the people depends . . . on the general opinion of the goodness of the government, as well as on the wisdom and integrity of its governor.

I hope therefore that for our own sakes as a part of the people, and for the sake of posterity, we shall act heartily and unanimously in recommending this Constitution.

NARRATOR: Dr. Franklin had indeed calmed the tempers of the delegates. He then moved that the remaining thirty-nine of the original fifty-five delegates sign the Constitution and record the signing of this momentous document "by unanimous consent."

FRANKLIN: Mr. President, since each state has at least one delegate who will sign, I move that we record that this document is in accordance with all states represented and is the unanimous consent of all states present. Your name shall go first, Mr. President.

JACKSON: "Done in convention by the unanimous consent of the States present the Seventeenth day of September in the year of our Lord one thousand seven hundred and eighty-seven, and of the independence of the United States of America the twelfth. In witness whereof, we have hereunto subscribed our names."

WASHINGTON: George Washington, President and deputy from Virginia.

KING: Rufus King of Massachusetts.

HAMILTON: Alexander Hamilton of New York.

LIVINGSTON: William Livingston, New Jersey.

PATERSON: William Paterson of New Jersey.

FRANKLIN: Benjamin Franklin of Pennsylvania.

WILSON: James Wilson, Pennsylvania.

READ: George Read, Delaware.

MADISON: James Madison, Jr., Virginia.

NARRATOR: One by one, all but three of the thirty-nine delegates from the twelve states represented made their way to the front of the convention hall to sign the document—delegates from New Hampshire, Connecticut, Massachusetts, New York, New Jersey, Pennsylvania, Delaware, Maryland, Virginia, North Carolina, South Carolina, and Georgia. Again the frail Dr. Franklin rose and spoke a bit wearily but triumphantly.

FRANKLIN: Mr. President, after these long, hard months of debate, we have at last framed a Constitution for our new nation.

WASHINGTON: We could not have accomplished this without you and the compromises you introduced. And when I am asked why the legislative branch of the government needs two houses, I shall point to our habit of pouring hot tea from a cup into a saucer to cool it. With two houses, one can check the other, as the hot tea is cooled by being turned from the cup to the saucer.

FRANKLIN: It is not, as I have said, a perfect document, but in years to come it can be and, I have no doubt, will be refined with amendments to make it better serve the needs of the people. At least we have a beginning.

NARRATOR: As the last of the delegates were putting their signatures to the Constitution, Dr. Franklin, observing from the side, spoke to a few of the delegates standing near him.

FRANKLIN: You see the picture of the sun painted at the back of General Washington's chair? Artists have always found it difficult to distinguish in their painting a rising from a setting sun. I confess that I have often in the course of the session looked at that behind the President without being able to tell whether it was rising or setting; but now at length I have the happiness to know that it is a rising and not a setting sun.

THE END

Paul Revere, Rider to Lexington

An important night in our nation's past

by Grace Alicia Mayr

Characters

NARRATOR
PAUL REVERE
ROBERT NEWMAN, *Sexton of North Church*
JOSHUA BENTLEY ⎫ *Sons of Liberty from Boston*
THOMAS RICHARDSON ⎭
JOHN LARKIN, *owner of Brown Beauty*
SERGEANT MOORE
REVEREND JONAS CLARK
JOHN HANCOCK
SAMUEL ADAMS
WILLIAM DAWES
DOLLY QUINCY
AUNT LYDIA HANCOCK
DR. SAMUEL PRESCOTT
MAJOR MITCHELL, *British officer*
JOHN LOVELL, *clerk to John Hancock*

NARRATOR: It is ten o'clock on the night of Tuesday, April 18, 1775. In Boston's cobbled North Square, British grenadiers and light infantry, called "Regulars," are lining up, ready to board transports at the shore of the Charles River. From his small house on the moonlit square, Paul Revere steals out and hastens to North Church. There he joins a man waiting for him in the dark—twenty-three-year-old Robert Newman, the church sexton.

REVERE: It's happened, Robbie! The British Regulars are moving out! Quick, up into the belfry with the signal for our friends across the river in Charlestown.

NEWMAN (*Breathing with difficulty*): I'm—ready with (*Inhales deeply*) one lantern—if they're coming by land—or two—if by water. (*Pauses for breath*) Which is it, Mr. Revere? One lantern or two?

REVERE: Two, Robbie. The Regulars are boarding riverboats by now. Hop to it, lad. I mark your heavy breathing. Not afeard are you, Robbie?

NEWMAN: Not afeard, sir. I'm winded. Redcoats are quartered in our house. (*Inhales deeply again*) I couldn't leave by the door, so I got out through an upper story window that opened onto a neighbor's roof. I dropped down into a side alley and made it here just before you did.

REVERE: Good lad! You're short-winded with good cause, but 'tis the supremely best cause for which we free-born men risk our necks tonight—the cause of liberty. May the flames of our two lanterns kindle hot fires of resistance against the tyranny and high-handed oppression of King George the Third!

NEWMAN: Mr. Revere, sir, what you say stirs me inside and makes my heart jump!

REVERE: It were better my words make your feet jump, Robbie. Up the stairs you go. (*Calling in muted tones after* NEWMAN) Whistle when you're there.

NEWMAN (*Whistling once*): Mr. Revere!

REVERE: Aye, I'm still here.

NEWMAN: From the tower I can see the *Somerset* sitting like a black vulture out there in the mouth of the river. You mind that. Her eyes are sharp.

REVERE: You think a man in a small boat crossing to Charlestown would be a juicy morsel, eh? Don't worry, Robbie. I'm not of a mind to be caught tonight of all nights, for I mean to be on the spot at the birth-hour of our American independence.

NEWMAN: Godspeed, Mr. Revere!

NARRATOR: But Revere has already darted out into the night. Through back lanes and narrow alleys he short-cuts toward the secret spot where his boat lies hidden, and Joshua Bentley and Thomas Richardson, both loyal Sons of Liberty, wait to row him across the Charles. Bentley and Richardson ease Revere's boat out into the river, perilously near to H.M.S. *Somerset,* the sixty-four gun British transport.

RICHARDSON: We'd best keep well to the offside of the *Somerset,* Joshua.

BENTLEY: Aye, out of range of lookouts, and Tom, keep your voice down. A mere whisper travels across water like the bellow of a bull.

REVERE (*Whispering*): We've no need to be asking for a spatter of gunshot to blast us out of the water.

BENTLEY: Soft, long dips of the oars now, Tom, with our backs into it. That's what's needed, eh, Paul?

REVERE: Speed too, Josh. By midnight the countryside must be roused, and I in Lexington. Tonight's business is dangerous and risky for us all, but the grievances under which our cruelly oppressed country labors will not be meekly endured any longer. Not only the lives of John Hancock and Sam Adams, but, in truth, the future of America may hang upon the success of my ride to Lexington this night.

BENTLEY: Does no one else ride express tonight?

REVERE: William Dawes was sent out earlier by the longer land route. One of us must get through to Lexington and warn Hancock and Adams. Our British Governor Gage would like to catch them in tonight's trap. He would also relish confiscating our Concord munition stores—a certain cannon in particular.

BENTLEY: We were told those munitions had been removed from Concord.

REVERE: True, they were, and well hidden miles away.

RICHARDSON: Then the Redcoats go on a fool's errand, searching for our guns and powder.

REVERE: Not if on the way they capture John Hancock and Sam Adams. No more loyal patriots are to be found in all thirteen provinces.

RICHARDSON: God forbid that such brave patriots should fall into Gage's hands.

REVERE: He would ship them to England to be tried and hanged for treason.

BENTLEY: Where'll we put in, Paul?

REVERE: Hold a bit. Lift your oars. We're near. Avoid wharfs. There may be river patrols about. Try for a landing in that cove over there.

BENTLEY: Back water some, Tom. Good. Now, let's glide in—close —closer. That does it. We've brought you to shore safely, Paul.

NARRATOR: Revere snakes his way through the brush to the road. The signals sent from the North Church belfry have been noted, and several men wait to tell Revere that British patrols cover the road to Concord, and perhaps prowl just ahead. Nearby a horse whinnies, and a slender mare is led forward by John Larkin.

LARKIN: The fastest mount in my father's stable, Mr. Revere. Brown Beauty's her name.

REVERE (*Appreciatively*): And a rare beauty she is, John.

LARKIN: She's sure-footed and tireless—courageous, too. Let me hold your stirrup, Mr. Revere. Up you go, sir.

REVERE: Gentlemen, I thank you. We'll do our best, the little mare and I.

NARRATOR: Revere touches the horse's flanks with his spurs and leans forward. Brown Beauty breaks into a run. Again and again, Revere rouses sleeping householders, shouting, "The Regulars are coming! The Regulars are coming!" then races on toward Lexington. Once he is forced to change course, when two British patrols come galloping after him.

REVERE: Come on, Beauty, we'll show them our heels. Go it! Ha, we've out-distanced the one, but the second means business. Here, we'll break into this marshy field. I know this soft wet turf, but I'll wager he does not. Thank God for your nimble feet, Beauty. There! Hear that splash? Our British friend has tumbled off into the icy stream.

NARRATOR: Never slackening his pace, Revere rides into Lexington and up to the door of the parsonage, where Hancock and Adams are hiding. Throwing himself off the mare, Revere suddenly finds his arms pinned painfully behind him and a musket stuck into the back of his neck. Sergeant Moore, who stands guard at the parsonage door, addresses him.

SERGEANT: State your business.

REVERE (*Struggling to free himself*): I must see John Hancock. I—

SERGEANT: The household is all abed, sirrah, and not to be disturbed.

REVERE: You dull-witted fog-brain! I'm Paul Revere, the express rider from Boston, sent by the Sons of Liberty.

SERGEANT: Paul Revere! Release him at once, men.

REVERE (*Loudly*): I must see John Hancock. Lives hang upon it!

SERGEANT: Not so much noise, if you please. I've had orders, sir.

REVERE: Noise! They'll have noise enough before long. The Regulars are coming.

SERGEANT: Tonight, sir?

REVERE: Before daylight. We've waited months for this chance. We'll show the British we're not colonial bumpkins but fighting Americans. Sergeant, let me through. (*Calling*) Mr. Hancock! Mr. Adams!

CLARK (*Muffled voice, as if from distance*): Who's that pounding on the door out there?

REVERE: I must see Mr. Hancock!

CLARK (*More clearly*): It's almost midnight. Who are you? What makes you think John Hancock is here?

REVERE: Look, man, we haven't time to waste arguing. Tell Hancock and Adams that Paul Revere must see them at once. It's a matter of life and death—theirs! The Regulars are coming.

CLARK: Revere! Yes, yes. Come in.

NARRATOR: The clock in the parsonage is tolling midnight as Revere follows Reverend Clark into the house. John Hancock is descending the stairs brandishing his sword, while Samuel Adams follows close behind, protesting every step.

SAMUEL ADAMS: Put up that sword, John, before you lop off somebody's ear.

JOHN HANCOCK: You heard, Sam. The Regulars are coming. We're going to fight at last. Where are my pistols? I must join the Minutemen.

ADAMS: John, don't be foolhardy.

REVERE: Mr. Hancock, sir, you and Mr. Adams must leave Lexington immediately.

HANCOCK: Leave! When any moment Lexington will be under British attack? No! I'm an officer of the Massachusetts Militia. Sergeant!

SERGEANT: Yes, sir.

HANCOCK: Sergeant, dispatch couriers. The militia must mobilize at once. Deputize boys under sixteen to spread the alarm.

SERGEANT: Yes, sir.

HANCOCK: Paul, how long would you say we'll have to wait?

REVERE (*Impatiently*): Mr. Hancock, the British troops left Boston two hours ago. At any moment they could arrive, and you and

Mr. Adams are—your pardon, gentlemen, but these are General Gage's own words—two arch-traitors and the first target for tonight. The second is the munition stores we had in Concord.

HANCOCK: Gage will search for them in Concord without success, thank God.

ADAMS: But here in Lexington Gage may succeed unless we leave as soon as possible. Be reasonable, John. It's our duty to the cause to escape before the British troops arrive.

HANCOCK: No! My duty lies here. Don't try to persuade me with your prudent reasons. I must stay and fight beside the brave men of Lexington. Besides, Aunt Lydia Hancock and Mistress Dolly Quincy are guests in this house. I can't abandon them.

REVERE: Both ladies will be safe enough within the parsonage.

HANCOCK: I will not run away. With this sword I mean to defend the principles I believe in. If blood is to be shed, let it first be shed here in Lexington—and if need be, let it be mine.

ADAMS: Brave words, John, but reckless and impractical. It is neither your duty nor mine to remain in Lexington tonight. We are both duly elected representatives to the Second Continental Congress. Our first duty is to be in Philadelphia on May tenth for the opening session.

HANCOCK: I intend to be there, but tonight I am—

CLARK: Gentlemen, if you please. Your argument has served no purpose that I can see except to disturb the ladies. I can hear them now in the upper hall. It has also almost drowned out the knocking I hear at the door.

REVERE: 'Tis Willie Dawes, most like.

SERGEANT: Reverend Clark, excuse me, sir, a second express rider from Boston has arrived.

REVERE: Willie? Is that you?

DAWES: Ah, Paul. There must have been British patrols behind every tree, but I left them scratching their noodles. That shows we Yankees can beat those British Doodles. (*Suddenly surprised*) What! Mr. Hancock and Mr. Adams—still here? Paul, haven't you given them the warning?

CLARK: Come in, man, and shut the door.

REVERE (*Confidentially, to* DAWES): Willie, they know, but Hancock refuses to save himself. Ah, there comes Mistress Dolly Quincy. Now there's a high-spirited lass, pretty as a picture and quick-witted too, for all her ribbons and laces. To Hancock she's the most beautiful girl in New England. I've heard he has the promise of her hand in marriage. Maybe she can persuade him to take Adams's advice and get out of here while the getting is good.

DOLLY: John, Sam is right. Leave at once!

ADAMS: Thank you, Mistress Dolly.

DOLLY: Why do you shake your head, John?

HANCOCK: Dolly, I had hoped that as my future wife you would argue for my wishes, not against them.

DOLLY: John, this is a matter of life and death, as I heard Paul Revere say, and it's not just your life and Sam's that you risk, but the lives, liberty, and happiness of us all in Massachusetts —maybe in all of America.

ADAMS: The stakes are very high, John. This is dangerous business.

HANCOCK (*Yielding somewhat*): I know as well as anyone the risks we all take. I have pledged to the cause my life and my fortune, for neither is worth a penny without that natural right of each of us—the right to individual liberty.

DOLLY: John, you're probably the richest man in Boston, the most respected and the most admired.

ADAMS (*Joining in quickly to support* DOLLY's *pleading*): The most generous with time and money for our cause.

CLARK: Benefactor of the church and friend to the poor.

REVERE: King Hancock to the merchants of Boston.

DAWES: Squire Hancock to the farmers of Massachusetts.

DOLLY: John, your life is precious to many people. For their sakes, escape quickly now while it is possible. For my sake, too, John, for one day we shall marry, and—

HANCOCK: Give me your hand, my love. Not one day, but soon. You've kept me dangling far too long.

DOLLY: Have I, John? Well, I don't want you dangling alongside Sam Adams on some gallows in England.

ADAMS: I don't fancy myself dancing a jig beside John on a British gallows, either. The mere thought of it turns me pale.

HANCOCK (*Won over at last*): Very well, I yield to you all. We'll leave. You too, Dolly. (*Calling upstairs*) Aunt Lydia, are you there?

NARRATOR: Aunt Lydia Hancock, who has been eavesdropping all the while from the second floor, calls down the stairs.

AUNT LYDIA: Johnny, I'm proud of you. You've come to your senses at last.

HANCOCK: How do you mean, Aunt Lydia?

AUNT LYDIA: You're taking the good advice of your friends.

HANCOCK: I'm a reasonable man, Aunt Lydia.

AUNT LYDIA: For once, Johnny, I'm pleased to see you are.

HANCOCK: Thank you, Aunt Lydia.

AUNT LYDIA: Come, Dolly. Help me pack our trunks.

DOLLY: In a moment, Aunt Lydia. I want to hear John's plans.

HANCOCK (*Assuming command*): Tonight we'll go to Woburn and then leave directly from there for Philadelphia, by-passing Boston.

REVERE: A wise decision, Mr. Hancock. While you were away from Boston, presiding at the Provincial Congress in Concord, the windows of your house were stoned and your lawn railing hacked to pieces by the swords of British officers. Boston is no place for John Hancock or his friends now.

HANCOCK: 'Tis fortunate then that none of us must return to Boston.

DOLLY: But, John, I want to go to my father's house in Boston.

HANCOCK: My love, you and Aunt Lydia must follow immediately after us to Woburn in Aunt Lydia's chaise.

DOLLY: La, sir, I am not yet under your control. I shall go home to my father's house.

HANCOCK (*Stiffly*): Madam, you shall not return to Boston so long as there's one British bayonet in the city.

DOLLY: I am not a child to be ordered about, sir. (*Calling*) Aunt Lydia!

HANCOCK: Run upstairs to Aunt Lydia, if you like, but you are my responsibility and I mean to protect you whether you like it or not.

ADAMS: John, the safety of many others is also our responsibility. When General Gage's men fail to catch us here in Lexington, and then fail to seize the munitions in Concord, they may take out their frustrations in an act of reprisal against the towns-people of Concord.

HANCOCK: We must warn Concord of this situation.

REVERE: I'll go, Mr. Hancock.

DAWES: I'll ride with you, Paul. Most like the way is heavily patrolled.

ADAMS: Good men. A safe ride to you both. There—I'll see you safely out the door. Then John and I can prepare for our journey.

NARRATOR: Minutemen are rapidly gathering as Revere and Dawes gallop off toward Concord, six miles away. They are barely outside Lexington—Brown Beauty pacing the run— when Revere spies a lone rider, trotting down a lane leading from a farmhouse.

REVERE: Willie, rein in. A rider! For a patrol, he rides openly.

DAWES: No skulking behind trees for him. He rides as if to enjoy the night air like a young man who's been a-courtin'.

REVERE: We can't take any chances, Willie. We'll challenge him with cocked pistols.

DAWES: Aye, Paul.

NARRATOR: The solitary rider shortens his reins to turn onto the Concord road, and rides into the ambush.

REVERE: Halt, or I'll shoot!

DAWES: Your name and business! That's my pistol against your ribs.

PRESCOTT: Gentlemen, you must be amateurs at this highway robbery business. I've nothing worth your stealing. I'm only a poor country doctor from Concord. Your obedient servant, Dr. Samuel Prescott, and had I my pistol in hand, I'd serve you properly, believe me.

REVERE: Your most humble pardon, Dr. Prescott. I'm Paul Revere. This is William Dawes.

PRESCOTT: The Boston express riders for the Sons of Liberty. Who hasn't heard of you both, Revere? But why stop me with pistols?

REVERE: You might have been one of the British officers on patrol.

PRESCOTT: On patrol, eh? So something's going on tonight. What is it?

REVERE: The Regulars are coming through Lexington for an attack on Concord in the morning.

PRESCOTT: Ha, then the Redcoats are in for a big surprise. They'll find plenty of resistance in Concord. The spirit of liberty never was higher than it is at present. You've come through Lexington, have you?

REVERE: Lexington has already been alerted, but householders between here and Concord must be warned with all haste.

PRESCOTT: Then I'll ride with you. I'm well known to the people in these parts. They trust me and will respond quickly to what I tell them.

REVERE: Good! Start with the house you just came from, Dr. Prescott, then ride as if the devil were at your heels—for he is! Let's go, Willie!

NARRATOR: So Dr. Prescott joins Paul Revere and Willie Dawes. From house to house along the Concord road the three riders gallop, shouting the fateful news. Halfway to Concord, however, Revere sights British officers charging down the road toward them.

REVERE: Holla, Willie! Dr. Prescott! We've been seen. Four mounted patrols ahead. Get off the road. Turn into this pasture. We'll separate and confuse them.

PRESCOTT: I'll dash across the pasture for a jump over that stone wall on the north.

DAWES: I'll go for the east wall, Paul.

REVERE: Come on, Beauty, we'll make for the woods across the field. If we're lucky we'll lose our pursuers there. Faster! Faster, girl! Good! Aha, one of us is safe—Dr. Prescott jumped wide and clear. He'll get to Concord. We're in luck, Beauty. The British patrols don't know the tricks of this kind of riding as we do. Oh-oh! Willie Dawes is reining his horse in too short! That's bad!

NARRATOR: Dawes fails to make the jump. He is thrown over his horse's head, but escapes by scrambling away on foot. Revere spurs Brown Beauty into the woods, but there he rides into an ambush of six British officers. Major Mitchell of the British Army seizes Brown Beauty's bridle and points his pistol at Revere's head.

MITCHELL: If you attempt to run, I'll blow your brains out. Your name, sir.

REVERE: Paul Revere.

MITCHELL: Paul Revere, indeed—the express rider for the Sons of Liberty in Boston. Aren't you the one they call Bold Revere?

REVERE: Aye, so I'm called.

MITCHELL: You're riding very late, Bold Revere.

REVERE: You ride very late yourselves, sir.

MITCHELL: We're searching for deserters from His Majesty's army.

REVERE: We well know how many desert—more and more every day are won over to the prospect of freedom here in a new land. But tonight you're not out after these deserters—you're patrolling these roads to prevent word from getting through to Concord about Gage's attack.

MITCHELL: You're much too well informed for your own good, Revere.

REVERE: Ha! Gage's plan has been known by the Sons of Liberty for days. I, myself, carried warning to Concord last Sunday. Tonight the countryside all the way from Boston has been alerted that the Regulars are out, heading this way. Let me tell you those Redcoats are in for a hot reception—hot lead if they fire on us.

MITCHELL: You rebels wouldn't dare resist His Majesty's troops!

REVERE: Try us! Minutemen stand ready now on Lexington Green, and they're far from the clod-hopping yokels you think they are. They are select members of the local militia—sharpshooting men and boys over sixteen who sleep in their clothes, ready for service at a minute's notice.

MITCHELL: Enough of this, Revere. Sergeant, take Revere's reins and lead his horse. We'll ride toward Lexington to investigate the truth of such wild tales of colonial defiance. Bold Revere, I won't hesitate to shoot you dead if you attempt to escape.

NARRATOR: In cold silence, Revere is escorted by his captors until they are within a half mile of Lexington. Then, suddenly, a blast of gunshot startles the riders. Brown Beauty rears. Revere clutches his saddle, readying himself for escape. The sergeant, however, thwarts Revere's attempt by holding firm to Brown Beauty's reins and forcing her into submission.

MITCHELL: What was that?

REVERE: The signal that the Massachusetts Militia is mobilizing.

MITCHELL: Militia mobilizing! So you Yankees do mean to fight. Men, Revere is just excess baggage to us now, but we can use his horse. Sergeant, your horse is tired. Cut the girth and bridle so he can't be ridden by Revere, and Revere's little rebel mare is yours.

NARRATOR: The British officers gallop off. Revere scrambles across pastures, over stone walls, through the graveyard to Lexington

Green. In the dark Revere hears the British fife and drum call to arms and sees the poorly armed Minutemen forming ranks. Just as Revere reaches the parsonage, John Hancock bursts out the door. Sam Adams follows, nods to Revere in surprise, but addresses himself to John Hancock.

ADAMS: Stop! John, you'll never make it across the green and back before Gage's troops arrive. I can hear the marching drums getting closer and closer.

HANCOCK: I must try, Sam. My trunk is there—the one made to fit the chaise in which we travel to Philadelphia. That trunk contains incriminating matter so treasonable that half of Massachusetts will hang if the papers fall into the wrong hands.

ADAMS: I know that, John, but send someone else. You can't risk going yourself, and I dare not risk going either. Here's Revere, by some miracle. Send him.

HANCOCK: Paul Revere? Here? Why, you're back safe from Concord!

REVERE: Aye, Mr. Hancock. We ran into trouble on the road, but your message has reached Concord by now. I—

ADAMS: Listen, Paul. Right now, Hancock's trunk is our problem.

REVERE: Where's your trunk, Mr. Hancock? I'll have it here in jig time.

HANCOCK: It's in a room above the stairs at Buckman Tavern. My clerk, John Lovell, is lodged there. He'll help you carry it.

ADAMS: Hurry, Paul. It's almost daylight.

NARRATOR: Revere races across the green through the lines of the Minutemen, who also hear the British drums and are preparing to stand their ground. Revere reaches the tavern just as day breaks. He calls up to a man who is watching from an open second-story window.

REVERE: John Lovell! I've orders from Mr. Hancock. He wants his trunk.

LOVELL: Paul Revere, isn't it? Come up.

NARRATOR: Revere rushes into the tavern, past the warm taproom hearth fire, up the stairs to the chamber where John Lovell waits for him with Hancock's trunk.

LOVELL: I've been expecting instructions since midnight when word first came that you, Paul Revere, had brought a warning. It's been like sitting on a powder keg. I'd have died before I'd let anyone take Mr. Hancock's trunk. But we'll never save it now. It's too late!

REVERE: We'll manage somehow. I've caught the strap on my side. Ready?

LOVELL: Yes. I've got this side. It's a heavy trunk. Watch the stairs. They're narrow.

REVERE: I'll go first. Let the weight of the trunk fall on my shoulders. Ugh! It is heavy. Guide me down until we're safely out the door onto the green.

NARRATOR: On the green, American Minutemen are now face-to-face with the King's troops. Revere and Lovell start through the American lines just as the scarlet-coated British commanding officer shatters the ominous silence with, "Disperse, you rebels! Disperse!" Revere urges Lovell on.

REVERE: Pay no heed, John Lovell. Look neither to right nor left. Just keep moving.

LOVELL: It's so quiet again.

REVERE: The calm before the storm. We're almost half-way. Take heart.

LOVELL: There! Listen! A shot was fired!

REVERE: There'll be more now once it's started. Can you move faster? Good! We're off the green and out of the line of fire here. Hancock will want us behind the parsonage to load this trunk onto his chaise. This way, John Lovell.

NARRATOR: Behind the parsonage, John Hancock is supervising the readying of his chaise. Dolly and Aunt Lydia watch from the parsonage. Sam Adams, mounted and holding the reins of Hancock's horse, sees Revere and Lovell.

ADAMS: At last! John, here's your trunk.

HANCOCK: Splendid, Paul. Thank you also, John Lovell, for your good care of my trunk. I'll show you where it fits into the chaise. Right there, see—snug and hidden—for all the world like a natural part of the chaise's backboard.

ADAMS: Hurry, John. Your horse is as restive as mine to get away from the racket of those British muskets.

HANCOCK: Give me my reins, Sam. Who fired first, Paul?

REVERE: Who can say? Lovell and I just kept moving as fast as we could, glad that no bullets hit us.

HANCOCK: Thank God for that. Dolly, I leave you and Aunt Lydia only because you insist.

AUNT LYDIA: I promise you, Johnny, that tomorrow my chaise and I shall bring Dolly Quincy to you.

HANCOCK: Dolly, do you agree?

DOLLY: Yes, John, I promise, too.

HANCOCK: Then John Lovell shall stay behind to ride with you as escort. Paul, I want you to follow Sam Adams and me. Give me a hand up, John Lovell. Thank you. Let's go, Sam.

DOLLY (*Softly*): God be with you, John, until we meet again.

HANCOCK: Goodbye, Dolly. Come along, Paul. If it's to be war, I'm for a vigorous defensive war. Powder and arms are the best measures we can take now. The time has passed for holding out the olive branch in hopes of reconciliation with the Crown.

REVERE: Lead on, Mr. Hancock. There's no turning back now. Our revolution has begun. American independence is here and now born!

NARRATOR: On this Wednesday morning, April 19, 1775, the American War for Independence has truly begun. Soon John Hancock and Sam Adams, accompanied by Dolly Quincy and Aunt Lydia Hancock, will roll south to Philadelphia and the Second Continental Congress. A few days later, John Hancock will be elected president of that unique assembly, and on August 25, he will marry Dolly Quincy. In Boston Robert Newman will be jailed by the British on suspicion of having hung the two lanterns in North Church belfry. Paul Revere will continue to serve the Sons of Liberty as a messenger, with two horses kept ready for his use. Brown Beauty will never be heard of again, but she has earned her place in American history by carrying Bold Paul Revere to Lexington on the fateful night of April 18, 1775.

THE END

A Birthday Anthem for America

The glorious past and the challenging future

by Lewy Olfson

CHORUS:

> Happy birthday, U.S.A.! You're now two centuries old!
> Through years to come may all your blessings grow a
> thousand-fold.
> Land of freedom, land of legend, land of liberty—
> What is our anthem all about? Our country, 'tis of thee!

LOW VOICES:

> What is America, that we should praise her?
> What is America, that we should sing?
> What makes our country so wonderfully special
> We want flags to fly and we want bells to ring?

HIGH VOICES:

> She is a land most rich and rare.
> She is a land most fine and fair.
> Filled with nature's wealth and grace,
> America is a lovely place!

1ST SOLO:

> Oh beautiful! for spacious skies, for amber waves of grain,
> For purple mountains' Majesty above the fruited plain.

CHORUS:

> She is a land of hills and mountains.
> She is a land of coves and canyons.
> She is a land of lakes and rivers.
> She is a land of fields and forests.

LOW VOICES:

> Rich in minerals, livestock, produce,
> Blessed with the splendor of changing seasons.

236

HIGH VOICES:

Vast and beautiful, wide and grand,
America is a lovely land.

LOW VOICES:

But what of pollution? What about waste?
Hasn't her beauty been spoiled and defaced?
How can we sing of a splendor so grand
When abuse and neglect are despoiling our land?

HIGH VOICES:

It's true that we aren't always careful and good.
It's true that we haven't done all that we could.
But in counting these graces Americans share,
We pledge to conserve them with wisdom and care.

LOW VOICES:

What else is America, that we should praise her?
What else is America, that we applaud?
What makes our country so rich and so splendid
That she should be honored at home and abroad?

HIGH VOICES:

She is a land of many peoples,
Of every creed, of every race.
All are equal, yet each is special.
She is a democratic place.

2ND SOLO:

Native Americans, early settlers,
Those who arrived by immigration,
From different cultures, with different backgrounds,
Combined to form a mighty nation.

CHORUS:

English, Spanish, Portuguese,
Greeks and Irish, Japanese,
Algonquins, Sioux, and Seminoles,
Swedes and Russians, Danes and Poles,

1ST SOLO:

Germans, Indians, Iranians,
Latvians, Dutch, and Lithuanians,

2ND SOLO:

Serbs and Slavs and Jews and Finns—
That's just the way the list begins!

3RD SOLO:

> Latins, Saxons, Semites, Celts—
> And practically everybody else!

CHORUS:

> From all around the world we're drawn.
> The list goes on and on and on.
> Yet wherever we come from, whoever we be,
> Here all are equal—here all are free.

LOW VOICES:

> But isn't there prejudice? Isn't there hate?
> How can we say America's great,
> When some people suffer injustice and need
> Because of their sex or their color or creed?

HIGH VOICES:

> It's true that there still is much work to be done
> Until all stand equally under our sun.
> But ours is a nation that's still on the move!
> We vow we'll do better! We pledge to improve!

LOW VOICES:

> What else is America, that we should praise her?
> What else is America, that we should shout?
> What makes our country so strong and dynamic
> We want the whole world to keep thinking about?

CHORUS:

> She is a land of truth and courage,
> Of strong ideals of liberty,
> Of human rights and human worth:
> The home of the brave and the land of the free.

3RD SOLO:

> Ours is a noble Constitution,
> Ours is a shining Bill of Rights,
> Ours is a true and great Republic,
> A way of life that holds great promise.

CHORUS:

> That's the word! The word we've needed!
> "Promise!" That's the special call!
> Our past was fine, our present's great—
> But our future will be best of all!
> So happy birthday, U.S.A.! We sing your praise in chorus,
> And gladly face the shining road that lies ahead before us!

THE END

Old Glory Grows Up

The history of our nation's flag

by Helen Louise Miller

Characters

FIVE SPEAKERS
GEORGE WASHINGTON
BETSY ROSS
NARRATOR
FRANCIS SCOTT KEY
VERMONT
KENTUCKY
COLUMBIA
UNCLE SAM
NEW MEXICO
ARIZONA
CONFEDERATE BOY
CONFEDERATE GIRL
ALASKA
HAWAII

BEFORE RISE: *On apron of stage is an easel bearing a large placard reading,* OLD GLORY. *Underneath this placard are seven date cards, arranged in order, so that each time a card is removed, another is revealed.* FIVE SPEAKERS *enter, wearing red, white and blue paper caps. As they reach center stage, they bow to the audience, and recite in turn.*

1ST SPEAKER:
  Good gentlemen and ladies,
  We've been sent here to say

We hope you will be patient.

There's been a slight delay.

2ND SPEAKER:

The costume for George Washington

We find is much too small,

Because the boy who plays the part

Has grown up much too tall.

3RD SPEAKER:

Last year the suit we had was right,

But George has put on inches.

And now the coat is far too tight.

In fact, he says it pinches.

4TH SPEAKER:

The trousers are a way too short.

The sleeves come up to here.

(*Gestures to indicate*)

The cotton wig and velvet hat

Perch right up on his ear.

5TH SPEAKER:

We'll do our best to hurry.

We hope it won't be long.

We'll sing while you are waiting

Our Yankee Doodle song. (SPEAKERS *sing verse and chorus of "Yankee Doodle."* NARRATOR *enters.*)

NARRATOR:

We're really very sorry

For causing this delay.

But now the costume's ready,

And we can start our play. (SPEAKERS *move left stage and remain there as a chorus.* NARRATOR *moves to easel.*)

We'll tell the story of our flag

Without a moment's loss. (*Removes first placard revealing date—1777*)

And now you'll meet George Washington

And Mistress Betsy Ross. (*Curtain rises.* GEORGE WASHINGTON *and* BETSY ROSS *stand at either side of a very large cardboard Colonial flag with thirteen stars arranged in a circle on the blue field. The field is a flannel board arrangement, which can be removed and replaced with a new field as the play progresses.*

Beside BETSY ROSS *is a small sewing stand or table, on which the other felt fields are placed so they will be available as needed.*)

BETSY ROSS: The flag is finished, General Washington. I trust it meets with your approval.

WASHINGTON: It is a beautiful flag, Mistress Ross. I am sure that the gentlemen of Congress will be pleased.

BETSY ROSS: I have tried to follow their orders, General Washington.

WASHINGTON: Everything is exactly right. On June 14th of this year, 1777, Congress voted that the flag of the United States should have thirteen red and white stripes, with a union of thirteen stars on a blue field.

BETSY ROSS: It was hard to arrange the stars. I first put them in three rows, but I liked the circle better.

WASHINGTON: You did well, Mistress Ross. We do not wish to place one state above another. Each one of our thirteen colonies is of equal importance. (*With his finger, he traces the outline of the circle.*) Then, too, the circle has no end, and there must never be an end to the glory of our country and our flag.

BETSY ROSS: That is a beautiful thought, sir.

WASHINGTON (*With a bow*): And a beautiful flag, Mistress Ross. I propose three big cheers for the red, white and blue.

SPEAKERS (*Singing chorus of "Columbia, the Gem of the Ocean"*):
    "Three cheers for the red, white and blue,
    Three cheers for the red, white and blue,
    The Army and Navy forever,
    Three cheers for the red, white and blue." (*Curtain closes.*
NARRATOR *removes the date card, 1777, revealing the date, 1795.*)

* * *

NARRATOR:
    The flag with only thirteen stars
    Remained the very same
    Until, in seventeen ninety-five,
    A change we must explain. (*Curtain opens on same scene, with* WASHINGTON *and* BETSY ROSS. VERMONT *and* KENTUCKY *enter, wearing baldric with name of the state.* VERMONT *carries a white stripe to be affixed to the flag;* KENTUCKY *carries a red stripe.*)

WASHINGTON: Our country is growing, Mistress Ross. Two new states have been admitted to the Union. I present Vermont and Kentucky. (*Gestures to them*)

BETSY ROSS (*With a curtsy*): Welcome to the United States of America. And now we must find a place for you in our flag.

VERMONT: The people of Vermont will be proud and happy to have a star of their own.

KENTUCKY: The citizens of Kentucky will always defend their star.

WASHINGTON: A circle of fifteen stars will be far too big for the blue field. (BETSY ROSS *removes field with thirteen stars and replaces it with a field of fifteen stars in five rows of three stars each.*)

BETSY ROSS: How do you like this design, sir? We will arrange the stars in five rows of three each.

WASHINGTON (*Viewing new flag*): Excellent, Mistress Ross, excellent.

VERMONT: If there are fifteen stars, there should be fifteen stripes. (*Attaches white stripe to the flag*) In the name of the state of Vermont, I add this white stripe to the flag of the United States.

KENTUCKY (*Adding red stripe*): This fifteenth stripe represents the people of the state of Kentucky.

WASHINGTON: May every stripe and star stand for America, sweet land of Liberty. (*Curtain closes as* SPEAKERS *sing the first stanza of "America."*)

*   *   *

NARRATOR:

So fifteen stripes and fifteen stars
Displayed in just this manner
Inspired the man who wrote the words
Of our "Star-Spangled Banner." (*Curtain opens on same flag with* FRANCIS SCOTT KEY, *holding notebook, beside it.*)

FRANCIS SCOTT KEY: My name is Francis Scott Key. It was this flag flying over Fort McHenry in 1814 which inspired me to write the poem in which I called it "the star-spangled banner." You all know the words, but let me read you my favorite lines. (*Reads from notebook as patriotic music is played in background*)

"Then conquer we must, when our cause it is just,
And this be our motto: 'In God is our trust!'"

And the Star-Spangled Banner in triumph shall wave
O'er the land of the free and the home of the brave!"
Today wherever the star-spangled banner is flown, there are
men, women and children to sing my song. But through the
years our flag has grown as our country has grown. There have
been many flagmakers who have changed the design of our
flag, but now to continue the story. The year is 1818. (FRANCIS
SCOTT KEY *exits, as* COLUMBIA *and* UNCLE SAM *enter.* NARRATOR
removes 1795 placard, revealing 1818 sign.)

NARRATOR:

Indiana, Tennessee,
Oklahoma, Maine,
Also Mississippi
Into the Union came.
Columbia and Uncle Sam
Now have a new decree
Of how the stars and stripes should look,
And how the flag should be.

COLUMBIA: Twenty states in the Union! That would mean twenty
stars and twenty stripes! And our country is still growing. It will
be hard to design a flag that will represent every new state.

UNCLE SAM (*Holding up document*): I have here an official Act
of Congress which solves our problem. It is dated April 4, 1818.
On this date the flag of the United States shall return to the
original design of thirteen stripes. (COLUMBIA *removes one red
and one white stripe.*) A new star shall be added for every new
state admitted to the Union. (COLUMBIA *puts up a field with
twenty stars.*)

COLUMBIA: Thirteen stripes and twenty stars—and America still
growing!

NARRATOR:

To twenty add another ten,
And there is room for more, (COLUMBIA *puts up field with
thirty-four stars.*)
Until, in 1861
Our flag had thirty-four. (NARRATOR *removes 1818 card and
reveals placard 1861-1865.*)

UNCLE SAM: The years from 1861 to 1865 were known as the War
Years and the flag was called the Flag of the Union. At this time
there were thirty-four stars in our flag, but only twenty states

remained in the Union. Eleven states had set up a government of their own with a new flag known as the "Stars and Bars." (CONFEDERATE BOY *and* GIRL *enter, each carrying a Confederate flag.*)

BOY: During the War Between the States, the Stars and Bars flew over eleven of our southern states, known as the Confederate States of America.

GIRL: The Confederate Flag was carried into all the battles of the War by the men in gray who fought under General Robert E. Lee.

UNCLE SAM: But when the War Between the States was over, the stars and stripes once more flew over both the North and the South, "one nation under God, indivisible, with liberty and justice for all."

SPEAKERS (*Singing "The Battle Hymn of the Republic"*):
 Glory, glory, hallelujah,
 Glory, glory, hallelujah,
 Glory, glory, hallelujah,
 Our flag goes marching on.
       (*Curtain closes.*)

*   *   *

NARRATOR (*Removing 1861-1865 and revealing 1912*):
 In 1912 the field of stars
 Had grown to forty-eight.
 As side by side two bright new stars
 Were added on that date. (*Curtain re-opens with* NEW MEXICO *and* ARIZONA *standing with* COLUMBIA *and* UNCLE SAM.)

UNCLE SAM: From the Indian Territory, New Mexico and Arizona are admitted to the Union.

COLUMBIA: Welcome to our newcomers from the great Southwest. (*Puts up field with forty-six stars*)

NEW MEXICO (*Affixing the forty-seventh star*):
 I place the forty-seventh star,
 With honor may it glow.
 And with this star I pledge the faith
 Of all New Mexico.

ARIZONA (*Placing forty-eighth star*):
 The cowboys and the Indians
 Who in this state do dwell

All pledge that Arizona
Will serve her country well.

COLUMBIA: The American flag now has thirteen stripes and forty-eight stars.

UNCLE SAM: It was this flag that was carried in World War One and World War Two. The American Flag with its forty-eight stars became the symbol of liberty to many other countries of the world. (SPEAKERS *sing "You're a Grand Old Flag," as curtain closes.*)

* * *

NARRATOR (*Exchanging 1912 for 1960*):
The story of the stars and stripes
Is not yet fully told.
We have another chapter
All ready to unfold.
For 1960 was the date
When two more stars appeared
To take their place upon the flag
Which we all hold so dear. (*Curtain re-opens on flag of fifty stars.* ALASKA *and* HAWAII *stand with entire company.*)

ALASKA (*Pointing to forty-ninth star*):
My star shines from Alaska,
The land of ice and snow,
The country of the totem pole
And sturdy Eskimo.

HAWAII (*Pointing to fiftieth star*):
My star shines from Hawaii,
The island of the flowers.
We're proud to join the U.S.A.
And make your country ours. (SPEAKERS *move into tableau with the rest.*)

1ST SPEAKER:
Good gentlemen and ladies,
We hope you understand
Just how the story of our flag
Has been prepared and planned.

2ND SPEAKER:
Remember how George Washington
Once had a suit too small,

We said he had outgrown it
Because he was too tall.

3RD SPEAKER:

America is growing, too,
It's bigger every day,
But we must not outgrow the flag
Of our own U.S.A.

4TH SPEAKER:

So every time we add a state
We add another star
To stand for people of our land
From regions near and far. (NARRATOR *removes 1960 card to reveal 1975-1976 placard.*)

5TH SPEAKER:

And so in 1975
These fifty stars behold,
And thirteen stripes of red and white
Within the flag unfold.

NARRATOR:

For as our country's growing
Old Glory's growing, too,
So let us pledge allegiance
And loyalty anew. (*All rise and pledge allegiance to the flag.*)

UNCLE SAM:

May God preserve America
And guard our liberty
And grant us peace and union
From sea to shining sea. (*All sing "America the Beautiful," as curtain closes.*)

THE END

Sing a Song of Holidays!

America's celebrations round the year

by Lewy Olfson

BOYS:
> Sing a song of holidays, sing a song of cheer.
> Sing of the red-letter days we have throughout the year.

GIRLS:
> Days of celebration, important to our nation,
> Sing in praise of holidays, and give a happy cheer.

ALL:
> January first is New Year's Day,
> A time when all Americans pray
> The year ahead will find us strong
> For all the tasks that come along.
> We hope one hope as each year starts:
> Peace in our world and peace in our hearts.

GIRLS:
> Then comes February! Breezy February!

BOYS:
> Freezy, wheezy, sneezy February!

ALL:
> But though the month is chill and gray,
> At least it brings us Presidents' Day.
> And Presidents' Day brings back again
> The thought of two of our finest men.
> They well deserve the fame they've won—
> Abe Lincoln and George Washington!

BOYS:
> April fourteenth reminds us, we have found,
> We're not the *only* Americans around.

GIRLS:

For that is Pan-American Day—
A day on which we proudly say
To all our neighbors south of the border:

ALL:

Thanks for harmony, trust, and order.

SOLO:

¡Saludos, amigos!

ALL:

A serious holiday ends the month of May.
Last Monday in the month—Memorial Day.

BOYS:

That is the day on which we humbly pause
To think of those we've lost in all our wars,

GIRLS:

The fighting men and women of our land
Who fell so that America might stand.

ALL:

They gave the greatest gift that one can give.
They gave their lives so liberty might live.

GIRLS:

No doubt you've all heard of the Betsy Ross story.
So let's give three cheers for our gorgeous Old Glory!

BOYS:

June fourteenth is Flag Day!
That bright, brassy, brag day,
When every American whose heartbeat is true
Says, "Cheers to the colors! The Red-White-and-Blue!"

ALL:

It's really a banner day, the fourteenth of June.
A "Star-Spangled Banner" day—our favorite tune!
Oh, long may that glorious banner yet wave
O'er the land of the free and the home of the brave!

BOYS:

What comes next
In our holiday text?

GIRLS:

America's birthday—
That's what's next!

BOYS:

> So send up the fireworks and light up the sky!
> Three cheers, three cheers, for the Fourth of July!
> Keep the flags and trumpets handy
> For every Yankee Doodle Dandy.

GIRLS:

> And celebrate in every way
> America's Independence Day!

ALL:

> In fourteen-hundred-and-ninety-two,
> Columbus sailed the ocean blue.
> Small were his ships, crude was his chart—
> But faith and courage filled his heart.
> And when his vessel bumped aground,
> America is what he found!

GIRLS:

> And October twelfth, we're glad to say,
> Is now known as Columbus Day.

BOYS:

> So praise Columbus! Cheer him! Shout him!
> Where would this country be without him?

SOLO:

> On the eleventh of November,
> All of America stops to remember
> Our veterans and the cause of peace,
> For which our efforts must never cease.
> Let us be silent. Let us all pray.
> Let us remember—on Veterans' Day.

BOYS:

> The next big holiday—now let us see.
> The next big holiday—what can it be?

GIRLS (*Softly*):

> Gobble, gobble, gobble!

BOYS:

> There's another holiday—but golly whiz!
> We can't seem to think of what it is!

GIRLS (*More loudly*):

> Gobble, gobble, gobble!

BOYS:

Perhaps our brains are coming unstrung.

It's right on the top of the tip of our tongue!

GIRLS (*Very loudly*):

Gobble, gobble, gobble!

BOYS:

Ah! Now we remember! Now we remember!

It comes the fourth Thursday in November.

That old but ever-living day—

GIRLS:

Of course! Of course! Thanksgiving Day!

BOYS:

This holiday was first begun

By Pilgrims in 1621.

They offered thanks, that Pilgrim band,

For the blessings they'd found in this strange new land.

And over their meager Thanksgiving feast,

They prayed that those blessings would be increased.

GIRLS:

As the Pilgrims did, so now do we:

We bow our head and we bend our knee,

And all of our gratefulness expressing,

We offer thanks, and we count each blessing.

ALL:

And then we rise for a special treat.

GIRLS (*Softly*):

Gobble, gobble, gobble!

BOYS (*Loudly*):

Let's eat!

ALL:

The days grow short, the nights grow drear.

The calendar comes to the end of its year.

But just before the year is through,

Christmas comes with a loud halloo!

GIRLS:

Christmas is not of American birth.

It belongs to people throughout the earth.

BOYS:

In every language, in every tongue,

The Christmas message of peace is sung.

ALL:

Yes, that is the message of Christmastide:

Peace and good will, the whole world wide.

GIRLS:

So sing a song of holidays, sing a song of cheer.

BOYS:

Sing of the red-letter days we have throughout the year.

ALL:

Days of celebration, important to our nation.

Sing in praise of holidays—all through the year!

THE END

George Washington, Farmer

Our first President at home

by *Aileen Fisher*

I

1ST BOY:

> "I think a farmer's life," he wrote,
> "the most enjoyable of all.
> To watch the wheat and barley sprout
> and see the trees grow strong and tall
> is best of all pursuits, bar none."
> He signed the words:

"G. Washington."

GROUP:

> And yet this man who loved the farm
> was quick to heed the call to arm:
> he stayed away four years and more
> to fight the French and Indian war.

II

2ND BOY:

> "The more I learn about the land,
> the better I am pleased," he wrote.
> "A farmer's satisfactions grow
> like crops . . . I'd happily devote
> my life to seeds and soil and sun."
> He signed the words:

"G. Washington."

GROUP:

> And then the Revolution came.
> Again his country made its claim.

He drilled the troops and held command—
eight years away from crops and land!

III

3RD BOY:

"No sight delights me quite as much,"
he wrote, "as farmland, thriving, neat.
I've added to my coat of arms,
quite suitably, some spears of wheat.
A farmer's work is mostly fun."
He signed the words:

"G. Washington."

GROUP:

But, once again, the years were spent
away from home—as President.
Two terms, eight years away again,
handling the strained affairs of men!

IV

4TH BOY:

"At last," he wrote, "I can enjoy
the shadow of my fig and vine.
At last I have my heart's delight:
a farmer's life again is mine.
But now my days are almost done . . ."
He signed the words:

"G. Washington."

GROUP:

Two final years of "heart's delight"
this Farmer had, who, overnight,
had heeded every beck and call
to do his duty, big or small . . .
though he loved farming best of all!

Victory Ball

Festivities at Mount Vernon

by Rowena Bennett

GIRLS:

> With candlelight, with candlelight,
>> So long and long ago,
> The windows of Mount Vernon,
>> All running in a row,
> Lit up the pillared porch and gave
>> The grass beyond a glow.

BOYS:

> The silhouettes of folk inside
>> Who danced on polished floors
> Were seen by those who came and went
>> Or watched from out-of-doors.
> The laughter that came floating forth
>> Was hale, they say, and hearty;
> The victory ball was not at all
>> Like Boston's grim tea party.

GIRLS:

> But those who sat to laugh and chat
>> Or rest from minueting
> Spoke low to General Washington.

1ST BOY:

> They said, We're not forgetting
> The way you weathered Valley Forge,
>> The way you fought each battle.

1ST GIRL:

> We're not forgetting anything
>> No matter how we prattle.

2ND GIRL:
> No matter how we dance about
>> And have our bit of fun—

2ND BOY:
> We know that we would not be free
>> To celebrate our victory
>> Except for Washington.

ALL (*Together*):
> We know that we would not be free
>> To celebrate our victory
>> Except for Washington!

Production Notes

AUTHOR OF LIBERTY

Characters: 6 male; 2 female.

Playing Time: 30 minutes.

Costumes: All the characters wear costumes of the Revolutionary period. Jacob wears working clothes. Jefferson changes coats as indicated in the text. Sophie adds a frilly apron to her costume.

Properties: Dust cloth, books, papers, portable desk (the desk may be represented by a small wooden box about one foot square and three inches high against which a board, about twice the size of the box, is propped at a slant), small doll, white tablecloth, lighted taper, note, paper knife, tray of food, tray with decanter and glasses.

Setting: The parlor is modestly but comfortably furnished in the style of the period. At right is a door leading to the stairway and down to the front door. The door is open. At left is a door to the bedroom which is closed. In the rear wall are two or three large windows. Upstage at center is a large table with the portable desk on it. On the portable desk are several sheets of paper with writing on them. On the table are several books and papers, a small doll, a paper knife and a lamp. Upstage from the table and facing downstage is an armchair. Downstage right is a large comfortable armchair with a small table near it. There are other chairs about the room some of which have accompanying small tables with lamps on them. On all the tables there are books.

Lighting: At rise daylight comes through the windows, but as the play progresses it fades out. The lamps are lit as indicated in the text.

INCIDENT AT VALLEY FORGE

Characters: 6 male; 2 female.

Playing Time: 30 minutes.

Costumes: Colonial costumes and uniforms for all the characters. The soldiers should be dressed very shabbily.

Properties: Sheet of paper, pieces of sewing, strip of white cloth, pair of boots, quill pen, sacks, boxes, crates, small bag for tea, ax, pistol.

Setting: A very simple setting may be used. For Scenes 1 and 3, a few chairs and a table may be used. For Scene 4, a few piles of boxes and sacks or crates to suggest a storeroom in the commissary. Scene 2 may be played before the curtain.

Lighting: No special effects.

PAUL REVERE OF BOSTON

Characters: 9 male; 7 female; 1 male or female for Reader.

Playing Time: 20 minutes.

Costumes: 18th-century dress.

Properties: Book for reader; nuts in shells, wooden bowl and knife for Paul's carving; letter, sampler, silver items, which include tray and teapot; necklace, lockets, bracelets, hinges, lengths of fabric, pipe for Mr. Revere.

Setting: Scene 1: Kitchen in the Revere home. There are a window with curtains to one side, a large fireplace upstage center with a mantel, several chairs suitable to the period, with one settle or wing chair near fireplace. There are accessories of the period such as candle molds, spinning wheel, candlesticks, gun over mantel, bed warmer and wooden bowl. Scene 2: Paul Revere's silversmith shop. The same basic set that was used for Scene 1. Instead of curtains the window has a sign, P. REVERE, SILVERSMITH. On mantel are pieces of silver: trays, candlesticks, bowl, etc. There is a counter stage right which has a silver teapot and tray on it. A bench is behind the counter. Scene 3: The same as Scene 2. Scene 4: Paul Revere's silversmith and hardware shop. The same basic set as in Scenes 2 and 3. There is another counter displaying jewelry, hinges, lengths of fabric, etc. A sign saying HARDWARE is added to the silversmith sign in the window.

Lighting: No special effects.

Sound: Horse galloping, clock striking twelve, as indicated in text.

257

AN IMAGINARY TRIAL OF
GEORGE WASHINGTON

Characters: 15 male; 3 female; as many
male and female as desired for
Citizens.
Playing Time: 30 minutes.
Costumes: Colonial dress. The Judge
wears a long black robe and a white
powdered wig. Other characters wear
appropriate costumes: fashionable
British suits, uniforms of British and
Colonial armies, American costumes,
etc.
Properties: British flag, bifocal glasses,
gavel, documents, parchment copy of
Declaration of Independence, book,
quill pen, Bible, letter. Witnesses and
Citizens may carry various posters and
flags, such as a sign reading, "No
Taxation without Representation," a
Vermont flag, etc.
Setting: A courtroom. There is a large
table at right, for Judge, with chair
behind it. Beside chair is the British
flag. There are several rows of chairs
in the gallery section, at left side of
stage. Two tables are placed in front
of the first row of chairs, for defense
and prosecution. At center is witness
stand, raised platform with chair on
it.
Lighting: No special effects.
Sound: "America the Beautiful," played
from a recording, and sung if desired,
as indicated in text.

ALL BECAUSE OF A SCULLERY MAID

Characters: 3 male; 5 female.
Playing Time: 25 minutes.
Costumes: Colonial dress. Dame Whiting's clothes are dark and severe
looking. Tolerance, Sarah, and Felicity
wear aprons over their long dresses.
Libby wears colorful clothing, and
carries a pouch bag. Chester wears
colonial breeches and jacket. Sam's
clothing is ragged and dirty. Oliver
wears a cape and a three-cornered hat.
Properties: Workbasket, full of patches
of quilt, thread, pieces of parchment,
shears, and a silhouette, for Felicity;
silhouette cut in half, for Libby:
chocolate pot with lid (an old-fash-
ioned tea or coffee pot will do); shears
and parchment; sheet of paper, sil-

houette for Chester; portfolio, for
Oliver; glass of milk, for Sam.
Setting: The stage represents a colonial
sitting room. At upstage center is a
fireplace with a mantelpiece, on which
are jars and vases that may be moved.
To the right of the fireplace is a small
chest in which the parchment and
shears are kept. At the center of left
wall is a cabinet or stand on which the
chocolate pot is prominently displayed. There are two low stools near
the fireplace, and a high stool at the
right. A highbacked chair for Felicity
and a settee complete the furnishings.
There are four exits: the doorway at
upper left leads to the garden; doorway at upper right leads to second floor; at lower right, to the scullery; at lower left, to the entrance of
the house and the road.
Lighting: No special effects.
Sound: Doorbell.

THE TRIAL OF PETER ZENGER

Characters: 22 male; 5 female; 1 male
or female for Narrator.
Playing Time: 35 minutes.
Costumes: Appropriate dress of the early
eighteenth century in Colonial New
York. Peter wears a printer's apron in
the printshop scenes. The Two
Women carry shopping baskets.
Sheriff has warrant in his coat pocket.
Properties: Paper and printer's mallet,
sheaf of papers, gavel, pad and pencil
for Clerk of Court.
Setting: Scene 1: Peter Zenger's printing shop, represented by a table down
left, with sheets of newsprint lying on
it. There are two chairs beside table.
Other printing equipment may be
added if desired. Scene 2: Courtroom.
Upstage center is the judges' bench,
and in front of it, at one side is a
small table for Clerk of the Court.
Down left is a table for Attorney General, and down right, a table for the
Defense. To right and at an angle is
the jury box—two rows of six chairs
each.
Lighting: Spotlights down left and down
right are used at beginning of play,
as indicated in text. Lights come up
full for courtroom scene.

THE BOSTON TEA PARTY

Characters: 3 male; 4 female.

Playing Time: 20 minutes.

Costumes: The girls are dressed in costumes of the Revolutionary period. John wears tight trousers and a long coat of the period. The two boys are dressed as Indians.

Properties: Embroidery for Abigail; knitting for Eliza; overnight bag; tea pot; plate of cakes; cups and saucers.

Setting: Living room of a home in Revolutionary times. At the back of the room is a low mantel over a fireplace. A section of the paneling in wall beside fireplace can be moved from behind scenes to give the effect of a sliding door leading to a secret passage. Above mantel is the portrait of a stern-looking gentleman, and on the mantel are brass candlesticks. A fireside bench stands in front of the fireplace. At the left is a window with white curtains. Doors are at lower left and right center. A small table with silver tea service, cups and saucers on it stands at upper right; a chair is placed in back of the table. Chairs are placed at upper left, lower left and right.

Lighting: No special effects.

MARTHA WASHINGTON'S SPY

Characters: 5 male; 2 female.

Playing Time: 20 minutes.

Costumes: Silas, Caleb and Sam wear battered mufflers, jackets, ragged pants and boots with cloths wrapped around them. Betsy wears a man's coat, a muffler, and a cocked hat. Benjamin is well dressed and wears a cocked hat. Washington is dressed in a greatcoat, a cocked hat and a muffler. Martha is also bundled up in a cape.

Properties: Musket.

Setting: No particular furnishings are required. Backdrop might depict a winter scene, with snowy trees, etc. A fence, snow-covered bushes, some logs, etc., might be placed around stage. Exits are at right and left.

Lighting: No special effects.

SUMMER SOLDIER

Characters: 12 male; 3 female.

Playing Time: 15 minutes.

Costumes: Colonial dress in Scene 1; Continental Army uniforms in Scene 2. Enlisted men's uniforms are worn and ragged.

Properties: Bundle of pamphlets for Hawker, coins, pamphlet for Paine; drum, quill pen, inkwell, paper, pamphlets.

Setting: Scene 1: A street in Philadelphia. Scene 2: Campsite of the Continental Army. A low stand and stool are down left.

Lighting: Scene 2 is dimly lighted.

MOLLY PITCHER MEETS THE GENERAL

Characters: 7 male; 1 female.

Playing Time: 20 minutes.

Costumes: The soldiers wear shabby uniforms of the Continental army. Charles, Frank, and Major Smith are dressed in officers' uniforms of the period. Washington in the first scene wears a cloak over his General's uniform; it has a large collar which can be turned up to hide the lower part of his face. Molly wears a long cotton dress with a full skirt and large apron. In Scene 2, the soldiers and officers are in same uniforms, but these are now dirty and disheveled. Washington wears a traditional uniform as General of the Continental army, and Molly wears a large soldier's jacket and soldier's cap, also too big.

Properties: Mugs, stirring spoon, ladle, kettle, spoons, handkerchiefs, papers and documents, plates, lantern.

Setting: Scene 1: A dimly lighted hut. There is a fireplace upstage center, from which hangs a crane with a large soup kettle suspended from it. There is a rough wood table against the wall, left, on which are a number of mugs, plates, spoons, and a lighted lantern. Two wooden benches form an angle in right corner, and a third bench stands in the shadow at the left, facing the fireplace. Scene 2: A clearing surrounded by bushes, with a log on the ground.

Lighting: The only light in the first scene comes from the lighted fireplace and the lighted lantern. No special lighting effects are required for Scene 2.

NAUGHTY SUSAN

Characters: 3 male; 4 female.

Playing Time: 10 minutes.

Costumes: Clothes of the Revolutionary period.

Properties: Samplers for Ann and Susan, cane for Grandmother, watch for Mr. Page.

Setting: The living room of a Quaker family in 1776. There are a table, several chairs for the adults and two footstools for the girls, also a bookcase filled with books and if possible a corner cupboard containing some simple china. Additional furnishings may be a spinning wheel, warming pan and copper or pewter bowls. In Scene 2 the table is set with dishes and silverware.

Lighting: No special effects.

Sound: Offstage bell, as indicated in text.

A GUIDE FOR GEORGE WASHINGTON

Characters: 3 male; 3 female.

Playing Time: 25 minutes.

Costumes: Washington and Captain wear worn Revolutionary army uniforms. In Scenes 1 and 3 they wear heavy, long, dark cloaks. Winchester is in plain uniform of the period. In Scene 4, he has white bandage around his head and his arm in a sling. Elizabeth is dressed in plain Colonial gown, while Mrs. Winchester wears formal gown covered by a full-length cape. In Scene 3, Elizabeth, as the Stranger, wears high boots, men's trousers and jacket and long cape. A cap is pulled low over her forehead. Maria wears maid's uniform.

Properties: Oil lantern.

Setting: Scenes 1 and 3: The banks of the Delaware River. If desired, a backdrop of a snowy landscape with evergreen trees may be used. Scene 2: The Winchester home. There is a curtained window up center. Doors are at back and at right. Colonial furnishings complete the setting. Scene 4: A small, sparsely furnished room with a chair and table. Exit is at right.

Lighting: In Scenes 1 and 3, the lights are dim.

Sound: Offstage pistol shot, as indicated in text.

HORSE SENSE

Characters: 3 male; 4 female.

Playing Time: 25 minutes.

Costumes: Colonial dress. Horse wears horse's-head mask or half mask, black sweater, slacks. Mrs. Locksley has spectacles in her pocket.

Properties: Cudgel, sugar lumps, cloak.

Setting: The workshop in Paul Revere's house, Boston. There is a fireplace at right, with a settee in front of it. A door at upper center leads to street; a door at left also leads outside, to stable area. At upper left, there is a cabinet holding silver bowls, trays, spoons, teapots, etc. At center there is a long wooden table with a bench in front of it facing the audience. At left of table is a rocking chair; at right of bench is a straight chair. There are silver engraving tool and teapot on table. Several silver spoons are in cabinet.

Lighting: No special effects.

Sound: Horse neighing, and thudding sounds, as indicated in text.

"WOOF" FOR THE RED, WHITE AND BLUE

Characters: 1 male; 4 female.

Playing Time: 10 minutes.

Costumes: Colonial dress.

Properties: Package containing squares of red, white, and blue fabric, stripes of red and white fabric and scraps of white shaped like stars; letter; small stones.

Setting: The street in front of Betsy Ross's house in Philadelphia. A picket fence with gate runs diagonally from up center to down right. Behind fence is Betsy Ross's house, with front door that serves as exit. Another exit is at left.

Lighting: No special effects.

Sound: Loud barking, as indicated in text.

TO TEST THE TRUTH

Characters: 7 male; 13 male or female for Narrator, Panelists, and Voices. Colonists and Unionists may be male or female.

Playing Time: 30 minutes.

Costumes: Three George Washingtons wear boots or shoes with buckles, knickers, white stockings, vests or long jackets with crepe-paper ruffles at cuffs and neck, powdered wigs, tricorn hats. Three Abraham Lincolns wear beards, dark suits and stovepipe hats. Corresponding dress may be worn by Voices of each period. Other actors wear everyday modern dress.

Properties: Cards marked with numbers 1, 2, and 3; cards marked with X.

Setting: Stage (or classroom) is decorated with red, white, and blue bunting, paintings of Washington and Lincoln and scenes from their lives, and Colonial flag. There is a sign reading TO TEST THE TRUTH on rear wall. Table and chair for host are up center. Table with four chairs for panelists is at right; table with three chairs for challengers is at left. Blank cards, marking pens, and holders for marked cards are on each table. Other chairs are at left and right for Voices, Unionists and Colonists.

Sound: Recording of "The Stars and Stripes," buzzer and bell, as indicated in text.

THE PETTICOAT REVOLUTION

Characters: 14 female.

Playing Time: 25 minutes.

Costumes: Queen Georgette wears a very elaborate regal dress, with wig, royal robe, and crown. The British Ladies have court gowns, wigs, and shawls. Lady Howe has silk slippers. In Scene 3, the British Ladies wear elaborate epaulettes on their shawls. The Messenger Girl has a panniered dress, scarlet dress coat, tricornered hat. The Minute Maids wear modest Colonial everyday dress, with aprons and lace caps. Martha Washington has a dark cape with epaulettes in Scene 3. Benita Franklin should wear hexagonal spectacles.

Properties: Scene 1: Fans, lorgnette, hand mirror, documents with seals, dispatch pouch, scroll paper, quill pen, ceremonial sword. Scene 2: Sewing items, embroidery items, knitting needles, knitting bags, yarn, wooden spoon, kite, rags for tail of kite, teaspoons, cups. Scene 3: Book, mop, brooms, rolling pins, pistol, dagger, chalk, smelling salts, lace shawl, lace handkerchief.

Setting: Scene 1: Queen Georgette's throne room. Down center there is an elaborately-decorated throne, and placed around it on the floor are stools and large cushions. Rugs, draperies, etc., may be added as desired. Scene 2: The parlor of a modest Colonial home. Chairs are arranged around a round table at center, and down right there is a fireplace, with a large kettle. Scene 3: The stage is bare, except for a small sign down right which reads, BUNKER HILL.

Sound: Appropriate background music, including a minuet, "Rule, Britannia," "Yankee Doodle," etc., as indicated in text. These may be recorded. Hoofbeats, as indicated in text.

Lighting: No special effects.

THE WHITES OF THEIR EYES

Characters: 9 male; 10 female. The number of cast members in pageant may be increased or decreased, if desired.

Playing Time: 20 minutes.

Costumes: Ordinary, everyday dress. Mr. Krick wears topcoat and derby.

Properties: Roll of green crepe paper, script, costume boxes, broomsticks, American flag.

Setting: The stage of Mr. Krick's theater. The stage is bare except for a few red and white streamers hanging at the back, and a table left, on which are records, record player and a telephone. A pile of broomsticks is on the floor near the table. A few straight chairs at right and left and a ladder at back may complete the setting. Exits are at right and left.

Lighting: No special effects.

Sound: Offstage hoofbeats, patriotic music, telephone bell, as indicated in text.

OLD GLORY GROWS UP

Characters: 5 male; 4 female; 10 male or female.

Playing Time: 10 minutes.

Costumes: George Washington and Betsy Ross wear traditional Colonial attire. Washington has a white wig tied with a black ribbon. Five Speakers wear red, white, and blue paper caps. Vermont is a girl in Colonial costume; Kentucky is a boy in pioneer outfit.

Francis Scott Key wears the appropriate dress of the period. Uncle Sam and Columbia wear traditional costumes. The Confederate boy and girl are in Civil War costumes; New Mexico and Arizona wear cowboy or pioneer outfits. Alaska is dressed as an Eskimo, and Hawaii in South Seas costume.

Properties: Seven large cards bearing the dates 1777, 1795, 1818, 1861-1865, 1912, 1960 and 1975-1976; red and white stripes for flannel board flag; notebook for Francis Scott Key; document, fields of fifteen, twenty, thirty-four, forty-six, and fifty stars, for flag; two Confederate flags; stars, for New Mexico and Arizona.

Setting: The stage is bare. On the apron of stage is an easel bearing a large placard labeled "Old Glory." Under the placard are date cards arranged in order. At upstage center is a large cardboard Colonial flag, with a flannel board field. Beside the flag is a table or small sewing stand on which the other fields are placed so they will be available as needed.

Lighting: No special effects.